THE NATURAL ORIGIN OF LANGUAGE

here) is precisely balanced by the wrongness of the later Wittgenstein. In his Notebooks of 1914-1916 (before he forced his ideas into the straitjacket of the Tractatus) his observations that "Language is a part of our organism and no less complicated than it", that names "themselves are connected; in this way the whole images the situation like a tableau vivant", "The name compresses its whole complex reference into one" and "Words are like the film on deep water"—would have fitted well into the theory presented here, had he not subsequently equally sharply asserted the arbitrary and conventional nature of language and the uselessness of seeking any philosophical enlightenment from it. The same category of authors, those stimulating by disagreement, would have to include Locke. Despite his denial of the possibility of innate ideas and his assertion of the arbitrariness of words, Locke's recognition of language as the great instrument and common tie of society and his careful discussion of the relation of words and knowledge have provided material used later in the book. Amongst linguists proper, Saussure and Sapir have been influential, in expressing so clearly ideas with which the present theory disagrees.

The positive debts can be referred to more briefly because evidence of them is apparent at many points in the book. Most important of all have been the ideas of Karl Lashley as a neurologist on the structural relation between speech, vision and action; his view that the rudiments of every human behavioural mechanism will be found far down in the evolutionary scale, that the problems of syntax and of the organisation of language are characteristic of almost all other cerebral activity, that temporal integration is found similarly in language, vision and action, and that spatial and temporal order appear to be almost completely interchangeable in cerebral action (with integration carried out hierarchically at a series of levels), are the direct foundation for the central argument presented in this book. One might repeat here his observation that "the study of comparative grammar is not the most direct approach to the physiology of the cerebral cortex yet speech is the only window through which the physiologist can view cerebral life . . . language presents in a most striking form the integrative functions that are characteristic of the cerebral cortex". Other important sources have been Lenneberg's pioneering Biological Foundations of Language with its discussion of children's acquisition of language as a maturational process within a critical period, Richard Gregory's stimulating ideas on the 'grammar of vision' and his speculation that language and vision are indeed based on common ground and the basic problems of both must be solved together. Last but far from least, Konrad Lorenz's broad approach to the development and integration of animal and human behaviour as well as his study of the vitally important process of 'imprinting', that is, genetically-programmed neurological development, making it possible for the cerebral structures of the animal (or human being) to be modified, after birth, to match the specific environment, social or physical, to which the individual is in fact exposed.

The chapter headings indicate in a summary way the 'articulation and concatenation of the whole system', the systematic development of the hypothesis from chapter to chapter, starting from the elementary units of speech, vision and action and progressing to the interrelation of sentence, visual scene and complex action. However, whether the theory seems probable. well argued and convincing depends not on the outline but on the detailed presentation and argument both in each chapter individually and in all the chapters taken together as mutually supporting each other. How readily the new view presented will be given a hearing, or accepted, is subject not only to the usual and often scientifically justified suspicion of the unorthodox—Locke remarks that new opinions are always suspected and usually opposed without any other reason but because they are not already common—but also to two special considerations, first that there is a powerful community of professional linguists whose careers and work have been founded on an assumption totally incompatible with the basis of the present hypothesis and secondly that there is no existing community of scientists or philosophers whose interests range as widely as the assumptions and evidence presented in this book require. We live in an age of specialists and sub-specialists. Even philosophers. who once took all life and all knowledge as their field now are often specialists only in philosophy in a narrow sense, in one corner of philosophy. There are no general 'natural philosophers' in the academic community, though there are psychologists, sociolinguists, neurolinguists, physiologists, whose specialisms ultimately can only be comprehensible as part of a total science of human nature. Perhaps the nearest successors to the 'ancient philosopher' who took the whole of nature as his study are to be found, as Monod suggests, among the biologists, or the sociobiologists—or amongst the exponents of artificial intelligence techniques. The most an author presenting a theory as wide-ranging as the present one can look for is that it should be treated on its merits, not dismissed out of hand. A theory of this kind must persuade; it cannot be cast in the form of a logical or mathematical proof. Hume, the great sceptic, at one point remarked that "a true sceptic will be diffident of his philosophical doubt". All that the author of the present work would hope for is that those reading it will be prepared, provisionally, to be diffident of their certainties—and particularly of the certainty so generally prevailing that words and language must be arbitrary and cannot be natural.

or 'invented' or 'random'. A system can be artificial without being random or unreasonable; see, for example, the system of the Morse code. A system can be social but constructed in accord with reason, as many important institutions have been. Saussure himself points out elsewhere that most important social institutions have at some point a natural base, so that to say that language is a social construct is not automatically to say that it is in some sense an arbitrary construct.

One suspects that most of those who discuss the nature of language and categorise it as arbitrary are confusing the current appearance of any language, as a collection of words which mostly have no obvious relation to their meaning, with the separate question of the historical origin of the individual words which go to form the present-day collection. It is not enough for Saussure to assert that language is arbitrary or non-natural because it is traditional since this leaves untackled the important question of the origin of the traditional link of word and meaning. It is not possible, without circularity, to argue that in its first origin the particular word was heard in use in speech—the tradition must have started somewhere, somehow. At one point, Saussure asks "How would a speaker take it upon himself to associate the idea with a word-image if he had not first come across the association in an act of speaking?"(17), but this is a puzzle which he has created for himself, to explain the historical first use of a particular word (we know the answer for some modern neologisms such as the origin of 'gas' 'paraffin' 'vaseline', as discussed by Potter(18)).

Those who speak of the cultural, social, customary origin of words and language might be reminded of the very relevant comments of Konrad Lorenz: "The undeniable fact that cultures are highly complex intellectual systems, resting on a basis of symbols expressive of cultural values, causes us to forget, given as we are to thinking in terms of opposites, that they are natural structures, which have evolved along natural lines"(19). Somewhat similarly, Hewes, after quoting the remarks of Tax extracted above on the arbitrary quality of cultural behaviour and language 'because it does not flow through the genes', points out that if culture and biology have always been separate domains, we have no way to explain how man's language capacity has been perfected.(20)

It seems absolutely clear that what is 'traditional' 'social' or 'conventional' can still be wholly or partly natural, or at the minimum natural in origin.

After all, there are obvious examples of what one would call 'conventions', styles of clothes, cookery recipes, matrimonial systems, methods of composing music, but for these one does not need to look very far to find natural bases or natural constraints on the forms which they take. Equally, one can easily identify obviously natural forms of behaviour upon which conventional, traditional or social elements have been superimposed. Eating is natural but there are conventions about the manner of eating; one chooses to eat in this way rather than that, even though in a sense both ways are equally natural. Even in the case of walking, which Saussure refers to as a clearly natural form of behaviour, there are different manners of walking, including some highly conventionalised ones such as marching, goose-stepping and so on. With the human being, the natural and the social are inextricably mingled in many forms of behaviour—and the essence of the convention or tradition may exactly be the adoption in a community of one particular form of behaviour out of several equally natural possible forms of behaviour. Shaking hands; and rubbing noses are equally natural as forms of contact and greeting, but our community prefers, by tradition, a hand-shake where the New Guineans may prefer a nose-rub.

Set against the range of words, often with imprecise uses, referring to the 'arbitrary' character of language are the various words used to express the opposite view. These include 'natural' 'biological' 'innate' 'genetic' 'physical' 'nativistic' 'instinctive' 'evolutionary' 'organismic' 'motivated' 'species-specific' and so on. It is fair to say that many of these are used with no more precision than the corresponding set of words grouped with 'arbitrary'. It is often difficult to decide what in a particular context is meant by 'natural'; all linguists tend to describe particular languages as 'natural' languages but this is only to distinguish them from invented universal languages (Esperanto, Interlingua and so on) or from the ideal or formal languages found in logic, philosophy or mathematics. Clearly this use of 'natural' implies no departure from the general view that all languages are arbitrary. So 'natural' tends to acquire its specific meaning in any context from the express or implied contrast with some opposed word: natural and artificial, natural and learned, natural and invented, natural and cultural and so on.

Given this, it is clearly not enough to assert that language or any aspect of language is 'natural' without specifying precisely the manner in which language is natural. 'Innate' is a more specific description than natural in hear any song by others of its species, it also develops an idiosyncratic song which is abnormal but diverges less from normal song than does that of the bird deaf from birth. The song of the isolated bird has a definite patterned morphology, made up of relatively pure and sustained tones, which however shows a progressive loss of species-specificity, that is, tends to diverge more and more from the norm for its species. To put the matter anthropomorphically, a songbird, like a child, must learn from other birds, if it is to vocalise correctly.

A vital further point, in which the process also resembles imprinting, is that the ability to learn the 'right' song is manifest only during a specially sensitive period of the young bird's life and at this stage it is highly selective. If a sparrow has played back to it both the song appropriate to its own species and that of another species, it will learn only the song appropriate to its own species. If the sparrow is allowed to hear only the song of a foreign species, it will ignore it and tend to develop a crude song, like that of a totally untrained sparrow, that is, the bird is tuned to learn certain sounds and not others. This is an indication of the precision of the genetic priming, since there is every reason to think that simply in terms of the anatomic mechanism required, the song patterns of close relatives should be within the vocal compass of the sparrow. Thus motor constraints on sound production do not provide an adequate explanation for the selectivity and instead we have to look to sensory processes involving the neural pathways for auditory processing, sensitising the bird only to certain patterns of sound stimulation (in rather the same way as the human infant is sensitised virtually from birth to discriminate speech-sounds from non-speech sounds).

There is obviously room for debate and much research on how the remarkable phenomena of bird-song development should be explained, neurologically and physiologically. Presumably there must be structures in the auditory system (including the neurological structuring serving the system) which embody information about the structure of appropriate vocal sounds, appropriate patterns of sound, which have a capacity to guide motor development. These 'auditory templates', as Marler describes them, are genetically specified only to an extent adequate to produce an approximation of the normal song for the species, though they are still sufficiently specific to focus the young bird's attention preferentially on the song of others of its species (if there is the opportunity to hear it) and thus to provide an explanation of the selectivity of this very special learning process. It is not irrelevant to note at this point that the selectivity of the learning process in bird-song extends not only to the basic sounds going to form the song but also to the groupings of sounds in phrases and the more extensive structuring of song in the complete melody.

It seems a natural and obvious transition in the light of the striking potential of the process of imprinting in the development of adaptive behaviour in birds and animals to consider how far the phenomena of first language learning in humans show features resembling, for example, those found in developing bird-song. Karl Lashley's firm conviction was that the rudiments of every human behavioural mechanism would be found far down the evolutionary scale and also represented in primitive activities of the nervous system. It is not a very daring venture down the evolutionary scale to look for similar mechanisms, similar physiological and neurological organisation in young humans and young birds or monkeys. If imprinting or some analogous process operates in language-learning, then one could conceive of language as a part-innate, part-environmentally determined system in its development. Readiness to learn a language would be a manifestation of a genetically-primed ability to select, as the mother tongue, one specific language from a range of equally possible languages.

Language learning by children would then be very much akin to learning of their characteristic song by birds, in that the actual learning of the song is developed by exposure to the song sung by others of the species, a potential which leaves room for a good deal of plasticity which can, on occasion, lead to birds learning songs inappropriate to their species. The 'imprinting' approach to language would also take as a parallel the visual learning of kittens as just described, which allows the environment to which kittens are exposed in the critical period to alter the permanent shape and functioning of the cortical visual apparatus. In all these cases, Lorenz's geese attaching themselves to humans rather than to parent geese, kittens learning to interpret visual environments in one way rather than another, birds learning one song rather than another, we have a demonstration of a basic capacity in the nervous system for multi-potentiality, malleability, contingent pre-tuning of the bird or animal to adapt itself to the particular character of the environment into which it is born and to adjust its behaviour (during a sensitive period) to improve its chances of survival in that particular environment.

of the non-arbitrariness of language, which makes imprinting possible, is its relatability to the structuring of perception (particularly visual perception) and to the structuring of the human capacity for action, a theme developed more fully in the next chapter. Perhaps the early Wittgenstein was wiser than he realised when he said. "The word falls, one is tempted to explain, into a mould of my mind prepared to receive it"(45).

Chapter II

Language Vision and Action

Chapter I has dealt with the fundamental issue, whether language should be considered to be an arbitrary structure, in the sense that it has no link to the physiological properties of man and that different languages existing in different human communities are the product of chance factors operating over long periods of time. The result of this being so would be not only that the lexicon and the grammar of any language would have no basis in biology, physiology or neurology, but also that the contents of the lexicon, the words of a language, and the grammar (or at any rate the 'surface' grammar) would have no direct relation with those matters which language is used to deal with. In particular, the word would have no relation of any kind with the percept; any sound-pattern could be used to represent any item of experience or thought. That is the extreme statement of the thesis of arbitrariness.

Chapter I has set out the arguments for thinking that such a thesis must be wrong, that it leads to impossibilities and inconsistencies, and in any case has led linguistics into a cul de sac, where man's major distinguishing ability, the power of speech, cannot be linked in any way to the course of human evolution; the origin of language cannot be explained and the ease with which children learn their language, ex hypothesi a totally arbitrary system, becomes incomprehensible. Chapter I has contended that the acquisition of language by children has to be based on an innate somato-sensory cortex, Hubel and Wiesel developed a refined technique for recording the activity of individual neurons in the visual cortex when the retina is stimulated in a defined way, with a spot of light or an illuminated pattern. Typically such a neuron can only be activated by light falling on a circumscribed area of the retina, defined as the receptive field of that particular neuron. The typical receptive field of a single cortical neuron on the retina has a narrow band of excitatory points, all lying on a straight line, surrounded by a wider field of inhibitory points, or vice versa.

These receptive fields for visual brain-cells at the retinal surface are the building blocks for the synthesis and perception of the complex visual world. Activation of specific cortical brain-cells requires highly specific shapes or forms to be presented at the retina, for example, the forms must be lines or edges with specific orientations of the lines and specific positions on the retina, Some categories of neurons are specialised to respond to angles or corners or to movements in one direction but not in another. A scheme of this kind that assumes a hierarchically ordered series of ascending connections at the different cell-levels in the brain explains many features of how neurons respond selectively to distinct stimuli, for example, to a bar of light, a corner or a square. At each stage brain-cells with relatively simple properties combine to deliver inputs to form fields of progressively greater complexity and visual content.

The main significance of these discoveries (which have been matched by the discovery of similar organisation in other sensory areas of the brain) is that the visual area of the brain, the cortex for vision, is now seen to be a highly specialised structure designed to factor out and emphasise the main features of optical inputs that are relevant in the perception of shapes and figures, that is, contours and their elements. Nevertheless the work is still at an early stage if one considers the massive complexity of brain-operation involved in effective perception. Hubel and Wiesel themselves have recognised that specialised as are the cells they have discovered in the cortex, they represent only a very elementary stage in the handling of complex forms, occupied with a relatively simple region-by-region analysis of retinal contours.

Despite the modesty of the researchers, perhaps even more important than the specific identifications made of neuronal response has been the evidence they have presented that visual processing is essentially a hierarchical operation. Cells at different levels perform different operations with the degree of complexity increasing at each level. Though later research has suggested that the relation between hierarchical levels is more complicated than was originally assumed, Hubel and Wiesel identified cells at several different levels, simple cells, complex cells, hypercomplex cells and higher-order hypercomplex cells. The first account was that simple cortical cells respond only to simple contours, for example, a line in a particular very narrowly defined retinal position; for complex cells, there are 'complex' receptive fields at the retina which mean that the cell may respond only to straight lines in particular orientations (sloping this way rather than that) and not to anything as simple as a spot of light, but, interestingly, the complex cell appears to respond to a line of the given orientation even when the position of the line on the retina is changed (to some extent the cell has extracted a general representation of a line with a given slope). There is less certainty about hypercomplex cells; these were said to be specialised to convey information about abrupt changes in the stimulus, such as when a line ends or changes its direction; hypercomplex cells were also said to be differentially sensitive to the length as well as the orientation of a contour. Higher-order hypercomplex cells were sensitive to two preferred orientations, 90 degrees apart, so that they were especially sensitive to the presentation on the retina of an angle; they responded best to a corner or right angle. Other cells, according to Hubel and Wiesel, had other specialisations: some were differentially sensitive to the distance of an object behind or in front of the point upon which the eyes were fixated; other cells were found to respond much more strongly to three-dimensional objects rather than to any two-dimensional stimulus shape. Despite the difficulties, and despite competing accounts of visual processing, Hubel and Wiesel's work (for which they received the Nobel prize) remains of central importance and it is not difficult. to imagine that as research continues, cortical cells will be found which are responsive to still more complex fields, collections of contours or shapes when they fall within a given area of the retina.

One final point from this research, namely, the remarkable emphasis placed in the system on the precise orientation of lines and contours. There seems to be an amazingly exact relation structurally between the cortical organisation and sensitivity to varying degrees of orientation, the perceived slope of the line. In one experiment, using electrodes implanted in the visual cortex, each time the electrode was moved forward as little as 25 or 30 micrometres (million of a metre) the optimal orientation (slope of the stimulating line) changed by a small step of about 10 degrees on average; the successive changes in orientation continued in the same direction, clockwise or counterclockwise, through a total angle of anywhere from 90 degrees to 270 degrees. In the normal cat, it was found that the preferred orientation of different cells was distributed all around the clock. Obviously there is something particularly vital for perception in the identification of the precise direction of lines seen in the visual field.

The general picture presented by Hubel and Wiesel's work on the elementary units of visual perception fits reasonably well with evidence from quite a different source, that is, the set of psychological experiments concerned with the mode of fragmentation of images stabilised on the retina. If an experimental subject is restricted to prolonged viewing of a particular shape or pattern (by techniques involving the use of contact lenses it is possible to keep the image of an external object immovably applied to one part of the retina despite any eye movements which the perceiver may make), it is found that the pattern perceived tends to undergo spontaneous changes (probably as a result of fatigue of the receptors). Eventually the shape or pattern may seem to disappear altogether but normally the pattern will tend to fragment, with parts of it disappearing and reappearing as a whole. This process seems to throw some light on what the visual apparatus treats as sub-units of any pattern, and so possibly on the character of the elementary visual units.

The disappearance of parts of the pattern in these experiments is not haphazard. Lines come and go as a whole, so that triangles lose one side at a time, while the letter T loses either its entire upright or its entire crosspiece. Parallel lines tend to disappear and appear together, even at considerable separations. Curvilinear figures often undergo simplification and gap-completion. Whenever possible, the fragmentation tends to produce meaningful patterns rather than nonsensical ones. A monogram breaks down into recognisable letters more often than into unnameable fragments; a word characteristically loses exactly those letters which will leave another definable word behind; the eye in profile disappears and reappears as a unit. For example, where the image stabilised on the retina was the word BEER, it fragmented in an orderly way first to PEER, then PEEP, BEE and BE. Where the stabilised image was HB, it fragmented successively into H B 3 4. Where the stabilised image was a face, it fragmented into a complete profile, then the eye, top of the head and nose, then the mouth and back of the head, and finally into a diminished profile of eye, nose and mouth.

When different shapes were projected, the speed and amount of fading and regeneration varied according to the nature of the figure. Meaningful figures faded less than meaningless ones; a profile face faded more slowly and remained longer than did a line alongside it. A letter with an irregular line across it remained when the line itself disappeared. Curved figures faded less than straight line figures. Certain parts of the outline of a square might disappear whilst others remained; in particular parallel sides tended to fade and regenerate together, and dots forming a continuous line also tended to fade together. Similar effects could be produced when the after-image of a bright figure was fixated in a dark room; in a circle with crossed diagonals, halves or quarters of the circle might disappear or both diagonals or the circumference of the circle. Words printed in capital letters faded less readily than did meaningless stimuli of the same general shape. Such complex effects, and especially the persistence of meaningful figures, must clearly have been related to visual processes in the brain, and the results in no way seem incompatible with the findings of Hubel and Wiesel of cortical cells with special sensitivities for particular contours and shapes.

In another field of work, artificial intelligence research into machine-vision and pattern-recognition, the selection of features for the computer analysis of complex shapes has been a prime problem. In one of the earlier and more interesting approaches to pattern-recognition, Selfridge's 'Pandemonium'(4), the selection of features to be examined was in the first place determined on common sense grounds, but the initial choice was verified by the usefulness in practical operation of the computer program of the particular features selected. Programs which were designed to look for elementary 'features' of a pattern and then combine in stages into a total percept were amongst the most successful in practice. The computer work on pattern-recognition has shown very clearly that extremely complex computational processes are required even for apparently very simple perceptual abilities, such as seeing a block, or seeing a straight line as a line. One approach has been to build up from the simplest level, starting with the identification of dots, then treating arrays of dots as configurations of lines and then treating configurations of lines as configurations of bars (which may then be combined into letter-forms or other more complex shapes)(5). Some of the most interesting work was done by Waltz(5) who showed how a process of mutual disambiguation can be applied to a complex array of lines and angles, so that his program was successful in interpreting line-drawings as representing a scene made up of a variety of blocks, distributed irregularly on a table. He gave his program prior knowledge of the possible interpretations of various types of line-junction, all of which out of context could be ambiguous. The problem he tackled was to find a globally consistent interpretation of the whole picture and in fact the program did surprisingly well even on quite complex pictures. The conclusion to be drawn from this work is not simply the astonishing complexity involved in the analysis even of the most apparently simple pictures but the value of a hierarchical, feature-identification approach, building up from isolation of the simplest possible elements, and constructing from them step by step more complex structures. There seems nothing incompatible between the approach which has proved itself of practical, though still restricted, value in machine-analysis of perceptual patterns, and the hierarchical and elementary-feature-based process of human perception which seems to be indicated by Hubel and Wiesel's work.

Apart from the evidence from neurological research and from study of the fragmentation of stabilised images, and the suggestive work on machine-vision, if, as a matter of common experience, one had to specify features likely to be used in the analysis of a visual field, they would certainly include lines (horizontal, vertical and oblique), junctions of two or more lines to form angles and corners, right angles and every size, position and orientation of angles (acute and obtuse), points or dots (presumably absolutely primitive since they can be put together to form any other feature of the visual scene), curved lines (convex and concave). In addition one might specify variations in brightness and darkness and in colour (areas of colour unbounded by lines as well as bounded areas). One might even list circles, squares, triangles and other more complex forms, and one could assume that in addition to the contour-elements in a scene. there would also be primitive relational aspects, relative sizes, distances and depths. The commonsense view would again seen not to diverge very far from what has so far been discovered in the scientific research referred to above.

Accordingly, if in the light of the above one had to specify elementary units of vision (and the safest basis might seen to be to rely mainly on Hubel and Wiesel's work) they might include:

1. Straight lines
2. Edges (lines separating a bright and a dark area)

3. Bars (dark on a light background)
4. Angles
5. Corners or right angles
6. Slits (light on a dark background)
7. Curves
8. Squares (possibly) and other more complex shapes (one researcher reported that a cell in the monkey's cortex only responded to display of a monkey's paw)

Apart from the contours to which cortical cells have been shown to respond, there are other relational aspects to which cells at different levels respond:

9. Orientation (especially of lines)
10. Discontinuity (end of a line or bar or a variation in direction)
11. Movement (some cells respond to both direction and rate of movement)
12. Location (simpler cells responded to location of the stimulus in the visual field but for most higher level cells what mattered was the particular contour or shape regardless of location).
13. Colour

It is fair to say that the assumption that the elementary features listed above are in fact those actually used in the analysis of visual shapes has not gone without challenge. Some would argue that the primary elements are not straight lines but angles and intersections (see Pomerantz(6)) on the basis of psychological pattern-discrimination experiments carried out with adult subjects. Whether this type of evidence, completely different from recording cortical cell responses to visual stimuli, casts doubt on the primacy of straight lines as elements is doubtful; it would not be at all surprising if adult human subjects taking part in the pattern-discrimination experiments were to use different perceptual strategies from those which are innate, or imprinted in the infant or the experimental animal. It seems highly likely that perceptual learning is superimposed on the innate processes of feature-detection from which percepts are initially constructed and that both straight lines and angles are rightfully to be included in the array of primitive visual units.

One final comment on the significance of the material presented in this section. The hierarchical scheme of visual perception, as Hubel and Wiesel themselves acknowledge, is undoubtedly not completely correct in detail and the only possible explanation. Rather it represents a useful hypothesis and an effective way of describing how the complex behaviour of cells in the visual system could be brought about. How the information is in fact used at later stages of the visual path is "far from clear and represents one of the tantalising problems of the future . . . From the elementary ability to respond to specific contour elements it is still a very far cry to mechanisms that can learn to classify shapes such as chairs and tables according to complex properties for which we cannot expect innate detectors to have developed during evolution. The main fact that emerges from the discovery of these specialised cells in the visual cortex is the profound preoccupation of the visual system with the contours of visual shapes. This suggests that contours play a special part in shape recognition"(7).

The preoccupation of the visual system with contour is one of the factors suggesting the approach adopted in this chapter, that is, one relating the elements of visual contour (as described) to the elements of action contour (discussed in the next section) and the contours of speech forms (considered as articulatory patterning).

Two more recent lines of vision research, those into distributed parallel processing and the use of sin-wave gratings to map the distribution of X, Y and Z neurons in the visual system, to some extent have challenged Hubel and Wiesel's findings as suggesting a hierarchical, feature—detection, visual process. Nevertheless, studies of eye—movements, saccades and fixations have not been invalidated and there seems no doubt that, at some level in the visual system, contour-elements are detected, combined and identified against stored schemas.

Natural Units of Action

The thesis presented in this book is that at every level there is an inevitably close relation, inter-digitation, between the structures and processes underlying language and those underlying perception and action. In the immediately preceding section there has been discussion of the elementary units of vision (as plausibly discovered in Hubel and Wiesel's research) which could be combined together by 'morphological' rules in order to produce more complex visual forms, and ultimately explain the characteristics of our total visual perception. In the present section the thesis is that in the case of bodily action, a similar line of analysis is appropriate, that is, complex actions of the human body (or of the animal body) are formed from elementary units of movement, elementary action, which are linked together in a systematic way in order to produce the total complex action. Thus we arrive at the same kind of analysis for action into elementary units, successive hierarchical stages and the syntactic construction of the total action sequence, as we postulate for vision and for speech. This is by no means a radical or novel idea. As for many of the more important insights into the parallelisms of behavioural structures, Lashley dealt precisely with this in his paper on "The problem of serial order in behavior"(8) in the Hixon Symposium. The whole article is of great interest but most relevantly one might quote the following section:

"Generality of the problem of syntax

I have devoted so much time to discussion of the problem of syntax, not only because language is one of the more important products of human cerebral action, but also because the problems raised by the organisation of language seem to be characteristic of almost all other cerebral activity. There is a series of hierarchies of organisation: the order of vocal movements in pronouncing the word, the order of words in the sentence, the order of sentences in the paragraph, the rational order of paragraphs in a discourse. Not only speech but all skilled acts seem to involve the same problems of serial ordering, even down to the temporal coordination of muscular contractions in such a movement as reaching and grasping. Analysis of the nervous mechanisms underlying order in the more primitive acts may contribute ultimately to the solution even of the physiology of logic. It is possible to designate, that is, to point to specific examples of the phenomena of the syntax of movement that require explanation . . . There are at least three sets of events to be accounted for. First, the activation of the expressive elements (the individual words or adaptive acts) which do not contain the temporal relations. Second, the determining tendency, the set or idea . . . Third, the syntax of the act, which can be described as an habitual order or mode of relating the expressive elements, a generalised pattern or schema of integration which may be imposed upon a wide range and a wide variety of specific acts. This is the essential problem of serial order; the existence of generalised schemata of action which determine the sequence of specific acts, acts which in themselves or in their associations seem to have no temporal valence . . . The problems of the syntax of

segment of speech. The invariance of the phoneme then is a derived one, related more to the structure of articulation, to the patterning of movement of the articulatory organs than to the quality of the sound as shewn in the acoustic record. Successive phonemes are merged in the sound stream; the articulatory gestures corresponding to successive phonemes are overlapped or shingled together, to produce a parallel delivery of information from which the hearer can construct the ideal sets of phonemes which went to form the articulatory programme of the speaker. This overlapping and combination of the articulatory gestures which phonemes, on this view, constitute, parallels very closely the ideas developed in the previous section of the chapter on the ways in which elementary units of action may be combined in a sequence and smoothed together to form a continuous pattern of action, in which it may then be difficult easily to identify the original component elements.

Both the evidence from child development and from the work of Liberman and his associates seem to make it plausible to take the set of phonemes as the elementary units of speech, properly to be matched with the elementary units of vision and the elementary units of action described in preceding sections. One might also quote here Ladefoged's(17) comment that modern linguistics is based on the assumption that speech is a sequence of discrete entities and even while one may accept the assertion of instrumental phoneticians that there are no procedures for isolating phonemes by acoustic traces, the status of the phoneme, analogous to that of electrons in physics, is every bit as real as any other theoretical entity in science.

Accordingly, in parallel with the elementary units of vision and action, one can now list the elementary units of speech-sound represented by the set of English phonemes:

Consonants

Bilabial: /b/ in 'bet' /m/ in 'met' /p/ in 'pet'
Labio-dental: /f/ in 'fan' /v/ in 'van'
Dental: /th/ in 'thin' /th/ in 'this'
Alveolar: /d/ in 'din' /t/ in 'tin' /l/ in 'let' /n/ in 'net'
/s/ in 'sin' /z/ in zoo
Post-alveolar: /r/ in 'red'
Palato-alveolar: /j/ in 'jet' /ch/ in 'chin' /sh/ in 'shin'

/zh/ in 'measure'
Palatal: /y/ in 'yes'
Glottal: /h/ in 'head'
Velar /g/ in 'goat' /k/ in 'coat' /w/ in 'wed'
/ng/ in 'sing'

Vowels

Short /ae/ in 'pat' /e/ in 'set' /i/ in 'sit'
/o/ in 'pot' /u/ in 'cut' /u/ in 'put'
/o/ in 'boat'

Long /aa/ in 'part' /ee/ in 'bear' /ii/ in 'beat'
/oo/ in 'port' /uu/ in 'pool' /uu/in 'purr'

Diphthongs /ei/ in 'bait' /ai/ in 'bite' /ao/ in 'bout'
/ou/ in 'boy' /au/ in 'howl'

The forms of the phonemes used above are based loosely on those in English Conversation Reader by P.A.D. McCarthy(18). For ease of reading the use of any less familiar phonetic symbolisation (such as the International Phonetic Alphabet) has been avoided. What matters is not the symbols used but that the sounds of the English set of phonemes are those in the words listed.

Systematic relation of elementary units of vision, action and speech

The preceding sections of this chapter have sought to determine on the basis of research in vision and phonetics and of the account of the syntax of action given by Lashley, what appear to be the elementary units of vision, action and speech which serve as the basis for construction, through a series of hierarchical stages and in accordance broadly with what might be described as syntactic rules, of the fully elaborated final visual percepts, complex actions and elaborated word-forms. The underlying argument has been that in human behaviour visual perception, action and language must be fully integrated with each other and one can reasonably look for evidence of the manner in which this integration is achieved at every level, including the level of the earliest stages in the formation of visual shapes, of action-routines and speech—forms. For vision, the elementary units were taken to be such features as lines, edges, corners, angles etc.; for action, the elements were taken to be the possible types and ranges of movement of the different parts of the body and for speech, the elementary units were identified with the set of phonemes familiar in traditional phonetics.

The task now is to suggest on what systematic basis these different categories of elementary units might, physiologically and neurologically, be associated with one another. There is no accepted body of research on which this systematic relation can be based and evidence, mostly anecdotal, of cross-modal linking of different sensory features in the established phenomenon of synaesthesia is not particularly helpful or relevant, except to the extent that it shows that in practical experience for a particular individual there can be a relation, for example, between the shape of a letter or number and a specific colour, that sounds can be matched regularly with colours and that in some individual brains neural connections must exist between systematic representations of different modalities of sensory experience. More generally, it is a matter of common observation that there can be a relation between speech and bodily action, in the usual forms of gesture associated with vigorous speech. Visual form can also be indicated by gesture, and deaf and dumb languages constitute a complete system for representing the content of spoken language by bodily action. Other indications that there are real relations between sounds and shapes come not only from onomatopoeia in the narrow sense but also from well-documented evidence of phonetic symbolism.

This section proceeds directly by proposing a particular scheme of equivalences between the elementary units of vision, speech and action. The manner in which the details of the scheme were derived and decided upon is described in detail in a previous book (The Physical Foundation of Language 1973). In studying the scheme of equivalences on the next page, the following points may be helpful:

1. The scheme shows in parallel in each of the three columns the visual, speech and action units which are to be treated as equivalent
2. The three sets of elements have been grouped into five categories. Each of the five categories of, for example, speech-elements is put in direct correspondence with a specific category of visual elements and a specific category of action elements

3. The five categories of speech-elements are identified as:

VOCALIC A E I O U AA EE II OO UU
(plus diphthongs)
MAIN CONSONANTAL B C D F TH G H
LATERAL S SH W X Z
CIRCULAR L M N R
PROJECTIVE ZH V CH J P T TH Y

4. The five speech-unit categories of vowels and consonants are matched with five categories of elementary visual units derived from the section dealing with vision earlier in this chapter, that is, lines, angles, curves and, more specially, a set of variations in the degree of accommodation for visual distance (variations in the ciliary muscles) and a range of positions in movement of the eyes as a result of rotation of the head.

5. The categories of speech and visual elements are matched systematically with a range of movements of the arm, drawn from the elementary units of action described earlier, namely, forward and upward movement of the unbent arm, raising of the arm bent at the elbow in a straight line, movement of the bent arm across the body, movement of the arm out from the side of the body (with a reverse movement sideways across the body) and finally rotation of the arm on its long axis. Verbal description of precise bodily movement is difficult; the reader is referred to the photographic illustrations of the exact arm positions associated with the different speech-elements contained in The Physical Foundation of Language.

A final comment: unavoidably the equivalences between visual units, speech units and action units suggested in the schema are speculative (though a careful attempt has been made to validate the suggested relations and when, as a practical matter, the elementary units are combined to form more complex shapes, words and actions, they give every impression of being empirically correct). Nevertheless, whether or not the particular equivalences suggested are correct, partially correct or totally incorrect, the thesis defended in this chapter, and in this book, is that there must be real correspondences at some level, physiologically and neurologically, between the elementary processes of vision, speech and action. All form part of one integrally organised body and brain, all depend on a central motor

primitive vocabulary are used for selecting examples of individual words in Part II for which the natural basis of the relation between word-form and word-meaning, in visual contour, action-pattern or body-movement, is presented.

The arbitrariness of words and the natural structure of the lexicon

Chapter I has discussed at length the traditional view that individual words are arbitrary and has argued that no part of language in fact can be wholly arbitrary, neither the forms of words nor the syntactic and grammatical structures by which words are joined together into phrases and sentences. But the difference of words between different languages has always been the root reason why linguists and others have virtually without a moment's hesitation taken it that language must be arbitrary. John Locke (1706 [1964]} in his Essay Concerning Human Understanding wrestled vigorously and extensively with the problems presented by the arbitrary nature of words. For him, words stood for nothing but the ideas in the mind of him that uses them ; but there are no innate ideas. 'To ask at what time a man has first any ideas is to ask when he begins to perceive, having ideas and perception being the same thing. Perception derives from sensation: When a man begins to have any ideas, is when he first has any sensation, which is such an impression or motion made in some part of the body as produces some perception in the understanding ... When the understanding is once stored with these simple ideas, it has the power to repeat, compare and unite them, even to an almost infinite variety, and so can make at pleasure new complex ideas ... It may also lead us a little towards the original of all our notions and knowledge, if we remark how great a dependence our words have on common sensible ideas, and how those which are made use of have their rise from thence, and from obvious sensible ideas are transferred to more abstruse significations, and made to stand for ideas that come not under the cognisance of our senses e.g. to imagine, apprehend, comprehend, adhere, conceive, instil, disgust, disturbance, tranquillity &c are all words taken from the operations of sensible things and applied to certain modes of thinking".(1)

Whatever view one may take of Locke's dismissal of the possibility of innate ideas or of his assertion that "since sounds have no natural connection with our ideas, but have all their significance from the arbitrary imposition of men . . . a man may use what words he pleases to signify his own ideas to himself", there is a great deal in the passage quoted above which seems founded on common sense and is fully compatible with the thesis advanced in this Part of the present Chapter. Locke himself came, somewhat to his own surprise, to a recognition of the significance of words for his philosophical enquiry: "When I first began this discourse of the understanding, and a good while after, I had not the least thought that any consideration of words was at all necessary to it" but he then found himself led into the still interesting and useful discussion of language contained in Book III.

Both in Locke and in the later extensive studies of Bishop Wilkins (1668 [1968]}, one can note some tinge of regret that words should be arbitrary and that there should be no natural relation between the structure of the world and the structure of language. Locke notes that there cannot be any natural connexion between particular articulate sounds and certain ideas, "for then there would be but one language amongst all men" and Wilkins (in his Essay Towards a Real Character and a Philosophical Language) comments rather sadly: "It were exceedingly desirable that the names of things might consist of such sounds as should bear in them some analogy to their natures; and the figure and character of their names should bear some proper resemblance to those sounds that men might easily guess at the sense or meaning of any name or word, upon the first hearing or sight of it. But how this can be done in all the particular species of things I understand not, and therefore shall take it for granted that this character must be by institution".(2)

A more recent, interesting, attempt to express how language and perception might be naturally related is to be found in Uhlan von Slagle's monograph Language, Thought and Perception (1974). He combines an approach derived from Kant and Humboldt with insights from gestalt psychology and proposes a direct relation of the structure of meaning to the structure of experienced reality. Language, he says, is "man's tool for adequately orienting himself in extra-linguistic reality, and one must look for a systematic correlation between the structure of thought and the structure of experience and reality . . . The drive is to overcome the dichotomy of perception and thought" and this he found in the contention that the immanent organisational factors of sensory fields are the immanent organisational factors of thought; semantic form classes correlate with perceptual forms; concepts are 'rules' of perceptual organisation, or rules of 'categorisation' of perception. The structure of information stored in the mind can be described in terms of the structure of the perception itself. The structure of sensory experience can be correlated with the structure of linguistic meaning and that of thought. The position he takes on the correlation of perception and conceptualisation "parallels the growing recognition by linguists of the interdependence of syntax and semantics in natural language. In each case, there is the underlying assumption that form and content are interdependent. "Linguistic patterning rests ultimately on extralinguistic patterning".(3)

The attempt in the first part of the present chapter, in the presentation and development of the concept of the Primitive Vocabulary, is to go some way towards meeting the objectives of Locke, Wilkins and Slagle, to demonstrate a natural relation between the structures of perception and action and the structure of the vocabulary of any language (on the argument that the full lexicon of a language is a structure built up round words relating to a concretely-based core of experience). In modern terms, the subject-matter of this part of the Chapter is essentially semantics, semantic fields, semantic structuring, the relation between the semantic groupings of words and the experiential grouping of perception and action.

Traditionally, the field of linguistics has been divided into phonetics, syntax and semantics—and semantics has tended to be the most neglected of the three, the section where the problems are greatest and the solutions least convincing. Often, linguists have concentrated on phonetics or syntax and ignored semantics. In any case, it has been very unusual among linguists to attempt to find or demonstrate any real operational relation between these domains of language study, even though, in practical experience, in speech 'performance' (as Chomsky would describe it) the three aspects of language are inextricably linked and mutually definitive and supportive. Linguists have tended to be more interested in syntax (or phonetics) and philosophers more interested (though at a very refined level) in semantics than in syntax. For many years, in this century, linguists were induced to believe (following influential authors such as Bloomfield and Sapir and the behaviourist psychologists) that 'meaning' (semantics) was none of their proper business and indeed hardly a respectable subject for study. This anti-semantic approach was initially at any rate demonstrated by Chomsky and his followers, even though gradually and covertly as time went on, it became necessary to introduce a larger semantic element (in the form of selection restrictions) into syntactic structures, to make more explicit allowance for the mutual interaction of syntax and semantics.

Outside the strict field of linguistics, rather more attention has been paid to semantic issues. Some of the most interesting work is in progress as part of natural language understanding programs in the field of artificial intelligence, the work of Roger Schank, Terry Winograd, Bobrow, Yorick Wilks and others and some reference to this will be made later. Apart from this, perhaps most relevant for this chapter has been activity of the general semanticists, the studies of semantic fields associated with Weisgerber (1962)and Trier (1931)(4), and discussed at some length(5) in Miller and Johnson-Laird's Language and Perception (1976)and John Lyons' treatise Semantics (1977)(6). Nevertheless, even the experts in the field would admit that the state of theoretical discussion of semantics is far from satisfactory and so far there has not been a great deal of practical value for understanding the real functioning of language which can be derived from it. As has been remarked by an expert in the field: "No one has yet presented even the outlines of a satisfactory comprehensive theory of semantics"(7).

Despite this rather discouraging situation, one can perhaps extract from the literature some probably valid and valuable points:

1. the general semanticists put as their chief principle that language and reality are related in the same way as a map is to the terrain to which it refers. Language therefore is not an image of reality; at best it is an image of the structure of reality. The second principle is that of incompleteness; the representations in language are always less than what is represented; the map inevitably ignores details of the terrain. The third principle is that of the self-reflexiveness of language; we use language to speak about language; we make judgments about judgments; we evaluate values. This process of abstraction can be removed in varying degrees from the level of the concrete event; multiordinal words have different meanings on different levels of abstraction.

2. the lexical items of a language form a coherent pattern. They are not as rigidly organised as rules of grammar but sufficiently patterned to enable each item to have a definable relationship with all the other items. Weisgerber and Trier would argue in this way that

lexical units should not be viewed in isolation; instead they form a closely knit and articulated lexical sphere, where the significance of each unit is determined by its neighbours, their semantic areas reciprocally limiting one another, the relation of lexical units being crudely similar to that of individual atoms in a complex molecule, where the displacement of one atom will to a greater or less degree affect the nature of the entire complex. It should be noted that there are imprecisions in the formulations of Weisgerber and Trier and what they say, in detail, is open to attack at a number of points but the principal emphasis of their work, the stress on the systematic structuring of the lexicon, and particularly of defined areas of the lexicon, has been stimulating and led to much more precise examination of the mutual interaction of meaning-elements.

3. Semantic structuring may fundamentally be innate with the ultimate terms of a semantic description such presumably biologically given notions as identity, time, space, body, movement, territory, life, &c; there may be a universal set of 'presumably innate' concepts which are expressed in all languages by affixation, suppletion, enclitic particles or word order. There may be an alternative possibility that the lexicon is organised with regard to the representational derivation of its entries: that is, the degree to which their meaning can be specified by sensorimotor images and contextual memories and associations; form-class semantic may leave its traces in the nervous system, facilitating thought in some directions, inhibiting thought in other directions.

This harvest of ideas on semantics drawn from a number of sources is perhaps not a very rich one. The general conclusion remains from this brief survey that as a field of study semantics is still far from well-developed and despite the volume of philosophical discussion of meaning and more recently of the mode by which semantics might be fruitfully incorporated in syntactic models of language, there is still rather little of solid value. One has to agree with Chafe(7) that semantic structure is the crucial component of language, so that modern linguistics has been like trying to describe milk-production while omitting the cow, and that much of the linguistic effort within semantics appears to have little or no relevance for a neurobiological study of language. Linguistics in fact has learned least about semantics.

Given the relative barrenness of academic discussion so far of semantics and semantic structuring of the lexicon, this Chapter experimentally adopts a quite different approach (which can however at some points be related to what has already been said). The approach is centred round the concept of the Primitive Vocabulary. The idea of the Primitive Vocabulary is that all language is built round a limited number of primitive words (used for referring to a limited number of primitive percepts, primitive actions and states, external or internal). The relation between the particular words in the primitive vocabulary and the percepts &c to which they refer can be established only by actual experience. The relation cannot be established by the mediation of other words, so that the Primitive Vocabulary represents the categories into which our 'naive' experience is divided, without reflection, without the discursive use of language and without second-hand communication of knowledge. The Primitive Vocabulary thus consists of the words which no one else can explain to us if we have not ourselves had experience of the percepts &c to which they refer; and this means that we cannot, without the actual experience, recognise a particular instance of a percept as belonging to the category named by a specific word. The initial set of words learned by a child is the prime example of what is described as the primitive vocabulary, that is it consists of words learned from the confrontation of the child with the object, the action or the event (normally accompanied by a direct or indirect naming of the object, action or event). The acquisition of words in the Primitive Vocabulary normally goes in step with, though occasionally follows, the formation of what could, in parallel, be described as the child's primitive perceptual repertoire, that is, those shapes, objects, things and relations that a child identifies first as its visual apparatus and experience develop.

The assumption is that the Primitive Vocabulary (and the associated primitive perceptual repertoire) are structured, that is organised, in terms of the sensory modalities involved, in terms of the frames of experience in which the objects or actions are normally encountered and in terms of the distinct physical frameworks to which particular objects or actions are directly related. This Primitive Vocabulary is set in contrast to the full lexicon acquired by the adult; the primitive perceptual repertoire is similarly contrasted with the much more extensive repertoire of perceptual and other experience acquired by the adult. To adopt one of the ideas of the general semanticists referred to earlier in the Chapter, the suggestion is that the Primitive Vocabulary maps on to the primitive perceptual repertoire in the same way as the full lexicon of a language (or of an individual adult) maps on to the complete perceptual repertoire inherent in the language or actually possessed by the individual adult.

Perhaps the most expeditious way of indicating what is meant by the Primitive Vocabulary is to present an illustrative list, an example of a Primitive Vocabulary. This is done on page 61 [moved to top of document] but before presenting the list, there are a few preliminary points which can usefully be made:

a. The idea of the Primitive Vocabulary is that it contains words whose meaning and understanding can only come from the direct confrontation so to say between the word as a patterned speech-sound and the specific experience (visual or action) to which it relates in the language used in the particular community, that is: we could not understand what in experience a flower might be without seeing a flower and being told that it was a flower; we could not understand what RED as a word means without seeing something red and being told that it is 'red';

b. There is no such thing as the absolute Primitive Vocabulary, in the sense that there is a defined minimum of words matching a defined minimum of items of perceptual experience but there is probably a near enough core primitive vocabulary which will be shared by all normal children and adults—body parts, body movements, colours, visual qualities. For a particular child (or adult), what in fact is contained in the Primitive Vocabulary depends firstly on the core items, secondly on the community environment in early years and thirdly on the particular family or social situation of the individual child in its early years: a Duke's child may well have a considerably different Primitive Vocabulary (and different repertoire of perceptual experience) from a dustman's child; the child of an Indian peasant will have a different Primitive Vocabulary (and primitive repertoire) from the child of a New York stockbroker and so on;

c. There may well also be, at first at any rate, a significant difference between the contents of a child's Primitive Vocabulary and the contents of its primitive perceptual repertoire; an infant will perceive and recognise a straight line, an angle or a circle but it does not follow that its parents will have told the child that these percepts are called LINE ANGLE or CIRCLE. An infant may also have inner perceptual experience, feel, think, know, without learning or being told that these experiences are named as FEEL THINK and KNOW. These gaps in the matching between primitive words and primitive percepts will normally be filled in later on and of course there can equally well be reverse gaps where an infant hears a word used without the matching percept to which it refers being presented to him;

d. Listing of the various words shown in the illustrative Primitive Vocabulary does not of course mean that all words listed are acquired together, though some words may be learned in groups. For each infant, there will be an individual order of acquisition of particular primitive words, though certain uniformities are probable in the order of word acquisition, particularly for functional words (as Roger Brown's observations suggest). For concrete words, the order of acquisition will depend on the order of actual experience of the objects referred to, which may differ between children and may be spread over a shorter or longer period;

e. Beyond what is presented here as an illustrative Primitive Vocabulary, there is a very much larger number (perhaps many times larger) of other primitive words (matching other items of primitive perceptual experience) where the understanding of the meaning of the word depends on conjoined experience of the word and the object or event. There is a mass of other words which cannot be understood mediately, that is by definition in terms of already familiar words;

f. One final obvious point: for individuals belonging to different cultures and climates, there will be words which are never found as part of their primitive vocabularies. ICE will certainly' not be in the Primitive Vocabulary of someone living on the equator and MONSOON will not be in the primitive vocabulary of a child brought up in England. Correspondingly, there may be a range of words in the Primitive Vocabulary of a child in one culture corresponding to a single primitive word in the vocabulary of a child in a remote culture: the familiar examples are the number of different words said to exist for different types of snow found among the Eskimos and the range of different words for animals, e.g. for camels found among the Arabs. The words forming a particular are not confined to common objects or even common percepts but extend over the whole of an individual's immediate, first-hand experience; they represent the irreducible elements in his linguistic mapping of his world.

THE PRIMITIVE VOCABULARY

SHAPES AND THINGS

Primary Visual	Body Parts	Animate	Food etc.	Near	Objects	Larger Scale	Time Aspects
DOT	FACE	MOTHER	WATER	CLOTH	PIN	SUN	TIME
POINT	EYE	FATHER	MILK	TOWEL	NEEDLE	MOON	BEFORE
LINE	EAR	BABY	SOUP	BATH	STRING	STAR	AFTER
EDGE	NOSE	BROTHER	EGG	BUCKET	ROPE	CLOUD	NOW
CURVE	MOUTH	SISTER	BISCUIT	RING	HAMMER	SMOKE	THEN
ANGLE	TOOTH	BOY	BREAD	BAG	AXE	STEAM	SUDDEN
CORNER	TONGUE	GIRL	MEAT	BOX	SPADE	MIST	SOON
SQUARE	LIP	CHILD	APPLE	BASKET	CAR	RAIN	
TRIANGLE	HAND	MAN	ORANGE	BRUSH	WHEEL	SKY	
CIRCLE	ARM	WOMAN	NUT	STOOL	BOAT	LIGHT	
HOLE	ELBOW	PERSON	FRUIT	CHAIR	SHIP	DARK	

Primary Visual	Body Parts	Animate	Food etc.	Near	Objects	Larger Scale	Time Aspects
BIT	WRIST	PEOPLE	POTATO	TABLE	SAIL		NIGHT
PART	FINGER	ANIMAL	BUTTER	BED	NET		DAY
PIECE	THUMB	DOG	SUGAR	LAMP	MONEY		EARTH
THING	NAIL	CAT	SALT	POT			WOOD
SURFACE	LEG	BIRD	CORE	PAN	LARGER		SCALE
LAYER	FOOT	HEN	PEEL	DOOR	LAKE		
FRAME	TOES	SHEEP	NEAR OBJECTS	HANDLE	HOUSE		SAND
SHAPE	KNEE	COW	BOTTLE	KNOB	PATH		WAVE
FORM	SHIN	HORSE	CUP	WINDOW	ROAD		ISLAND
SIZE	THIGH	PIC	SPOON	CEILING	WAY		RIVER
LUMP	HEAD	FLY	FORK	WALL	STREET		
HEAP	NECK	BEE	KNIFE	FLOOR	ARCH		AUDITORY
PILE	HAIR	ANT	PLATE	ROOM	BRIDGE		THUNDER
BALL	CHIN	FROM	SAUCER	STAIRS	GARDEN		WINDS
BLOCK	CHEEK	WORM	SHOE	FIRE	FIELD		SOUND

THE PRIMITIVE VOCABULARY

SHAPES AND THINGS

Primary Visual	Body Parts	Animate	Food etc.	Near	Objects	Larger Scale	Time Aspects
POLE	FOREHEAD	SNAKE	SOCK	FLAME	TREE	VOICE	
TUBE	BEARD	CLAW	DRESS	COAL	GRASS	NAME	
BRICK	BODY	TAIL	COAT	ASH	FLOWER	WORD	
COLOUR	CHEST	HORN	SHIRT	STONE	PLANT	AIR	
SHADOW	BACK	FEATHER	HAT	SCISSORS	BRANCH		
SPACE	BELLY	FUR	CLOTHES	PAPER	STEM		
MIRROR	SKIN		BUTTON	BOOK	BERRY		
	BREAST		HOOK	PEN	SEED		
			PENCIL	ROOT			
			LEAF				

MOVEMENTS AND ACTIONS QUALITIES AND RELATIONS

Primary	Body Parts	Arm	Whole Body	Complex	Visual	Other	Relational	
IS	SUCK	HAVE	ACT	WORK	BRIGHT	HARD	TOP	ACROSS
MOVE	DRINK	HOLD	STAND	PLAY	DARK	SOFT	MIDDLE	THROUGH
CHANGE	BITE	TOUCH	SIT	MAKE	BLACK	SMOOTH	BOTTOM	AGAINST
BEGIN	EAT	STRETCH	LIE	WASH	WHITE	ROUGH	SIDE	OPPOSITE
END	LICK	KEEP	SLEEP	COOK	RED	STICKY	LEFT	PARALLEL
STOP	CHEW	LET	REST	SEW	GREEN	STRONG	RIGHT	SOME
START	BREATHE	PUSH	COME	COVER	YELLOW	WEAK	FRONT	SEVERAL
JOIN	BLOW	PULL	GO	READ	BLUE	STIFF	BACK	ONE
FLOW	SWELL	PUT	WALK	WRITE	GREY	LOOSE	BEHIND	TWO
SEE	YAWN	GRIP	RUN	DRAW	BROWN	SOLID	HERE	MANY
LOOK	SMILE	GRASP	SLIP	COPY	BIG	HEAVY	THERE	ALL
SEARCH	LAUGH	GET	FALL	SEND	SMALL	LIGHT	THIS	THE
FIND	SNEEZE	GIVE	STEP	LIKE	WIDE	DRY	THAT	A
SEARCH	LAUGH	GET	FALL	SEND	SMALL	LIGHT	THIS	THE
FIND	SNEEZE	GIVE	STEP	LIKE	WIDE	DRY	THAT	A
LOSE	COUGH	TAKE	JUMP	WANT	LONG	WET	NEAR	SAME
HEAR	KISS	CARRY	KICK	NEED	SHORT	HOT	FAR	LIKE
SMELL	CRY	BRING	SKIP	PAIN	NARROW	COLD	OVER	DIFFERENT
TASTE	CALL	LIFT	CLIMB	HURT	POINTED	SWEET	UNDER	ME
LISTEN	TALK	SHAKE	TURN	FEAR	THICK	SOUR	BETWEEN	YOU
	SAY	SPREAD	SWIM	TRY	THIN	BITTER	AMONG	HE
	TELL	FOLD	ROLL	WILL	BENT	LOUD	BY	SHE

MOVEMENTS AND ACTIONS QUALITIES AND RELATIONS

Primary	Body Parts	Arm	Whole Body	Complex	Visual	Other	Relational	
	SING	HIT	MEET	MAY	STRAIGHT	QUIET	WITH	IT
	SHOUT	THROW	LEAD	THINK	ROUND	SLOW	AND	WE
	SPEAK	TWIST	DRIVE	KNOW	FLAT	QUICK	OF	THEY
	ASK	RUB	FIGHT	LOVE	HOLLOW	STILL	IN	
		MIX	ATTACK	MUST	FULL	HUNGRY	ON	WHAT
		CRUSH	CATCH	CHOOSE	HIGH	TIRED	OUT	WHO
		BREAK	DROP		LOW	SICK	OFF	HOW
		SMASH	DANCE		DEEP	OLD	AT	WHY
		CRACK	WAIT		SHARP	YOUNG	ABOUT	
		SPLIT			CLEAN	GOOD	TO	
		PIERCE			DIRTY	BAD	FROM	
		PRICK					UP	
		CUT					DOWN	

The list described as the Primitive Vocabulary is, as has already been noted, only one among many possible primitive vocabularies though the proposition is that some primitive list of this kind is the starting point for every individual's acquisition of language. The presentation of a specific illustrative list of this kind, however, allows one to consider a number of points, to raise a number of questions:

1. Why should the particular words included in the list figure in it?
2. How is this concept of a primitive vocabulary related to other uses of semantic primitives, in a variety of fields of study?

3. What kind of internal structuring does a list of this kind display both in terms of meanings and in terms of the grammatical classifications of the words included in it?

4. How is a list of this kind related to the development of a child's repertoire of perceptual experience (and experience of action)?

5. By what processes can the field of application of words included in the list be extended?

6. More generally, what is the relation between a Primitive Vocabulary ('core' vocabulary) of this kind and the full vocabulary acquired by an adult, the full lexicon of a particular language?

7. What significance should be attached to the scope for the metaphorical use of words included in the Primitive Vocabulary or of other words subsequently added to form the adult lexicon?

8. In what sense can one treat words included in a Primitive Vocabulary of this kind as natural, that is as having a non-arbitrary relation between the sound-structure of the word and its meaning?

Selection of the five hundred or so words which figure in the illustrative Primitive Vocabulary has been guided by a number of principles. First of all, the essential qualification for inclusion of a word in the list is that it should not be possible for the meaning of the word to be understood by definition in terms of other words; though some broad indication of the meaning of one of the words may be given by using more evolved parts of an individual's vocabulary, the way in which a child learns the meaning of 'saucer', 'sit', 'finger' is by actual experience. Locke commented on the impossibility of indicating to a blind man the sensation associated with the word 'scarlet'; the nearest one might come to it, he thought, might be 'something like the sound of a trumpet', but this would still be far from understanding the concrete meaning in experience of 'scarlet'. Not all the words included in the Primitive Vocabulary are ones for which an object can be indicated by pointing, handling, hearing or smelling; some words are understood as associated with a particular facet of experience: 'bad' or a particular use of language: 'What?' No parent explains to a child 'This is what 'what' means'; or 'bad' is defined in the following way. The learning of words such as these is as much a part of the child's lived experience as its learning of the meaning of 'cat', 'chair', 'black' and so on.

There is nothing particularly new, of course, about an attempt to identify a restricted, primitive list of words, for linguistic research or other purposes. In

the investigation of unknown or little known languages, it is commonplace
for the field investigator to make use of a restricted basic vocabulary. For
example, the interesting work done by members of the Summer Institute
of Linguistics into the genetic relationship of groups of American Indian
languages Comparative Studies in Amerindian Languages (ed. Esther
Matteson et al 1972(10)) was based on restricted word-lists which, for the
different languages, ranged between 100 and 300 words. Morris Swadesh
(1972)(11), for work in support of glottochronological theory, used a
basic vocabulary list containing 100 words. The constructors of Basic
English(12) confined themselves to 850 words (including many words for
commercial applications which would not be suitable for a primitive list
of the kind with which the discussion in this chapter is concerned). In the
field of artificial intelligence, there has been intense discussion of the extent
to which knowledge structures can be built up from extremely limited lists
of semantic primitives. Yorick Wilks (1977)(13)proposed that some 100
semantic primitives would suffice; others, e.g. Roger Schank (1972)(14)
have made do with very much smaller numbers. An illustrative Primitive
Vocabulary containing nearly 500 words is thus of a respectable size and
may serve as a basis for useful discussion of some of the issues which have
been noted above.

The items included in a primitive vocabulary of this kind fall naturally into
a number of distinct categories; the list can be structured in various ways.
Most obviously, the words are divided between those referring to shapes
and things, movements and actions and qualities and relations. More
broadly, one might say that the items in the list divide into those which
are specifiable in spatial terms and those which are specifiable in terms
of time, and that relational words, as well as words relating to objects or
movements, can be referred primarily to space or time relations. Another
basis of structure of items in the list is the sensory modality with which a
word is primarily associated: things seen, heard, felt, tasted, smelled, felt
internally, and so on. Another basis of arrangement of items in the list is in
terms of the specific physical structures of which the items normally form
part or in which they are experienced, for example, parts of the body are
naturally grouped together as are movements of those body-parts, objects
found in a room or a house can be grouped together as can be objects in
the external landscape, whether the smaller-scale landscape of street and
neighbourhood or the larger landscape of field, wood, lake, sea and sky.
Objects can be classified in terms of their size or use as instruments, as

parts of sequences of activity or types of occupation, furniture, clothing, utensils. Against this wide variety of possibilities of classification of the items to which the words in the Primitive Vocabulary relate one can set the traditional groupings of grammar, the analysis into parts of speech, nouns, verbs, adjectives, prepositions, adverbs, pronouns; the traditional classification has a rather arid and academic air compared with the groupings and structuring of words in the Primitive Vocabulary given by experience. Though MOUTH may be classified as noun, DRINK as verb and SWEET as adjective, the real experiential grouping of the items is as part of one process for the child, for example, drinking a glass of milk or a cup of tea, and this sort of analysis is closer to that suggested by Fillmore(15) in his case grammar, to the concept of selection restrictions used in transformational grammar and to the frame approach suggested by Minsky(16) in artificial intelligence and Roger Schank's (1980) approach in terms of 'scripts', that is extended descriptions of the kinds of setting in which particular words are likely to figure. This issue, of the way in which the lexicon is naturally and operationally structured, as an aspect of the process of speech comprehension, is one to which it will be necessary to return later. It is of particular importance because the suggestion will be that the express or implicit structuring of items in the Primitive Vocabulary (and of the parallel items in the primitive repertoire of perceptual experience) is the foundation for the organic structuring of the total lexicon of any individual adult in the extreme, of the total lexicon of any given language. What is clear however at this stage is that the traditional analysis into parts of speech has only a rather distant relation to the natural structuring which the set of words in the Primitive Vocabulary displays; in English, the same word may readily serve as verb, noun or adjective; adverbs and prepositions are often only with difficulty distinguishable; parts of speech normally associated with distinctions of space are often used, with little complication, to refer to distinctions of time. Consideration of the practically effective structuring either of the primitive vocabulary or of the full lexicon will require a pretty radical reconsideration of the formal or real significance of traditional parts-of-speech categorisation.

Not much perhaps needs to be said about the relation between a child's primitive vocabulary and the development of the child's repertoire of perceptual experience, which has been the subject of such close study by Piaget and his assistants. The effective acquisition of a word by a child must proceed in step with the maturing of its sensorimotor capabilities and the meaning attached to a particular word may broaden or narrow as the child's experience of perception and action extends. Individual words may receive a wider extension: 'mother' (initially one person in a particular relation and to some extent itself a generalisation from the separate occasions on which the phenomena of 'Mother' manifest themselves) may gradually become a word referring' to 'mothers in general'; the mother of that other child as well as the mother of the individual child; there is a quite natural extension of a word from referring to one particular percept to referring to a class of similar percepts. 'Chair' may initially be one chair and later on 'any chair'. Words included in the Primitive Vocabulary are thus not all necessarily at the same level of concreteness or abstractness, particularity or generality. Apart from the implicit generalisation in each individual word, there may be words which are already classes of classes; e.g. 'colour' may refer to any of red, green &c and indeed the child may in fact acquire the word 'colour' as 'a set of colours', crayons, or a colouring book. Nor will the acquisition of words necessarily match that of the theoretical class-order. 'Clothes' as in bed-clothes or the child's own clothes may be a functioning item of experience, a usable word, before particular types of clothes, whether these are 'sheet', 'blanket', 'dress' and so on. The word 'fruit' and the experience 'fruit' may come before the acquisition of words for individual fruits. The schemes proposed in more abstract approaches to semantic features, the hierarchical ordering of words and concepts, may simply be irrelevant for the mode in which in fact a child, or an adult acquires the elements in his Primitive Vocabulary. The reality is that every word is an abstraction from the multiplicity and individuality of perceptual and action experience and acquisition of particular words may proceed, in temporal order, either from the more specific to the more general or from the more general to the more specific (as the entomologist, for example, proceeds from 'ant' and 'bee' in his primitive child's vocabulary to the hundreds of thousands of specifically distinguished ants and bees recognised in his professional career. Theoretical semantics so far has generally disregarded this vitally important aspect of the growth of the individual's semantic structure, his knowledge structure.

Some indication has already been given of how words forming part of an individual's primitive vocabulary can gradually and naturally acquire a wider range of application, as the individual's experience itself develops. Most simply, apart from extending the word 'chair' to apply to any chair rather than just one particular chair (that is to any item sharing some broad

extensive mapping of perceptual experience. Words originally applied to single percepts or actions can be applied to a range or class of percepts and actions; simple words can be applied to refer to structurally similar aspects of experience (a primitive form of metaphorical extension of the use of words). Words referring to percepts first experienced as objects can be used as indications of action, nouns converted into verbs or adjectives; there can, in English, be a rich grammatical extension in the application to experience of a range of words. By these simple processes, the range of perceptual experience covered by the words in the list can without difficulty be extended many times over, possibly by a factor of ten or even a hundred;

2. Still confining oneself to words in the illustrative Primitive Vocabulary, one can extend their range of application by the straightforward process of composition, by putting together two words in the primitive list, some new percept can be identified or some specialised variant of a known percept indicated. From the word LEG, one can form, with other words in the Primitive Vocabulary, a whole range of words: TABLELEG, CHAIRLEG—simply by combining words falling in the same broad category of shapes and objects. Even more extensive combinations can be derived from putting together words referring to objects and words referring to movement, action, quality or relation, e.g. BACKDOOR, BACKSTAIRS, BEDSIDE, CATCALL, OVERSEA, UNDERCOAT and so on; obviously a very large number of combinations and permutations of the words in the Primitive Vocabulary is possible;

3. Then there is the set of minor variations in word-form, part of the process normally described as derivation, which may allow each word in the Primitive Vocabulary to develop into a whole family of words; there is, in English, a large number of bound morphemes (which might well be included in their own right in the Primitive Vocabulary) which are highly productive in yielding new applications of meaning from existing words, for example, prefixes such as RE—or UN-, suffixes such as—ER,—NESS,—ING,—LESS. These bound morphemes may provide particular applications of words in the Primitive Vocabulary, mark changes in grammatical function, or in fact generate words with quite distinct meanings, where the relation to the earlier primitive meaning is more remote.

4. From the three types of process described, it is apparent already that from a Primitive Vocabulary of about 500 words, many thousands more words can be derived and that, for the most part, these new words and new applications will still be closely linked to the perceptual structuring underlying the categories into which the Primitive Vocabulary naturally divides. At a guess, something like 5000 or 10,000 words may be readily derived in these ways from the original 500. Perhaps even more important, the area of perceptual experience covered by the available vocabulary (restricted though it still is) is likely to have increased by a much larger factor still. This is still only a small way from the initial 500 words of the Primitive Vocabulary to a reasonably typical adult vocabulary (though the words available may already be adequate for the greater part of the language-communication needs of the typical member of the community).

5. The next major extension of the vocabulary (which may in fact of course proceed in parallel with the extension derived directly from the words of the illustrative Primitive Vocabulary) comes with the addition of what are essentially other Primitive Vocabulary word-forms, words related to discrete items of experience, which may be old and familiar or novel. All the words for birds, animals, fruit, trees, minerals, fish, insects, flowers come into the vocabulary as primitive elements. A camel, just as much as a cat or a dog, has to be seen before the word can become a functioning part of someone's vocabulary. Some of the names of animals may, in the Saussurean sense, be completely opaque, non-self-explanatory; others nay be apparently combinations of preexisting word forms, such as BLACKBIRD, even though the identification of the particular bird cannot be derived from the combination of the two apparently familiar words. At this stage in the continuing growth of the Primitive Vocabulary, we are still chiefly concerned with words not borrowed or deliberately introduced as learned terms into the English language, words which for the typical English-speaker are thought of as native. Note that in parallel to the expansion of the individual adult's Primitive Vocabulary (in the sense defined), there is also a continuing growth in the so-to-say collective Primitive Vocabulary of English, as new items of experience come to be named; even a word such as 'television' is thought of as primitive, an object of experience rather than a word understood by definition.

Insofar as the new items acquired are essentially extensions of the Primitive Vocabulary, they are not isolated but will find their place in the field-structure into which the Primitive Vocabulary divides; they will have a direct perceptual base and will not be learnable by the intermediation of other words i.e. it will still remain the case that experience of word and percept conjoined is essential, though extension of the perceptual repertoire can all the time, and will all the time tend to, proceed in advance of the corresponding extension of the lexicon in fact comprehended and usable by the individual.

6. How much progress then has now been made from the small initial vocabulary to the full adult vocabulary? or to the full English lexicon? Allowing for the application of processes of composition and derivation, the possible variations in grammatical use of individual words, it is now quite possible that the total available vocabulary may have reached something like 25,000 to 40,000 words or even more, certainly reasonable progress towards the typical adult vocabulary though still a long way short of the contents of any substantial English dictionary. The next great step forward in the size of the English vocabulary comes from a feature particularly marked in English as compared with most other languages, its extraordinary readiness as a historical fact to take in words from other languages (French, the Germanic languages, Latin, Greek) and often to naturalise them, to use them in parallel with or to supplement English words not far removed from them in meaning. Sometimes there is no English equivalent—the word TELEVISION has already been mentioned—but sometimes the words introduced seem almost duplicates of already available English words, so that the effect has been more to allow a finer discrimination of perceptual experience by the differentiation of the English and the foreign word. See for example the range of colour-words introduced from other languages. Some of the words borrowed into English in this way are, one may say, elements in the Primitive Vocabulary of the originating language; others, as borrowed into English, in every respect operate as primitive words e.g. one cannot know by definition the perceptual meaning of the word BEIGE. But where the borrowed words are not themselves primitive words in their original language, they will have been indirectly derived from the primitive vocabularies of the originating language. For example,

JUSTICE comes from a Latin primitive word JUS, INDECISION from a combination of Latin primitive words equivalent to UN-, OFF and CUT (IN DE CAEDERE). Meanings of derived words such as these in English are generally not primitive; their meaning can be explained by a string of simple English primitive words; the motive for their introduction into English often has been allow the compression into a single more concise form of a complex set of actions, percepts, events, relationships. Such words are for convenience rather than essential but they represent an extremely important new principle in the generation of the English lexicon, as compared with the development directly from the English primitive vocabulary. Such words survive because they are useful; no one, without a rather lengthy use of other words, could by immediate contemplation of a word such as MISDEMEANOUR, rather than a definition, arrive at a precise view of its meaning or use. The process by which the particular word MISDEMEANOUR becomes attached to a particular area of experience is complex, historically and intellectually, but no doubt it could plausibly be attributed to the operation of what the general semanticists would describe as their third principle, the self-reflexive potentialities of language, the creation of new words to refer to groupings or strings of existing words. One final comment on the significance of this type of borrowing for the expansion of the English lexicon: the driving force for the addition of words to the lexicon comes from the ever-growing extent of individual and collective perceptual and intellectual experience, the growth of knowledge in all its forms, science and technology, knowledge of the world and of societies. Perception for the individual and for the community is open-ended and language has to keep growing to match it.

7. Starting from the small initial Primitive Vocabulary of some 500 words, one has proceeded to a vocabulary of some 25,000 to 40,000 words by processes of derivation, composition &c applied to primitive English elements and beyond this one has an immense accession to the vocabulary from the introduction of words originating in the primitive vocabularies of other languages and from the application of composition, derivation, prefixation and suffixation to these words. And note that what has been borrowed from other languages includes not only particular simple or compound words but also word-elements, bound morphemes,

for manipulating thought, constructing scientific theories, evaluating literary forms, describing the subtleties of the human mind and character, elaborating philosophies and religions. These two great blocks of the lexicon, the more immediate perceptual block and the abstract block, are knitted together, organically related to one another through the absolutely basic neurological process of metaphorical transformation. Metaphor is not a linguistic device primarily but a perceptual device; it is the manner in which our perceptual system extracts from the multifarious patterns of reality analogies of structure, uniformities of organisation between things and events which may at first seem quite distinct. The metaphorical process as it operates uniformly to extend language and perceptual experience to match each other is only the last stage in the great hierarchy of physiological and neurological processes by which the eye and the ear, the visual and auditory apparatus and brain, extract from endless apparent diversity of form the definite, patterned persisting objects, sounds, events and actions from which our world is made. At the humblest level, the visual and neurological processes which from the endlessly varying appearances of any single visible object (at different angles, in different lights, in different positions and relations), the brain identifies this structure (and records it) as A CHAIR or A TREE (however many different sorts of chair or tree there may be), is the same category of process as that by which a political theorist identifies a persisting society, a lawyer the structure of a legal system, or a linguist the persisting inherent ordered structure of a language.

Most briefly, the metaphorical process (of language and perception) unites the Primitive Vocabulary and the total lexicon, the primitive perceptual repertoire and the total range of human experience.

The natural origin of individual words in the extended Primitive Vocabulary

The first part of this Chapter has discussed how what is described as the Primitive Vocabulary (that is: words whose meanings can be acquired only from perceptual experience and not by definition in terms of other words) forms the core of the total English lexicon and communicates a specific structure to the total lexicon, reflecting the origin of words as sound-forms matching the familiar features of experience, the different aspects of human behaviour in action, perception and language. So far, the chapter has argued that on the largest scale, the lexicon is structured by the physiologically and neurologically derived features of actin, perception and language. The present, second part of the chapter complements the first part by presenting an account of the way in which the sound-structure of each individual word in the extended Primitive Vocabulary gives either a direct representation of the percept or action referred to or at least a helpful clue or cue to the meaning of the particular word, the contention being (as set out in Chapter III) that there are necessarily direct physiological and neurological relations between the patterning underlying action, perception and articulation and that the combination of elementary sounds to form a particular word derives from and represents the elements in visual processing or in action which go to form a perceptual contour or a contour of action related to the meaning of the word. The final section of this Part of the Chapter demonstrates specifically in relation to a variety of words drawn from the illustrative Primitive Vocabulary on page 61, the exact manner in which the sound-structure of the word and the visual or action contour of the percept, action or event are related.

However, before these specific illustrations of the links between individual words and associated visual or action contours can be presented, there is an important intermediate stage. At the end of Chapter III, a scheme of equivalences between the elementary units of vision, action and speech was set out, that is the isolated elements in each modality. But the words we may have to deal with related to complete percepts, distinct actions, defined shapes and objects. One has to bridge the gap between the presentation of the elementary units (the individual sounds &c) and the formation of groups of elementary sounds into words, groups of visual elements into shapes. and elements of bodily action into complete types of action. At one stage Saussure(20) spoke about the need at some future time for a new science of combinatorics, the principles on which elements can be formed into larger unities, and it is precisely this which has to be tackled in the present part of this Chapter. The matter is one of great difficulty: in vision research, progress in pattern-recognition and the construction of patterns from elementary visual features has made less progress than was at one time hoped for; in speech research, whilst there has been intense research in phonetics (the isolable elements of speech-sound) there has been much less attention devoted to the principles of the combination of phonemes, the merging of phonemes into the integrated structure of the word; in relation to the organisation of bodily action, the position if anything, is even less encouraging. In Chapter III, Karl Lashley's(21) pessimistic assessment of the progress made in the syntactic analysis of action, of voluntary movement, was quoted and much less is known than one would wish about the manner in which the intention to perform a bodily action is translated into the actual physical action.

Nevertheless, an attempt must be made to tackle these difficult matters. The order in which they are treated is the same as that adopted in Chapter III, that is first the construction of visual forms from elementary visual units, secondly the formation of more complex actions from the elementary units of bodily action and thirdly the formation of individual words from the combination of the elementary speech-sounds (the phonemes). The construction of visual forms

This section considers the basis on which in perception the visual system extracts from the light falling on the retina particular shapes, forms and objects, as a second stage building on the initial identification in perception of the isolable elementary visual units discussed in Chapter III. The whole subject is extremely complex and no definitive results have yet been reached in the massive research programme which has been under way for many years. There are some preliminary points which can usefully be made, however:

1. The concern of this section of the Chapter is not with the general organisation of the visual field (the classic analysis by the Gestalt psychologists &c of the division of the perceived scene, by semi-automatic processes, into Figure and Ground, the total-field characteristics which the visual constancies of size, shape, depth, colour &c seem to derive from or the interrelation of distinct items in the visual field. These are matters more relevant for the comparison of 'visual scene' and 'sentence-structure' which is dealt with in the immediately following Chapter V. The emphasis is on the individual visual shape, from the point of view not so much of its recognition in practical experience but of the manner in which the individual shape is formed, derives its structure from more elementary units. This emphasis is chosen because the comparison of critical interest is with the overall structure of the word, the sound structure formed from elementary sound-units (and again not primarily with the recognition of the word in the complex, always abnormal conditions of ordinary speech);

2. So far the problem of shape recognition in ordinary vision has remained unsolved, though there have of course been a number of theories, not least those stimulated by Hubel and Wiesel's discovery of receptive cells in the visual cortex which respond selectively to various stimuli (as more fully described in Chapter III). As has already been noted, it is still a far cry from the elementary ability to respond to specific elementary contour elements (the elementary visual units) to mechanisms that can learn to classify shapes such as tables and chairs, according to complex properties for which one cannot expect innate detectors to have developed during evolution. However, a great deal of work is in progress, not only in the field of the physiological bases of vision but in that of pattern-recognition, machine-vision, in the field of artificial intelligence and useful clues towards the way in which shape-construction and shape-recognition may operate are gradually being gathered;

3. There is no reason to believe that there is any single, unchanging mode of construction and recognition of visual shapes either throughout the life of the individual, from infant to adult, or necessarily between one adult and another. There seems every reason for assuming that the visual apparatus will exploit. all the modes of shape exploration that are open to it, and the overlap and redundancy between different modes will offer real benefits: in terms of the reliability of perception, the accuracy of perception under distorted or difficult conditions and so on. If there are several ways of forming a view of what a particular shape represents, the chances that the shape will be correctly identified will be substantially increased and the effectiveness of perception, as an instrument serving the organisation of action, correspondingly increased; it is possible that in the development of perceptual experience, there can be a move from initial reliance on the identification of specific elementary visual units to form percepts towards use of much more shortcut methods when familiar percepts have become stored and labelled by words in the central nervous system. In this way, a new much more rapid process of recognition is made available to the adult than is available to the infant or child. In much the same way, whilst a child, in reading, may first identify a word by taking each letter separately, the adult reader learns to recognise whole word-shapes, and so makes possible very much greater reading speeds;

4. What at a minimum seems clear, as a result of research into the perception of visual shapes, is that there are two vital elements. The first is that visual perception is an intensely active process, depending on the construction of particular percepts from unceasing movement of the eyes, in saccades and fixations, pursuit and search movements of the eyes, movement of the eyes in accommodation by adjustment of the ciliary muscles, and change in direction of gaze as a result of co-ordinated movements of the head. As Lashley said: "I have come to feel that the problem of scanning underlies many other problems of neurophysiology. Visual perceptions are rarely based upon a momentary stimulation of the fixed retina . . . most of our perception of objects is derived from a succession of scanning movements, the succession of retinal images being translated into a single impression of form."(21) Neisser, after quoting these remarks, commented that this act of translation of a succession of 'snapshots' into a single form has hardly ever been studied but is evidently among the most fundamental cognitive processes so that, under normal conditions, visual perception is an eminently constructive act: "The individual snapshots are remembered only in the way that the words of a sentence are remembered when you recollect nothing but its meaning: they have contributed something which endures"(22)). The second vital element in the perception of visual forms is the profound preoccupation of the visual system with the contours of visual shapes which suggests that contours play a special part in shape recognition (and hence in shape construction). Children gradually develop the ability to follow contours, and contours retain their importance in the recognition of novel shapes throughout adult life.

After these rather extensive preliminary comments, the reader may look for a systematic statement of the accepted processes of shape construction and recognition by the visual apparatus. No such generally accepted account exists but it may be right here to quote one of the more interesting, and ambitious, accounts of the process of visual shape perception, that in Sommerhoff's wide-ranging book Logic of the Living Brain(23) from which some of the preliminary material above has already been drawn. The following outline of possible mechanisms for shape recognition (based on a tracking of contours, generally relying on central vision—that is the fixation of the perceived object in relation to the fovea) is drawn from him:

1. At the lowest level, we have the 'primary analyzers', the wired-in detectors; for particular contour features such as for bars in particular orientations, bars stopped at one end, angles &c. We cannot assume of course that the wired-in detectors discovered by Hubel and Wiesel are the only ones; there may be more complex analyzers not yet discovered. At some level of complexity, we must reach a point where a particular feature is no longer 'innately' detectable but requires visual exploration and learning;

2. For these higher levels of complexity, learning processes are required which, initially at any rate, depend on the outcomes of exploratory activities such as contour-following. To pass from knowledge of the salient contour features or elements of a shape to knowledge of the shape as such we need knowledge of the spatial relations between these features or elements. On the reafference principle (that is: the process by which the visual apparatus derives information from its own self-generated movements), the brain can factor out information regarding the spatial relation between particular contour elements by moving the eyes from contour element to contour element while registering at the same time the nature of the eye-movements required. It can do this either by scanning the contour elements in their proper serial order (contour-following) or by jumping haphazardly from salient element to salient element. Either method would yield the required information. To register the outcome of these movements is in effect to compile a list of the characteristic properties of the contours in question, that is of the shape formed. The movement information required could be derived either directly from the oculomotor apparatus (movement of the eyes &c) or from corresponding internal attentional processes.

3. In continuous contour-following, the characteristics of the contour are represented by a family of permitted eye-movements; this representation is invariant in respect to the translation of the object within the visual field. And indeed if only the relative directions and relative magnitudes of the movements were registered by the brain, the resulting representation would also be invariant with respect to the size and orientation of the image i.e. a process by which one would arrive at the record of a constant visual percept (somewhat analogous to the lines of constant orientation (though varying retinal position) identified by Hubel and Wiesel's complex cells in the visual cortex). It perhaps ought to be noted here that

'contour-following' itself is not a smooth process; it proceeds by a series of jumps, saccades, from one point of fixation to the next, and the record of a shape derived from contour-following would thus take the form of a succession of these irregular eye-movements in straight lines from one point to another.

4. Given a sufficiently comprehensive exploration of the shape by the eye, the aggregate of the registrations of the eye-movements forms an adequate neural basis for categorising the shape according to the mutual relations between the continually recognisable elements (lines, curves, angles, terminations etc.). It is difficult to see why the brain should not avail itself of such records. The attentional responses with which we inspect one portion of a stimulus after another must take a form which corresponds to the shape and other attributes of the object. Internalised versions of these responses could therefore serve as bases for the internal representation of the objects.

5. If, as perceptual learning progresses, a sufficient sample of these classifying outputs can become conditioned to any particular projections of the shape, then the mere occurrence of that projection in due course permits instant recognition of the shape i.e. recognition without prior exploration (in the same way as wired-in detectors for elementary units such as straight lines allow their instant recognition by the young animal). The system as it stands eventually permits the shape in any projection experienced during learning to trigger a characteristic set of expectations about what stimulus the fovea of the eye will receive following any one of a number of possible movements of the eye. The complete set of these shape-expectations constitutes the 'model' that is activated in the separation of the figure from the ground and the act of recognition (and in the associated act of naming of the perceived object).

The above account, drawn from Sommerhoff, is unavoidably somewhat complex and it may be helpful to summarise at this point what seem to be some of the points of more direct relevance for the hypothesis being presented in this Chapter, that is, the direct structural relation between visual shapes, word-forms and action-contours. Contours are very important for recognising shapes and initially shapes appear to be recognised by the elementary features they contain and the eye-movements involved in transition from one elementary feature to another;

a. recognition of a shape (in visual search) seems, as Lashley says, to involve readiness to recognise a motor sequence, starting from some line or angle in the picture and then scanning adjacent lines. Eye-movement and shape-perception seem to be interlocked, mutually dependent processes; one might say that we perceive visual shapes through movements of the oculomotor apparatus, the eyes, the turning of the head, the adjustment of the ciliary muscles for focusing; the interaction between movement and perception seems to remain reciprocal;

b. the key question is how the succession of retinal images resulting from scanning is converted into a single stable impression of form. The structure of percepts at first appears to be formed from the elementary visual units but these units may be assembled into higher-level sub-groups. What seems to be involved is both an elementary feature-detection system for shape-recognition (as used in some computer programs for vision) and, at a later stage in human development, with perceptual learning, a 'template' or 'schema' matching system, with which can be associated the permanent labelling of visual shapes and objects provided by word-forms.

Looking ahead to the section of this part of the Chapter dealing with the formation of words from elementary speech-sounds, one can relate the discussion to the vital importance of the contour of the word-shape, formed from elementary units of speech-sounds, parallel to the elementary units of vision, and chained together into a more complex structure by the succession of movements of the articulatory organs necessary for the production of the word, the characteristic pattern of movements identifying the stable word as the characteristic pattern of eye-movements identifies the stable visual shape. In parallel to the visual template or 'schema' developed for familiar shapes and objects, one has auditory and articulatory 'templates' and 'schemas' for familiar words. For both vision and speech, there is a parallel progression, by hierarchical stages, from the simplest to the most complex forms.

The construction of action-forms

Chapter III attempted to identify the elementary units from which more complex forms of visual shape, action and speech-forms are constructed. The immediately preceding section of this Chapter has attempted to give

so much in terms of the acoustic trace but in terms of patterning at the level of the neuromuscular system controlling the distinct articulation of different phonemes, and providing for the integration into smooth sequences of (permitted) combinations of phonemes. The argument will be that the constraints on the formation of word-structures from particular combinations of phonemes which are as a practical matter observed in English are not accidental or conventional but reflect underlying biases and constraints on the combination of articulatory movements, and at a higher level on the patterning of neural commands for words. Whether or not speech is comprehended by a kind of reverse process to that for speech-production as Liberman suggests with a good deal of plausibility, the form of words actually available in a language must depend on the permissible combinations and permutations of the required adjustments of the articulatory organs (and there may be neurological as well as anatomical factors which bias any particular language towards the use of one set of phonemes rather than another or towards the use or avoidance of particular combinations of phonemes in forming the words of the language.

In a sense the problem of speech recognition, speech comprehension, is a quite different one from and much less fundamental than that of speech production, the formation of phonemes into word-structures. Speech becomes audible because of the impact of the variation in the air-stream from the lungs (as modIfied by adjustments of the vocal tract) on the pressure-patterns in the external air, the medium of distance-communication, but the acoustic patterns in the air so produced are, to speak in a rather extreme way, simply a by-product of the "controlled gestures of the vocal organs"(27) (Ladefoged's phrase) by which speech is produced, physiologically and neurologically; the events taking place in the individual are the sequencing of the neural impulses to the muscles which control the shape and movement of the various elements which go to form the bodily speech-apparatus, There is an essential identity of central nervous control of speech-movements and other types of voluntary movement. It is a reasonable hypothesis that the production of speech involves sequences of movements similar to those of rapid typing, or playing the piano. If one takes this essential identity to its logical extreme, one could in fact analyse the production of speech, the control and patterning of movements of the articulatory organs, simply as one sub-species of the general problem of the neural and muscular control of voluntary movement of all kinds, a sub-division of what I have earlier described as 'action-organisation' as a part of total human behaviour.

Approached in this way, the analysis of the formation of word-structures from the elementary units of speech-sound (that is the phonemes as representing unitary organisations of positions and movements of the articulatory organs) can readily proceed in parallel with much of what has already been said about the formation of visual shapes from elementary units and action-routines from elementary units of bodily action (the unit movements of the mobile parts of the body). The concept of contour is just as important and informative for considering word-formation as it is for the formation of visual shapes or action-routines; others have noted the profound preoccupation of the auditory system with articulatory contours—and one might link this with what Brain(28), in a general discussion of the relation of physiological speech mechanisms and the aphasias referred to as the tendency for the system to operate with what (following Head and Holmes) he termed 'schemas' not only auditory phoneme-schemas but also central word-schemas, word-meaning schemas, sentence-schemas and motor phoneme-schemas. What is in vision constituted by the formation of contour-elements into unique discriminable patterns is in speech formed into unique discriminable articulatory patterns (with speech comprehension as a process of 'breaking the code" which the translation of successive phonemes into acoustic variations represents).

When phonemes are linked together to constitute a word, this process is more than a simple addition: a word constitutes a unity or pattern at a higher level of organisation, with Head's word-schema playing the same part in the recognition of the word as the phoneme-schema does in the recognition of the phoneme. A word is perceived as a whole which is something different from the sum of its parts. The relation of invariance for words and phonemes, derived from the unique patterning of articulatory movement, the ideal form which may be translated in varying ways depending on the immediate circumstances of the position of the articulatory organs and general anatomical factors varying from individual to individual, is no different in character from the invariance for visual shapes derived in some such way as that suggested by Sommerhoff, as described in the earlier section of this chapter, from the elementary information provided about the sequences of movements of the eye-muscles in tracing contours and identifying elementary features.

The recognition of the word (or phrase) in continuous speech-sound and of the simple or complex object in the stream of visual stimuli seems to involve the same problems and require some of the same solutions; in each case, some version of the Figure/Ground mechanisms seems to operate, with a known form being brought sharply out by enhanced contrast from the background, remembering that in the case of heard speech-sound, the word has to be detached, isolated, not only from other words, other patterning of speech-sound, but also from ancillary sound (dialect, emphatic and attitudinal variations) and more generally, from the whole flow of non—speech sound in progress at any moment. The word-object has to be identified in the 'auditory scene' (that is the total play of sound of all kinds on the basilar membrane of the ear at any one time) in the same way as the visual shape-object has to be identified in the visual stream playing on the retina. The fact that instrumental acoustic research shows that neither the phoneme nor the word is necessarily identifiable by segmentation or distinct markers in the acoustic record (in terms of frequency or intensity) is really no more surprising than if one recorded similarly the equivalent components of the light-stream, the intensity and frequency of the dots of light, and found that there was no mechanical operation of segmentation which allowed one directly to identify the diversity of objects represented in the stream. Acoustic research has shown simultaneous cueing (multiplexing) for phonemic and syllabic features and clearly the phenomena of figure and ground, the visual constancies, indicate that there can be simultaneous cueing for distinct aspects of the visual scene.

In the case of both speech recognition and visual perception, there clearly must be elaborate decoding processes, to recover from the crude acoustic and visual stimuli the structures from which they were originally derived, in the speaker or in the objects from which light has been reflected. The subtleties of the process of decoding, certainly in the case of speech, appear to be very considerable, though substantial progress has been made in identifying them. A great deal of this work has been done by Liberman(29) and his associates at the Haskins Laboratories. Given the inexplicitness of the acoustic record, the listener appears to use the inconstant sound as a basis for finding his way back to the articulatory gestures that produced it, and thence, as it were, to the speaker's intent. Perception depends on inferences unconsciously drawn about the originating patterns of articulation. Indeed, it has been suggested that in the same way as the eyes are used to scan a visual scene, to extract information from the periodic fixations on salient points, so the hearer's articulatory apparatus in some way is used as a basis for scanning the information provided in the sound-stream. In the process of decoding; as Liberman(30) pointed out at the 1975 New York Conference, silence may be as indicative as sound; the gap in the acoustic record for the stop consonant because it provides information that a total closure of the vocal tract was made necessary for the production of the stop consonant, and the hearer has in this way been given his clue to the articulatory patterning of the speaker. Variations in acoustic shape may not simply indicate presence or absence of phonemes or syllabic fragments but encode the order of phonemes to allow one to distinguish e.g. the word DAB from the word BAD.

There has been some direct evidence of the invariance of the phoneme (and beyond that of the invariance of the word) in terms of articulatory patterning from electromyographical research techniques. Liberman recorded that when two adjacent phonemes were produced by spatially separate groups of muscles, there were essentially invariant tracings in neural signals to the muscles (the EMG record) from the characteristic articulatory gestures for each phoneme, regardless of the identity of the other. When the temporarily overlapping articulatory gestures for successive phonemes involved more or less adjacent muscles that controlled the same structures, they found essentially identical EMG signals for the initial consonant but the EMG signal for the following phoneme involving the same feature of the articulatory structure might show substantial changes from its characteristic form. In the onsets and offsets of EMG activity in various muscles, the researchers found a segmentation like that of the several dimensions that constitute the phoneme i.e. one could find in the neuromuscular record where the phoneme boundaries must be, a matching of the contour of a word from a succession of phonemes, in a way quite unlike that found in the acoustic record. This seems clear evidence of the fundamental relation between word-structure form and the sequencing of articulatory movements, that is a relation between the word as a unit in speech and the action-routine in bodily movement as a sequencing of changes in the muscles involved in any particular bodily action. But the fact that in each case the combination of individual elementary patterns of muscle-movement is bound to alter the specific expression of the pattern in the sequence so that B at the end of a word is formed differently from B at the beginning of a word, or a grasping movement with the arm stretched out may be realised differently from a grasping movement with the arm contracted, does not in any way run counter to the basic hypothesis that complex actions or complex speech forms are built up from a flexible and smoothly integrated set of elementary units, initial patterns of articulation or bodily action, in much the same way as, in the Hubel and Wiesel approach, complex visual forms may be built up hierarchically from elementary visual units, invariant elementary visual patterns.

This Part of the present Chapter has set out to explain how it is possible and plausible that, quite apart from unity of structuring given to the Primitive Vocabulary, and beyond that to the total lexicon by the origin of the word/meaning relation in the fundamental characteristics of human behaviour, human perception and human action, the individual words in the extended Primitive Vocabulary, the structures formed from the elementary speech-sounds, can have a natural origin, a natural relation between the sound and the meaning of the word because of the underlying physiological and neurological parallelisms between the processes of visual perception, bodily action and speech. The chapter will conclude with a detailed presentation of the manner in which the sound-structure of a variety of words selected from the Primitive Vocabulary indicates in one or another way real features of the percepts, actions or qualities to which the words relate. Before this detailed presentation, it will be useful to sum up exactly what seems to emerge about the parallelisms and relationships of the physiological and neurological processes of vision, action and speech from the three sections of the chapter just completed dealing respectively with the construction of visual forms, the construction of action-forms and the construction of word—forms. The important points (which contribute both to establishing the plausibility of the equivalences between word-form, visual contour and action-contour presented in the concluding section of the Chapter and to explaining how such equivalence can be possible) can be listed as:

I.   The mode of construction of a form, whether a visual shape, an action-routine or a word-form, is a quite separate matter from the research issue of how such forms are recognised when they are, typically, presented as part of a continuous stream of visual information, an unbroken sequence of activity or a continuous stream of speech-sound (or more generally of sound of all types). In a rather special sense (different from that used by Chomsky) one can distinguish between 'competence' in vision, action or speech, the elements and structures which make these faculties possible, and 'performance', that is the functioning of vision, action and speech in all the special circumstances of the real world, in conditions of obscurity, distortion or confusion.

II. Because one can postulate elementary units of vision, action and speech and the manner in which these elements might be formed into larger structures, visual shapes, action-routines, word-structures, this does not mean that throughout the individual's life, from infant to adult, the shapes perceived, the action-routines used or the words formulated must on each occasion be formed de novo from the elementary units. The growth of experience of vision, of action and of speech, clearly provides the individual with more efficient processes, with 'templates' and 'schemas'' representing more complex visual, action or speech-structures (no doubt represented in the cortex at some level higher than that so far reached by Hubel and Wiesel's researches), which can be used directly both to increase the speed and effectiveness of perception, to allow the more rapid construction of complex chains of actions and to form whole words directly into complex sentence-forms. For vision, action and speech, there is not a choice between a feature-detection (or a feature-construction) process from elementary units and a 'template-matching' scheme, for production or comprehension; vision, action and speech will use whatever methods are most efficient and best adapted to the circumstances of actual experience. A word, a visual shape or an action-routine, can in their turns be treated as whole units, to form even more complex structures;

III. What emerges from the detailed consideration of the processes underlying vision, action and speech is the overriding importance in behaviour of the organisation of movement, of the central co-ordination neurally of complex sequences of movements which may relate in a parallel way to movements of the eyes (the oculomotor apparatus) in seeing, to movements of the parts of the body and the body as a whole in the organisation of action or to movements of the vocal organs, the articulatory apparatus in speech. The highest level of control of bodily skill is now thought to be mediated by a set of motor schemas or motor programs that can be executed with a wide variety of initial positions of the muscles and organs involved and of the local environments. Vision, action and speech are all examples of highly skilled human activities, and the probability is very high that they are organised and executed in very similar ways, by neural structures which in their formation and manner of operation are closely similar. Everything points to a central role for the motor cortex, not only in relation to bodily action but also to visual perception and speech; and this coming together in the brain of the structures for planning complex action in these different forms provides a possible, and a probable, basis for the detailed interrelation between visual forms, action-forms and word-forms, which is the central hypothesis of this Chapter. Such a relation between patterning at the cortical level would allow one to understand how it is that the structure of visual shapes and action-routines, which everyone would accept as natural and not arbitrary in any sense, can he related to the structures of words, which traditionally have been thought to be wholly arbitrary, despite their inexplicably close relation in consciousness with the percepts and the actions to which they refer. Penfield has remarked that "the image of how to speak a word is really a pattern of the motor complex required to produce the word"(31) and in this precise fact one should look for the naturalness of language and for the appropriateness of the structure of the individual word for the meaning it has (the visual shape or object, the action-contour).

ANNEX TO CHAPTER IV

The structure of the illustrative Primitive Vocabulary in terms of the types of visual or action contours to which the word-structures are related; and examples for a selection of words from the Vocabulary of the specific relation between the particular word-structure and the particular associated visual or action contour

The earlier parts of this Chapter have described how the total English lexicon can plausibly be thought of as built from a Primitive Vocabulary of words known directly from the developing experience of the child or adult and not by way of explanation or definition in terms of other words. On page 61 a list was provided as an illustrative Primitive Vocabulary showing the kinds of words which might be acquired in this way. The second part of the chapter has attempted to describe how from elementary visual units, elementary units of action and elementary units of speech-sound, more complex forms are built up, visual shapes, action-routines and individual words, and has emphasised the physiological and neurological common elements underlying these processes of construction, for vision, action and speech so that it is plausible that there should be direct physiological and neurological relationships between the motor-patterns, the schemas, in the central nervous system, primarily the motor cortex, governing the production of the complex patternings of bodily movement (eye—movement, bodily action, articulation) which go to form the processes of visual perception, bodily action and speech. Chapter III had earlier proposed that this relationship, one of close equivalence, could be found at the most elementary level and at the end of Chapter III a table was presented, a scheme of detailed equivalences, between the visual units identified by Hubel and Wiesel, the elementary units of action of mobile parts of the body and the elementary speech-sounds (phonemes).

The purpose of this Annex is to bring together this general argument and evidence in a practical demonstration of the manner in which the appropriateness of individual words for their meaning, the naturalness of individual words, can be derived from the relation between their structure and the visual contours, the contours of action and other features of perception and action necessarily associated with the particular speech-sounds used and the order in which those sounds are arranged in the individual word.

This Annex does not set out to explain or justify in detail the particular way in which the sound-structures of the individual words give rise to or are associated with the particular visual or action contours which indicate their meaning. That is a lengthy matter which has been dealt with elsewhere. A careful explanation of the process by which elementary units of speech-sound are combined and matched with combinations of elementary units of bodily action or vision is contained in The Physical Foundation of Language (1973).

The Annex deals with two matters: first, it explains how the words in the Primitive Vocabulary (on page 61) can be classified in terms of visual or action contours associated with each of them, as a consequence of the particular sound-structure of the individual words, Secondly it sets out specifically for a substantial sample of words drawn from the Primitive Vocabulary the character of the visual or action contour associated with the particular word which constitutes the natural bond between the sound of the word and its meaning. Practical verification of the validity of the relationships for the individual words chosen is something that can only be taken a limited way at this point. The reader will have to rely on his own efforts to decide whether or not the relationships proposed for the individual words seem plausible and helpful.

Classification of the Primitive Vocabulary in terms of associated visual or action contours

The list on page 61 contains rather less than 500 words. The broad classes into which these are divided is already indicated in the list; beyond that, against each word there is a letter or letters set which refer to the particular type of action or visual contour associated with the sound-structure of the individual word. The following paragraphs describe more fully the meaning of these classifications and the general characteristics of the structure of the Primitive Vocabulary when one analyses it in terms of the number of words found in each class.

The first broad classification is into:

Shapes and Things
Primary Visual
Body Parts
Animate
Food etc.
Near Objects
Larger Scale
Auditory
Time aspects
Movements and actions
Primary
Movement of body parts
Arm actions
Whole body actions
Complex actions
Internal actions and states
Qualities and Relations
Visual Qualities
Other Qualities
Relational

Some notes on the interpretation of these categories may be helpful:

1. Primary visual includes words which seem to have a simple visual contour
2. Animate extends to include a few parts of animate creatures (the category body parts relates to parts of the human body)
3. Food &c includes a few parts of edible things
4. Near Objects consists largely of objects found within a room or within a house (though some items are classed here purely for convenience e.g. ship, boat, car)
5. Larger scale could be divided into two sub-categories, near landscape (things outside of but near to and on the scale of the house) and larger-scale landscape features
6. Auditory contains a few items where the mode of perception seems clearly to be auditory rather than visual
7. Time aspects this is a list which could be considerably extended but it is a difficult group which obviously needs further consideration
8. Movements and actions Most of the categories are self-explanatory. The list does (somewhat inconsistently) include a few stative verbs; where IS (AM or ARE) and similar verbs should be placed is a rather arbitrary decision
9. Complex actions These refer to actions involving instruments or specific external circumstances or goals
10. Internal actions and states It is arguable in several cases whether words in the list should be treated as referring to internal actions or internal states. Some could equally well be either (and a good deal of philosophical discussion has been devoted to the attempt to decide whether they are state or action)
11. Spatial qualities and relations These divide into positional and directional (mostly positional) but the distinction is not a clearcut one.

In terms of the numbers of words in each of the main categories, the analysis straightforwardly is as follows:

Primary Visual	33 words		
Body Parts	34		
Animate &c	32		
Food &c	17		
Near Objects	66		
Larger scale	40		
SHAPES AND THINGS			222 words

AUDITORY
7 words

TIME ASPECTS
8 words

Primary movement	17		
Movement of body parts	24		
Arm actions	34		
Whole body actions	30		
Complex actions	12		
Internal actions states	14		
MOVEMENTS AND ACTIONS			131 words

Visual qualities	32		
Other qualities		32	
All Qualities			64 words

Spatial relations			39
Other relations	22		
All relations			61 words

QUALITIES AND RELATIONS
125 words

TOTAL PRIMITIVE VOCABULARY   486 words

The above gives a broad first analysis of the composition of the illustrative Primitive Vocabulary in terms of the common-sense classifications into which the different words in the list on page 61 have been grouped. However, the reader will have noted that against each word in the list a letter or letters has been set, and these are intended to indicate more precisely the kind of visual or action contour (or other perceptual characteristic) associated with the sound-structure of each word. Taking a couple of obvious cases, the two words SUCK and LICK are put in the category of 'movement of body parts' and have the letter A marked against them; the A simply means that the kind of contour or action associated with the sound-structure of these words is straightforward bodily action. It seems self-evident that the words SUCK and LICK, by virtue of the sound-elements of which they are formed: and the way these sound-elements are in fact produced, are very closely associated with the actual actions of sucking and licking; if one says either of the words carefully and emphatically, one finds that in the very action of saying them, one comes very close to performing the specific actions which constitute the meanings of the words. Of course, for many of the words in the list, the relation between sound and action or visual contour is less immediately apparent and the letters set against each of the words are intended as a guide in each case to the associated effect.

The following shows the significance of the different markings placed against each word in the illustrative Primitive Vocabulary:

— V this means that there is a visual contour associated with the sound-element. going to form the word, which resembles or at least gives a cue or clue to the percept to which the word refers

— A Similarly this means that there is an action or action-contour associated with the sound-structure of the word. So, for SUCK, as already referred to, the marking is A because the action of sucking is clearly associated with the saying of the word

— P This means that there is a Pointing action directly associated with the saying of the word. This is, not surprisingly, the kind of action particularly associated with words referring to parts of the body: EYE EAR NOSE

— SH :This means that the action associated with the sound of the word is an actual showing of the part referred to. For example, the simplest indication of HAND is to hold up the hand, and the sound-structure of the word is associated with that action

— VP This indicates that the contour or action associated with the sound of the word combines visual and pointing elements, with the form first indicated V for visual, appearing to be the more important

— PV :This is the reverse of the previous mark, that is the Pointing element appears to be more important than the visual element in the associated contour or action

— S :This means that associated with the sound-elements going to form the particular word is a sound typical of the thing to which the word is related e.g. most obviously the word THUNDER has associated with it a sound imitating thunder

— SR this means that associated with the word-structure is a sound referring to the percept or thing to which the word relates e.g the word BEE has associated with it the sound of a bee buzzing (see for example BUMBLE-BEE and HUMBLE-BEE, clearly onomatopoeic word-formations in the traditional sense)

— AR Similarly this means the associated action refers to the percept or thing to which the word related. For example, associated with the sound-structure NEEDLE is not a contour indicating the shape of a needle but the action of a needle used in sewing

— PA This means that the associated contour or action for a word has both a primary Pointing element as well as more a general action element. In the case of HAT, for example, there is a combination of a pointing action with an action of putting on or taking off a hat

— VA This means that there is a combination of a visual contour associated with the word and an element of action. For example, the word FLOWER appears to have associated with it both an indication of the general shape of a flower and of the action of plucking a flower

— SV This means that there is a combination of a sound and a visual element associated with the word-structure. For example, SAND has a sound associated with it of the sea-shore (no doubt part of the typical effect of the fricative S) as well as an indication by a visual contour of an extent or surface

— CVS this means that there appears to be a complex contour or action associated with the sound-structure of the particular word and that this complex includes visual and sound elements. This seems to be the case for DOG and BIRD, and it would not be surprising that this should be so since both the visual contour of a dog or bird and the sound that each of them makes are obvious clues to the nature of the thing perceived.

— CSA Similarly this means that the complex contour or gesture includes sound and action elements. An example, again an unsurprising one, is the word HEN, where the sound element seems to be primary

— ASR This means that the contour or action has both action and sound elements which refer to the percept or thing to which the word-structure relates. So the word SNAKE has both an action element related to the movement of a snake and a sound element

(apparently deriving from what Firth described as the 'sibilant' phonetic quality of the initial S)

— I This means that the action or contour associated with the word refers to am internal state or activity. For example, the word BITTER has associated with it a mouth-action which relates to the reaction to a bitter taste

— PI This means that the action or contour associated with a word has both a pointing element and an internal state or activity which is referred to. For example, the word THINK has associated with it a Pointing to the head (a very familiar gesture) as well as an awareness of an internal state or activity

— IA This means that there is a combination of an internal state or activity and an external action, both represented in the sound-structure of the word. So LOVE has associated with it an internal state or activity and an external action of clasping or holding

— AI This means that the external action component seems to be more important than the internal state or activity. For example, in the case of the word CHOOSE, the external action seems to be one of picking between objects but there is also an internal awareness of the state or activity of choosing

— ? This means that so far applications of the equivalences and rules for the combination of elementary units described in the previous book has not made it possible to arrive at any plausible identification of the contour or action &c associated with the structure of the particular word.

Following this explanation of the significance of the markings placed against each word in the illustrative Primitive Vocabulary, it is possible to make a number of supplementary points:

1. The classifications in terms of the associated visual contour or action apply in the same way to all the words in the list, regardless of whether or not they would normally be treated in grammatical terms as nouns, adjectives, verbs, prepositions, adverbs or conjunctions, &c. So, the adjective HEAVY is marked AR—that is, the word has associated with it an action reference to the meaning of the word; similarly the noun PENCIL is also marked AR, again because it has an action associated with it referring to the use of a pencil (not

a visual contour of a pencil). Again, the preposition TO is marked PA, that is it combines a pointing element and an action element referring to movement in a direction, just as, already indicated, the noun HAT is marked PA because the word-structure contains both a Pointing and an action element.

2.   The main categories of contour or action associated with words in the list are clearly Visual, Pointing and Action with, not surprisingly, most of the V markings relating to Qualities and Shapes and Things, most of the P markings relating to body parts, prepositions and pronouns, and most of the A markings relating to movements and actions. But the divisions are by no means clear-cut. Some words with which one might, at first sight, expect to find associated visual contours. are, on examination, found to be indicated in other ways. For example, the sound-structure of FROG does not relate to a visual contour but to a combination of an action element and a sound element. The word HEAR has associated with it a pointing action, very similar to that associated with EAR. MEET as a word is marked VA, that is the word refers to a visual indication of meeting, not to an action.

3.   The small selection of words relating to Time are of particular interest. Some time-words have associated with them a pointing element, pointing forward or backward, an obvious transfer from spatial reference to temporal reference. Others seem to involve action referring to the meaning of the time-word e.g. NOW is marked AR and seems to involve an action with the arm moving sharply to point straight upward, as distinct from THEN, also marked AR, where the arm moves similarly but to point forward from the vertical. It is difficult to decide whether time-words should be marked P or AR; they seem to refer to a temporal frame of reference modelled on a one-dimensional spatial frame of reference, so that points in time are distributed along an imaginary line

4.   A small class of words, but an important one, is included in the list referring to internal states and activities. In these cases, it is not just an assumption that the sound-structures of the words make this kind of reference but it is proposed that the sound-structure of the words has a specific felt relation to the internal meaning of the words. Certainly this is likely to be the case for words referring to emotions which have associated with them changes of physical state e.g. SAD, GLAD, TIRED.

5. The class of interrogative words is somewhat difficult to categorise and they have been marked I?. Associated with words such as HOW WHY WHO seems to be a specific attitude, some particular internal state of organisation.

6. Also of interest, of course, are those words where so far it has not been possible to identify the contour, action, &c associated with the sound-structure of the word with any plausibility or confidence. Such words in the list include TIME SPACE COLOUR SHADOW SHAPE FORM SOON EARTH BY WITH AND OF AMONG IS, together with a miscellaneous collection of other more specific words DRY WET CLEAN DIRTY BEGIN LOSE WAIT BIT PIECE THING STOOL CHAIR CAR BOAT SOCK COAL ASH PAPER BUTTER SUGAR SALT SHEEP—with some more significant words such as MAN WOMAN BOY GIRL MOTHER FATHER BABY BROTHER SISTER ANIMAL. Perhaps most important of these are those words referring to family relationships &c, some of the functional words and some very general words TIME SPACE THING FORM SHAPE COLOUR. Further study is obviously needed of the possible implications of the sound-structures of these words.

7. Finally, in analysing the Primitive Vocabulary, it may be informative to sort out precisely how the words in the list divide up between the different categories of associated contour, action &c which have been identified above. Out of the 486 words in the list (including the doubtful cases), 128 refer to action as the sole element or an element in the natural character of the word, 132 to visual contour and 79 to pointing or showing the percept or thing referred to. If one adds together all the words where the sound-structure seems to indicate some form of action reference i.e. including items of pointing and showing, the total is 249, that is, more than half the words in the illustrative Primitive Vocabulary derive the naturalness of their meaning from some associated action, some reference to action. The corresponding figure for words where there is some kind of reference to visual contour is 144. Comparatively, words with some association with sound are rather few, 55 in total, and there are 26 words with some internal reference. From this analysis emerges the dominant role is played by action-patterns in determining the sound-structure of words found in the Primitive Vocabulary, and of course it must be remembered that even where a word is marked

as associated with a visual contour, that contour in fact is formed either by a movement of the eyes in scanning the percept or by a representation of the visual shape in terms of movement of the arm and hand. Examples drawn from the Primitive Vocabulary of the natural relation between the sound-structures of individual words and their meanings

Although the 500 or so words in the illustrative Primitive Vocabulary have been classified above in terms of the type of visual or action contour &c associated with the sound-structure þf each individual word, very little has so far been said about the specific character of the visual or action contour associated with the sound structure of individual words (though a few incidental examples have been given). This concluding section of the present Annex explains more specifically for a substantial sample of words drawn from the Primitive Vocabulary the form taken by the visual or action contour derived from the sound-structure of individual words and serving to indicate or give a clue or cue to the meaning of the particular word. The sample of words selected comes from the different main categories which have already been described, that is, words where the associated visual or action contour relates to action directly pointing to or showing, to visual shape, to internal activity or state, to sound directly, to time aspects or to complex combinations of visual, sound and action contours.

The sample of words selected in these different categories are:

WORDS CLASSIFIED BY CATEGORY

Action Complex	Pointing Showing	Visual	Internal Pointing	Sound	Time Aspects
YAWN	EAR	EDGE	THINK	THUNDER	NOW
LICK	HEAR	CIRCLE	KNOW	CALL	THEN
TOUCH	EYE	HEAP	ME	SPEAK	WHEN
PUT	I	CUP		CRACK	BEFORE
PUSH	HAND	HOOK		LAKE	
HIT	HAIR	LAMP		RAIN	
GO	THAT	ARCH		HEN	
SEW	THE	FALL		COW	
NEEDLE	A	WIDE		FIRE	
WORM	YOU	NARROW			
POINT	IT	THICK			
UP	THIN				
MEET	HIGH				
SAME	CLAW				
HAMMER	BOUGH				
BIRD					

The illustrations for the next two classes, Internal and Sound, are less obvious than the preceding ones:

Internal Pointing Words

THINK The external aspect of the action associated with the word, is the hand being drawn in so as nearly to touch the upper forehead with the fingers placed together (a very usual gesture for thinking). Besides this, there seems to be an internal state or activity associated with the sounds forming the word. The action associated with THING seems to be very similar—so perhaps a THING is something thought (see Latin REOR—think and RES—thing)

KNOW Very similar position of the hand, in relation to the head, to that for THINK, with a somewhat different Internal component

ME The hand points towards the mouth or face, with an accompanying internal feeling (which is not apparent for I)

Sound words

THUNDER This has associated with it the making of a sound clearly meant to imitate the sound of thunder. See other straightforwardly onomatopoeic words such as DING DONG, BANG, WHIZZ (and onomatopoeic words for THUNDER in other languages eg. Malay GUNTOR)

CALL This involves stretching the arm forward and outward with the sound of a call (some relation to a clearly onomatopoeic word like CAW)

SPEAK Again the stretching of the hands forward is accompanied by voice-sound

CRACK This is a combination of an action (of breaking something) with a flat sound, like SMASH

Time aspects

NOW This is associated with a short upward movement of the hand indicating spatially a time-concept

THEN A movement similar to that associated with THERE but a shorter, forward indicating movement

WHEN A more emphatic movement than for THEN, apparently with some characteristic internal aspect, aspect of feeling, similar to that for other interrogative words

BEFORE A forward indicatory action, again as a result of transfer of reference from spatial position to temporal position

Complex words

BIRD Largely a sound-word but there is also an element of visual indication, perhaps of movement of the wings

HEN This seems to combine an indication of the characteristic sound made by a hen with action reflecting the equally characteristic movement of a hen

FIRE This combines an indication of the rushing sound of a fire, with an indication of flames rising

LAKE This combines an indication of an extent or stretch of space (of water) with some sound of wind, over water

RAIN This combines an indication of the sound of raindrops, with some visual indication of the lines of rain falling.

NB: It is much harder to be sure about the actions and shapes associated with the complex words in the Primitive Vocabulary, to describe them satisfactorily or to indicate clearly how the actions, sounds &c are formed as a result of the structure. of the words—but the broad indications given above seem, as an empirical matter, reasonably reliable. There is a whole field of study to be explored of how speech-sounds indicate or model but do not imitate obviously and simply types of sound other than speech-sounds. Many names of birds appear to indicate, in the sound-structure of the words, the characteristic cry or call of the bird—but not through direct imitation which would involve using types of sound outside the accepted range of human speech-sounds, that is the available set of phonemes.

Chapter V

Sentences Visual Scenes
and Complex Actions

The initial hypothesis of this book, as set out in Chapter II, was that there is an extremely close and necessary relationship between action-organisation in the human individual, perception and language—and that this integration, physiologically and neurologically, should be manifest at every level, from the Stage I of the elementary units of action, vision and speech, through the more extended forms represented by action-routines, visual shapes and word-structures in Stage II, on to the complexity of the sentence, the visual scene and the complete action in Stage III, dealt with in this Chapter—and of course beyond that to the unending, continuous fully integrated stream of behaviour, activity, perception and speech, that constitutes the normal life of the human being. Chapter III attempted to identify the elementary units in this hierarchical system, and Chapter IV described how these elementary units might be combined into more extended forms, and in particular how words are fully natural in two senses, both in the structure of the sound-elements of which they are composed and in the mode by which the vocabulary, the lexicon, both of an individual and of a language, is built up from the Primitive Vocabulary and the primitive perceptual repertoire, those things which can be learnt only in experience, and which, by their inherent structuring, in reality and through the vital process of metaphorical transformation, go to serve as the basis for massive extension of the English lexicon beyond the concrete to the whole realm of abstract language, used for the highest flights of human thought and creativity.

At this stage, in the process of tracing the interlinking of action, perception and language, the task becomes more difficult because the complexity of the material grows geometrically rather than arithmetically. The combination of the thousands of available words into sentences must be a more difficult matter to analyse than the combination of a few elementary visual units into some simple shapes, or 30 or 40 speech-sounds (phonemes) into the available individual words. If 30 or 40 different elementary speech-sounds in this or other languages can make in practice half a million or a million words in English (and an unthinkably large number of distinct words if one considers together all the languages of the world), what kind of scale can one apply to the combinations and permutations available of the total mass of words? Chomsky and others have argued that a characteristic feature of language is that it is open-ended, generative, and this is true in the sense that human experience, perception and action, is endless in the forms it can take, the sequences that can be created; language, the mass of the words and the organising rules of syntax taken together, has its role in its ability to keep pace with this huge growth of experience; language has to be such that, as the general semanticists would say, it is capable of mapping an empirical and intellectual terrain that is forever growing more extended and more complex.

How then, at Stage III in the examination of the hierarchical development of action, perception and language, can one best tackle this overwhelming complexity? Linguists and others have applied simplifying approaches; some have simply ignored in practice the prime feature of language, that its purpose is meaning and that it should be directly relatable to the lived world; they have concentrated on the arid bones of syntax in a traditional sense—sought to modernise the ancient, traditional formulations of grammar and give them a more modish, modern dress. Others—philosophers—have on their side abandoned the attempt to see the central, total role of language in thought and philosophy and have concentrated on attempting to clear minor areas of the conceptual jungle, the natural language approach to the analysis of the use of individual words. Some of those who have, at the linguistic or philosophical level, concentrated on semantics have even said that syntax is 'dead' as a subject—but they are as wrong as those who say that nothing but syntax matters. Language, as it functions, unavoidably and awkwardly for those who would like some simple theory, depends on the union, the interpenetration, of syntax and semantics (in the framework provided by the acoustic and auditory expression of the language-medium).

The approach in the present chapter is guided by the following principles or positions:

I In an article under the title' "Scientific perspectives and philosophical deadends in modern linguistics" Luria (one of the most distinguished Soviet researchers into language and thought) said: "We must look for the roots of basic linguistic structures in the relations between the active subject and reality and not in the mind itself. Language is thus a system of codes used to express the relations of the subject with the outside world."(1)

Somewhat similarly, George Lakoff in "Some Remarks on Artificial Intelligence and Linguistics" said that assumptions of current linguistics which now seemed to him wrong were that "we can speak of the 'language faculty', an autonomous entity, independent of sensorimotor and cognitive development, perception, memory, attention, social interaction, personality and other aspects of experience" . . . and that "linguistic structure is independent of linguistic function"(2). The view in this book (developed in this Chapter in relation to the sentence) is that the structure and functioning of the sentence have a natural or semi-natural origin, as have words and phonemes; that this natural origin is to be found in the structures and functioning of other human behavioural systems, specifically those for perception and action—and that the study of the interrelationship of the structures and processes underlying language, vision and action can help one to understand not only how language functions but also perhaps to some extent how vision and action are organised (since their organisation is reflected in the organisation of language).

II Obviously, as has already be on noted (and one can refer back again to the remarks of Miller and Johnson Laird on the linking of words and percepts to the whole conceptual structure) there are unmeasurable complexities involved when in effect the whole meaning-structure of the individual, his whole knowledge-structure, has to be brought into a specific relation with his ongoing experience (the union of the temporal order, in the syntax of vision, action and speech) and of the simultaneous' many-dimensional structure into which his action-skills, perceptual experience of the world, his lexicon of words and meanings, are formed). But one must find some thread for winding one's way through the labyrinth of grammatical forms, syntax, morphology, semantic structure, the illocutionary and performative functions of speech, and so on. The vital thread to hang on to is the understanding that action, vision and language are biologically, and evolutionarily unified—and that the structures of language take the forms they do because language must serve the needs of action and perception. This is a view close to that expressed by Malinowski(3) and, following him, by Michael Halliday(4); for them, using language is itself an action, like other actions; language is multifunctional: in its structure it mirrors the real categories derived from the practical uses of the child and 'the primitive man' (though I would prefer to refer to the 'primitive elements in language').

III The working hypothesis is that the structure of a sentence must be related in a definite way to the structure of an action, of an intended action, of a perception of a scene or action, or even of the perception of language itself (as used by oneself or by others to reflect or encode action and perception). What is given in the sentence is a collection of words drawn from the total lexicon, together with some specific grouping and ordering of those particular words—that is: in the sentence one is given what Chomsky would describe as the surface structure. The surface structure is a fact; the nature of any underlying deeper structure is a theory or a supposition. Surface grammar is concerned with the evidence of language (spoken or written) as it is—and no deep grammar which is not transformable into the surface-grammar and which does not allow a systematic presentation of the characteristics of surface-grammar can be worth much: it is the acoustic stream into which the surface-structure is converted that has to be decoded by the person listening to a sentence and the hypothesis in this book is that the underlying 'deep structure" is not just some other organisation of words, phrases, kernel sentences, re-write rules, but the real physiological and neurological 'deep structures' underlying the processes of visual perception and action-organisation. Word-order, the grouping of words in phrases, the surface-organisation of the sentence into subject/predicate/object/adjunct etc., are not the 'icing' on the cake, the frills thrown out by the transformation of a purely linguistic deep structure, but essential elements in the 'coding' and 'decoding' process of the sentence; word-order is a vital part of the total resources for signalling in a language, even though different languages may make different uses of this particular coding resource against other coding devices, such as inflection, concordance, intonation. Just as different languages make different selections from the range of natural word-structures available to indicate percepts or action (items of experience), so different languages make different selections and use in different combinations features of the total signalling capacity that the human speech-process makes available (a subject developed more fully in Chapter VI which considers directly the comparative application of the hypotheses, broad and detailed, so far developed in this book in relation to the English language).

IV The central problem of this Chapter (of all linguistics) is how it is, why it is, that a particular collection of words, put together in a particular order, grouped in a particular way, should produce a single, coherent, unique, total meaning? What are the methods by which it serves to produce the total meaning? what determines that the sequence should have this total specific meaning rather than that? Traditionally, grammar has devoted itself to parsing, that is allocating an accepted description within the framework of the traditional grammar to each of the words or each of the word-groupings in a sentence. 'Parsing' in this sense is now something which can be done by machine, has been done by computer programs in various ways but parsing as such amounts to very little if it is simply a matching of individual words with items in a conventional list or set of grammatical categories. To understand a spoken sentence, we need to be able to do very much more than parse it—what we are looking for is a correct solution of the decoding problem that any individual sentence constitutes. To say that a solution of the sentence is correct is to say that it fits into some larger structure, either external or internal to the person perceiving who frames the sentence or to the person who comprehends the sentence; what the sentence says, or means, must be relatable and must in fact be related by the speaker and the listener to the organisation of the real world of perception and action. But our ambitions for finding a correct solution must be defined and, in reality, limited; an infinite variety of distinct sentences is possible and an individual uses and hears an incalculable number of sentences related to his experience from moment to moment. We cannot hope to solve correctly, in any definitive way, the way in which a particular sentence gains its full real meaning, in the particular circumstances in which it is spoken or heard—we would need to know more than we possibly could about the content and organisation of our own intellectual and perceptual experience, that of the person speaking or listening to us and the world-context in which the sentence is framed. But this does not mean that we can do nothing of importance in this linguistic examination. We have to distinguish between a general solution to the problem of the total meaning of the sentence (or for that matter to the problem of the total interpretation of the visual scene) and a particular solution (for a particular sentence or scene). A general solution would specify the steps and processes involved in extracting a specific meaning from any sentence—the way in which the narrowing-down of the possible semantic values of the words included in the sentence-cluster proceeds in step with the narrowing-down of the possible relations, functionally, between the items in the sentence, as a result of the ordering-rules applied to the word-string and the sub-groups of words within it, including the rules which provisionally indicate which words ought within the sentence to be formed into distinct sub-groups.

This general solution would, unavoidably, have to refer to things so far unspecified, and which may for ever be unspecifiable (if one accepts the view of Ragnar Granit(5) quoted in the last Chapter on the ununderstandable final complexity of the human brain)—the overall structure of the total vocabulary/conceptual store, the organisation. of memory, the ongoing reference-frame of personal experience and the immediate external environment, the relation between hearer and speaker, the frames of motivation, expectation and intention, the preceding language and experiential exchanges between hearer and speaker, the individual experience of hearer and speaker with the individual words used and with the subject-matter to which the sentence refers. Nevertheless, though it would be burdensome and perhaps impossible even in the simplest case to specify everything going to determine the particular solution to the particular sentence, the attempt to postulate a general solution fairly economically would be a worthy and valuable one—and it is hoped that this Chapter will make some contribution towards that general solution.

V The conviction on which the material in this Chapter is based is that some gain in understanding cam be made from attempting to deal in parallel with the processes underlying the structuring of continuous speech (the sentence), continuous visual perception (the visual scene) and continuous activity (the complex action sequence). At a minimum, a parallel discussion of the sentence, the visual scene and the complex action should increase the understanding of how each process functions. At a higher level, the comparison should demonstrate the isomorphism of sentence, visual scene and complex action. In the discussion, we can proceed either from language to vision (and action) or from vision (and action) to language—but as a practical matter we can follow both courses: that is reflect, in parallel, on what is known about the processes underlying speech, vision and action. Insofar as the structuring of language, at the syntactic level, is more apparent to us, (or we think it is), then our knowledge of the functioning of sentences may offer pointers to aid understanding of the functioning of the visual scene in perception and of the planning and execution of the action-programme. The hope is that various, quite precise, equivalences, between speech, vision and action as processes can be observed or postulated and that closer examination of those equivalences will help to advance our overall understanding of the interrelation of speech, vision and action. Certainly, it is true that neither visual research (physiological or neurological or by computer in the field of artificial intelligence) nor research into the organisation of action have advanced as far as one would wish (as Chapter IV brought out rather emphatically) nor, on the linguistics side, has the study of syntax and semantics made as sure progress as some might suppose, so that there can be no easy matching of research results from the three distinct areas. The argument and the material in this Chapter are therefore bound to be tentative and suggestive rather than final and sharply focused—but the attempt to see a coherent unity emerging from the bits and pieces of experimental evidence, to distinguish some clearer contours and shapes at present hidden in the theoretical fuzz (as some AI exponents might describe it) seems to be worthwhile. This Chapter itself, and indeed the whole book, is, at an abstract level, a search for the best interpretation of the theoretical scene, the most coherent interpretation of the stream of discourse (the river of discourse) about vision, language and action. Literally, in Greek, 'theory simply means seeing and, in Latin, 'perception' means grasping—this Chapter attempts to see and grasp the structure that underlies the functioning of language. The effort here (one of a kind that Hegel might have appreciated) is to use language to express the perception of the structure and functioning of language as a central part of total human action, total human behaviour; and at the same time to derive the distinctive character of language itself from the perception and action which it seeks to express.

Following this rather extensive statement of the principles or propositions guiding the general approach in this Chapter, it may be helpful to be more specific about the structure of the remaining part of the Chapter and the kinds of material and issues to be dealt with in it. In linguistics, in dealing with the sentence, one quickly finds that every aspect involves every other aspect, word-meanings, sentence-patterns and types, segmentation into clauses, phrases and word-groupings, grammatical parts of speech, inflection, word-order; in no time at all one can lose sight of the main drive of one's theory and become deeply involved in detailed exploration of subsidiary parts of the whole. The same is true of the many facets of research into visual perception, the elements in the visual scene, the relation of figure and ground, the disambiguation of complex contours, the order of scanning, visual search and pursuit movement of the eyes, the visual constancies as features of the total organisation of the visual scene.

Undoubtedly, the same general observation is true of the analysis of any complex activity, even though less research has been done and the distinct aspects of total activity are less well-identified. Quite clearly then, there is a substantial problem, in exploring the implications of the theory that the processes underlying speech, vision and action are interrelatod at the syntactic as well as the semantic level, in deciding hew best the material available should be ordered, how most logically and informatively the different aspects of vision, action and speech should be tackled. And there is an equally great problem in deciding what concrete results one ought to look for from the discussion in this chapter: should they be conclusions about the functioning of speech, vision and action or should they be suggestive parallels and equivalences or should they be pointers for further thought and research?

Beyond this, as if the possible degree of complexity involved is not already sufficiently large, one has to remember that the analysis so far in this Chapter, and in earlier Chapters, has very largely proceeded in terms of one language, English—but the problems one wants to tackle are those of language generally, a multiplicity of languages with widely differing syntactic systems as well as differing lexicons. As a practical matter, one must attempt first to arrive at a clear view of how a general theory and its detailed development apply to one language, before going on to consider the complications required to apply such a theory to languages of very different types. Accordingly, this Chapter continues to concentrate on the joint problems of syntax and semantics for English and reserves until the next Chapter the attempt to tackle the comparative implications of the general theory that language, perception and action are behaviourally integrated.

Having put on one side for the moment the comparative issue, this Chapter, somewhat similarly to the patterning of Chapters III and IV, first deals separately with vision, speech and action at the Stage III level of complexity, then attempts to identify important aspects of research into the functioning of each activity, brings those different aspects together in what one might describe as a table of equivalences in syntactic/semantic functioning, and discusses each main type of equivalence to see how far what is known about speech throws light on vision or action and vice versa and then returns to the central issue of the Chapter, namely what sort of general solution can be postulated for the solution of the visual scene and the sentence, how does one arrive at, in general principle, a unique, coherent and total comprehension of the meaning of an individual sentence or the content of an individual visual scene. The separate sections which follow, on this basis, are:

1. The concept of the visual scene The concept of the complex action The concept of the sentence The interrelation of those broad views of scene, action and sentence
2. A table of equivalent aspects of research into the visual scene, the complex action and the sentence and discussion of the different groups into which these equivalent aspects can be placed 3. The 'general solution' of the problem of the interpretation of the visual scene and the sentence.

The concept of the visual scene

This Chapter deals with the application of the hypothesis on the relation between perception and language at the Stage where visual shapes are formed into complete scenes and individual words are formed into complete sentences; the sentence and the detailed visual scene are taken as corresponding levels of construction and complexity. The attempt is to see how far a systematic examination of the mode of construction of a visual scene, from the elementary units discussed in Chapter III as formed into more complex visual shapes in ways considered in Chapter IV, can be applied to or throw light on the construction and analysis of the sentence. In a succeeding section of this Chapter, the contrary procedure is followed; a close examination of what is known from linguistics research about the analysis and construction of the sentence to see how far that may reciprocally throw light on the analysis and construction of the visual scene.

But neither 'visual scene' nor 'sentence' are self-explanatory or necessarily clearly understood concepts. In the literature, there has been pretty extensive discussion about the way in which 'scene' and 'sentence' should be described or characterised; hence the present section of the Chapter concentrating on the concept of the visual scene. There are some preliminary points to be made: first of all, when one thinks of a particular 'visual scene', of course what one has in mind is the scene as we have already perceived it; we have already carried out, unconsciously, the complex processes of analysis of the visual stimuli falling on the retina, grouped the units of stimulation into elementary units, lines, contours; then formed these into specific shapes or objects (whether quickly recognised because familiar, or novel), reached automatically conclusions about which are the significant figures in the scene and which the less important background, noted the qualities of the figural elements and their positional relationships and so on. As we normally use the words, 'visual scene' means for us a sample of our perception of the external world; some have described the scene as the unitary organisation of visual information within one pulse of the psychological present—the extraction within this period from continuous stimulation of information we can relate to the structure of our previous perceptual experience and to our current purposes and actions. The visual scene in this sense is one of the snapshots which the visual apparatus keeps taking of the real world (as the real world makes itself manifest bathed in a flux of light-energy). The manner in which we perceive the instantaneous visual scene is not necessarily something specifically human—all the research evidence is that the laws governing the organisation of elements of the scene into coherent units of figure and ground, the determination of the similarities of visual form and the whole organisation of the visual field are fundamentally the same for the bird, the rodent and the man; the pattern-recognising systems used by organisms as diverse as pigeons, octopuses, cats and monkeys are likely to have much in common.

The second preliminary point is related to the first: the real visual scene is not our interpretation of what we see but the ordering and structuring implicit in the light-energy at any point stimulating the mosaic of receptors in the retinas of our eyes (in the same way as at any moment the real 'auditory scene' (if one can invent the phrase) is the stream of variations in the frequency and pressure of the movements of the air acting upon the receiving mechanisms of the ear). As was noted in Chapter IV, in relation to the formation of visual shapes and word-forms, there is an important distinction between the problems of the mode of construction of the visual scene (as perceived) or of the sentence and the practical problems in real experience of recognition of the structures contained in the stream of light-energy (or of sound). There is a problem of 'decoding' the information in the total stream of light or sound to arrive at the visual scene or sentence, as there is a problem of decoding to arrive at the individual shape or word, or even at the elementary unit of vision or speech-sound. At this point in the Chapter one is more concerned with the broad features of the construction of the visual scene (or sentence) rather than with the complex problems of recognition, of decoding of the scene or sentence (which are discussed more fully in the concluding section of the Chapter).

So, as a matter of simplicity in thinking about the "visual scene', one can start from the familiar and proceed to the more complex. The visual scene can be thought of, initially, as a static scene, rather like a picture in a frame (though the frame in reality is one formed from time as well as from space)—or perhaps as one 'frame' in a stretch of colour-film. The static visual scene is something of an abstraction (though a useful abstraction to start from) since the whole of vision in fact is impregnated with movement, concerned with observing movement and derived from the constant movements of the visual apparatus. The static visual scene is an idealised and generalised version of the process of integration that in fact takes place at every level of the visual system as information flows in from receptors to converge, for example, on one ganglion cell or one cell in the visual cortex to bring about a single specific change of state in the particular cell affected.

The static visual scene is an abstraction in another sense; in reality, in our ordinary experience, there are no separate, marked-off visual scenes, no separate auditory scenes, but a super-unified overall perceptual scene (which takes in what is seen, heard and felt externally as well as what is felt, thought and intended internally). But, as a practical matter, we cannot tackle everything at once—we can only start even the most tentative approach to the total complexity by starting with the preliminary construct of the (somewhat artificial) 'visual scene'. To make the discussion more concrete, one could start from a typical simplified visual scene—a static scene say of a landscape. In such a scene, a stretch of countryside, there will be a given range of colours (which in fact simultaneously influence each other and react on each other in our visual apparatus), there will be large familiar shapes—clouds, hills, trees, roads, cattle—as well as small detail close at hand. Some of the shapes in the scene will be interpreted as three-dimensional objects, trees, cows, and others may be thought of as two-dimensional or apparently two-dimensional e.g. variations in the colours on a stone wall, a pattern on the flank of a cow; within the total scene, if we wish, we can note typical contour-elements going to form the objects in the scene: straight lines, angles, curves, spots' or blotches of colour, curved lines, possibly circles or squares.

Also in the scene will be the relations perceived between the different shapes and masses: relative sizes of cloud and cow and tree, the nearness or distance of particular objects, the relative placing and directions of objects in the scene, the degree of sharpness or unclarity with which particular objects can be perceived, the arrangement of the objects in the scene—from low down to high up, from left to right, from near ground to far distance—the occlusion (partial obscuring of some objects in the scene by other objects), the perceived physical contact of objects, the attachment of parts to the whole object, the horn or tail to the cow, the man standing on the path, the bird on the branch, the stone in the grass; the relative lightness and darkness of different parts of the scene, and of the scene overall (the sky and the landscape). There will be other relationships within such a scene: well-known easily recognised elements, more doubtfully-recognised elements, thoroughly unclear elements, with a progression in perception of the scene from the sharp line for some objects or areas to blur and shade for others. Implicit in the scene will be the perspective organisation of the lines forming it, the direction of light and shading and shadow.

This rather lengthy detailed description of the composition and' relationships in an extremely commonplace static visual scene is intended to bring out how many different aspects, how many different relationships, are in fact involved in perception of even the simplest of visual scenes'. Such a scene, however ordinary, is far removed in its complexity from what one might describe as the primitive visual scene. The most primitive scene no doubt is an area of diffuse, even illumination with nothing in it—the uniform greyness of fog. If into this truly primitive scene one introduces the simplest possible element, a dark spot or a bright spot, one immediately also introduces a whole array of aspects of structure and relation—the location of the dot in the scene, high or low, to the left or to the right, the degree of sharpness or fuzziness of the dot. And as one brings in more detail, one also requires more structuring, more specification of relationships. With two dots, there are new relations between their size, their relative brightness, their relative position and the direction which an imaginary line joining them would follow. As the number of dots increases (and this of course is essentially what happens in the visual stream as it actually exists and stimulates the retina), the visual system starts to organise the dots into meaningful elementary contours, lines, angles, corners—and if enough information is provided, into shapes and objects. The scene grows rapidly in complexity with the amount of detail introduced; it starts to be formed not simply into a two-dimensional array of detail but into a three-dimensional system—and the different objects and items in the scene start to form themselves into groups; the perception of one object or group affects the perception of others; all the material in the scene starts to become organised into a coherent, total interpretation of the scene, as a result of the interaction of the material available in the scene (the selection from the repertoire of perceptual objects and contours) and the ordering rules which relate the features found in the scene—that is as a result of the interaction of one might describe as the 'semantic' (the familiar, meaningful, single items in the scene) and the "syntactic" (that is the grouping, ordering and relating) aspects of the visual process.

Once one has proceeded from the absolutely primitive visual scene to the commonplace but much more complex static visual scene represented by the kind of landscape described earlier in this section, there is a vastly greater degree of complexity that can be introduced into the 'visual scene' as one starts to consider other types of scene. The range of 'frames' within which a scene is formed may vary; at first one may have familiar, almost stereotyped settings of the kind described in Chapter IV in relating the Primitive Vocabulary to what was described as the primitive perceptual repertoire; the scene may be set within a room, out of doors, in the street, in the countryside, with human content or animate content. The scene may no longer be a wholly static one; there may be continuous movement of items within the scene, cows grazing, clouds moving, trees waving in the wind. There can be scenes which are themselves as a whole in continuous movement, like the views from the windows of a railway train. All these scenes involving movement bring in of course the directional aspects of movement, the rates of change of speed of movement, progressive change in perspective organisation, shifts between the positions of objects in two or three dimensions: distant objects coming nearer, moving to the left; near objects growing larger and so on. Once movement is introduced, there is almost an unlimited degree of complexity in the organisation of the scene; the decoding problem of perception grows rapidly and what has been described as the 'syntax' of the scene correspondingly becomes more complicated.

Besides movement, there are other important sources of complexity in the visual scene. Visual scenes may have associated with them and require for their interpretation, other non-visual material, the association of auditory or other sensory material, the bell ringing in the country church, the dog barking in the field, at the simplest level, but perhaps most important there is the aspect of the physical (and intellectual) relation of the seer to the scene. There are scenes which present themselves for manipulation—a chessboard, or scenes not influenceable by the perceiver (the TV screen—other than to switch it off), scenes seen from a railway carriage window; scenes related to a plan of action—a walk through a wood in the country. The 'visual scene' in fact is not an isolated static element in perception; scenes are related to one another: they may be juxtaposed in space or time—turn the head to the left and see a different but related view of the landscape. Look from the television screen out of the window and see a scene immediately following in time but in content completely unrelated to what has just been perceived.

Perception in fact moves on from visual scene to visual scene. In ordinary movement, perhaps a large part of the elements remain constant between two successive visual scenes and the perception is concentrated only on the novel items in the sequence (the Gestalt idea of the 'common fate' of items moving in a uniform way is still of value as a clue to the type of movement and the persistence of the objects concerned)—but nevertheless there are great complexities in the geometrical analysis even of such types of movement. As we move physically away from a given visual scene it shrinks in size and in effect becomes included as one element in a successive larger visual scene (much the same happens when we use a telescope or a microscope but here a small element of the present scene is drawn out of the primary visual scene). With other forms of change in relation to the visual scene, there is an internal reordering of the relations between elements in the scene e.g. if one walks round a display in a museum, a historical grouping in a waxworks, or if one turns one's head to look round the room. The processes of perception have to extract the changes in relationship between the successive scenes whilst preserving as far as possible the identification of the elements, the shapes, objects, which form the substantial content of the scene. Even if one for the moment disregards thought about the visual scene as external or internal (imaginary, remembered), actual or possible, present, past or future, referred to oneself or to someone else's point of view, the overwhelming complexity of organisation is apparent, the scale of the decoding process to achieve successful perception is clearly immense and the degree to which an explicit 'syntax' of vision might exceed in its intricacy any syntax so far suggested for language is obvious.

Nevertheless, despite all this daunting complexity of the perceptual process, mankind has in fact developed a language-faculty which can cope effectively with moment-to-moment experience of visual perception and beyond that can relate talk about perception to talk about all kinds of human action, human thought and human feeling. Somehow then the problem of correlation of the syntax of vision and the syntax of language has, in evolutionary terms, been solved—and what this Chapter is concerned with is finding pointers to the way in which the achievement has been possible.

The concept of the complex action

Chapter II described the direct dependence of perception on the needs of the action-organisation of the human or animal and the immediately preceding section has attempted to explore the complexities involved in the construction and organisation of the 'visual scene', which itself may include elements of observed action or form part of a sequence of action. Vision provides a large proportion of the total information upon which effective voluntary activity depends. The kind of information that successful activity requires depends very largely on the way in which sequences of complex activity are planned, made-up from the available primitive action elements or learned action sub-routines and adapted both to the state of the external environment which the voluntary action is intended to affect and to the momentary state of the individual human being as he prepares to carry through a sequence of actions; that is his bodily posture, the positions of his limbs, his actual physical location in the environment in which he is operating or his relation to the objects which he may intend using as instruments of his action or the objects or animate creatures (perhaps other human beings) towards which his action is directed. Insofar as (as explained in Chapter II) in evolutionary terms and as part of total human behaviour, the structuring of voluntary action determined the kind of structure that effective visual (and other) perception should have, and insofar as the required structure of visual perception had a determining influence on the content and form that language would need to have to serve as an effective medium for communicating the content of perception, a close examination of the structure of the manifold forms which voluntary complex actions can take ought to provide some useful insights into the syntactic and semantic organisation both of perception and of language.

Each of the preceding chapters has dealt with aspects of the organisation of action at the successive levels; Chapter III attempted to identify the elementary units of action in terms of the range and types of movement available for the parts of the human body and the human body as a whole, the straightforward movements of arms, hands, legs, head, trunk; Chapter IV considered action at the next stage, the way in which the elementary units of action might be combined into simple familiar action-routines, such actions as hitting or throwing. But in real life human behaviour is not made up of isolated, individual action-routines—hitting, throwing, turning, standing and so on—but of combinations of complex actions, carried through in specific external and internal situations, aiming at specific goals, specific physical changes in the surrounding environment or in the relationships of specific objects, creatures, other humans. The complex action is not just a type of action but a specific sequence of actual movements organised into a unity both in time and in the space within which the action takes place; the complex action needs as essential parts of its construction not only elements formed from action sub-routines but also the actor, the individual who initiates the action, the specific parts of the body used in executing the action, the instruments used—the stick or stone grasped, the tennis racket or the steering wheel of the car, the direction and object of the action, the person or thing affected and intended to be affected by the action. The complex action requires highly involved relational aspects (similar to the relational aspects of a visual scene but much more extensive); the assessment of relative weights, forces and directions, speeds and distances, the specific determination of the acceleration and deceleration of the muscular movements required of the parts of the body used in executing the action.

For us as human beings, action in all its forms seems the most natural, the best-known, the most simply understood aspect of our total behaviour, of our life from moment to moment. Essentially, all the forms of behaviour that we can observe in human beings, in ourselves or in other animals, are types of activity (on closer analysis patterns of skeletal movement): walking, running, ballet dancing, playing the piano, playing tennis or cricket, driving a car, writing a letter, reading a book and even, of course, the act of speaking itself. Even when at first sight the particular action seems a more simple one, the hitting, or throwing which in the last Chapter were treated as action sub-routines, the incorporation of this simple type of action in a real stretch of activity, in a real situation, makes the whole process much more complex. Roberts, in his study Neurophysiology of Postural Mechanisms, illustrates the complexity of even simple real actions by describing what is involved in catching or throwing a ball or some similar object as an executed action; he points out that the same muscles may at different times be called upon to perform very different kinds of tasks which he characterises by the terms SET HOLD and DRIVE—and the different modes of use of the muscles may be combined in varying ways. So "in the act of catching, the modes of setting and holding are combined in sequence. The catching limb is first moved to a chosen position and it is then called upon to hold that position in spite of the impact of the object that is to be caught. To reduce the damage inherent (in the absorption of the large forces imposed by the sudden deceleration of the caught object) this is achieved by arranging for the catching limb to give at the moment of impact, thus allowing time for modest braking forces to achieve the desired change in momentum. The act of throwing may be regarded as the converse of catching. Here the task is to impart momentum rather than to absorb it. Throwing is achieved by a combination of drive and set. During a change from one selected limb position to another, the relevant muscles develop more force than that just needed to overcome resistance. The excess force accelerates the limb as well as any attached masses (the object to be thrown), which thus acquires momentum so that they continue in motion after the muscular action has ceased"(6).

The more complex the action, the larger the number of elementary units of action, action sub-routines required to execute it and the more complex the syntactic organisation of the total action. Even as apparently an unvigorous an action as writing involves the regulation of many muscles throughout the entire body; if one hand is engaged in writing, adjustments are needed in the trunk muscles to alter the distribution of support forces as the hand moves over the paper. The head moves on the neck as the eyes follow the line of writing, and so on. Whenever we deliberately move any one part of our body, we involuntarily also make compensatory and auxiliary adjustments elsewhere in the body—background changes in activity, essential for the support of voluntary movement. Any movement may be thought of as a change in posture—or one may distinguish the general, usually unconscious, postural changes as the background against which the voluntary movement in formulated. That is, one has, in the organisation of voluntary activity, a clear analogy to the distinction made in vision, by equally unconscious and automatic processes, between Figure and Ground, the figure carrying the main meaningful content of the perceived visual scene, as the pattern of voluntary action carries the main practical significance of the total change of the individual's momentary bodily organisation.

Bartlett illustrated this in terms of the way in which one makes a stroke at tennis or cricket: "How I make the stroke depends on the relating of certain new experiences, most of them visual, to other immediately visual experiences, and to my posture, or balance of postures, at the moment. The latter, the balance of postures, is the result of a whole series of earlier movements, in which the last movement before the stroke is played has a predominant function. When I make the stroke, I do not, as a matter of fact, produce something absolutely new, and I never merely repeat something old. The stroke is literally manufactured out of the living visual and postural 'schemata' of the moment and their interrelations"(7). This description (which, structurally, at many points resembles very precisely the kind of description one might make of the processes involved in actually speaking a sentence or observing a visual scene in a particular context) reminds one that in normal human behaviour not only is there no sharp distinction between the intended, voluntary pattern of complex action and the postural background, but also that there is no sharp distinction between the state of action, the execution of the particular complex action, and a state of what is usually described as inaction. What in fact we have is a continuous stream of action, just as we have a continuous stream of perception. Because all the time the human body is acted on by persisting forces (obviously the force of gravity but also other forces in the environment, wind, the movement of external objects), even the absence of overt voluntary activity implies the maintenance of a particular posture by the continued application of appropriate forces. Standing still, lying down, sleeping, resting (indeed virtually every state other than deep coma or death) require action, organisation of the neuromuscular system to produce movement or prevent externally-induced movement. Organisms are not passive objects upon which stimuli impinge to produce behaviour; the activity of the nervous system of most animals is in a state of constant flux and the fate of any particular stimulus is largely determined by the pattern that happens to be present in the nervous system when it arrives. Because the complex action has to be performed against a constantly changing internal background, the postural organisation at any moment, and in a constantly changing set of external circumstances, skilled action cannot be simply a matter of habitual sequences of change in particular groupings of muscles; for example, as Lashley points out, handwriting retains its essential characteristics, even when produced by combinations of muscles never previously employed for the purpose. Handwriting is specified as a generalised sequence of movements in relation both to overall bodily organisation and an internalised co-ordinate system constituting the organisation's orientation to its environment. Any complex action has a syntax which can be described as 'an habitual order or mode of relating the expressive elements to a generalised pattern or schema of integration which may be imposed upon a wide range and a wide variety of specific acts. just as in language, Lashley points out the syntax organises into specific sequences the expressive elements which the individual words constitute. Parallel in the organisation of voluntary action to what Pribram describes as the 'image of achievement', the patterning expressing the elements required for the execution of the specific complex act, one can set the 'image of meaning', the patterning expressing the total content of meaning to be conveyed through the syntactic organisation of the available semantic material. What more specific points can one usefully extract from the discussion above of the complexities of the organisation of action? Perhaps the following:

1. In neurophysiological terms, there is still virtually no understanding of the mechanisms underlying the initiation of the simplest voluntary movement—reaching for a pencil, clasping one's fingers together (as Lashley pointed out many years ago)—but this does not mean that one cannot describe and analyse the overt manifestations of complex actions, the elements of which they appear to be formed, their sequencing and adaptation to the environment (internal to the individual and external) within which the actions are in fact executed; one can in fact make a parallel distinction between the overt construction of a complex action and the practical physiological problems of its execution, to that already drawn between the construction of a visual scene and its interpretation or

decoding from the given visual stimuli or the distinction between the mode of interaction of syntax and semantics in the formation of a sentence, language competence (to adopt Chomsky's term), and the much different problems of the decoding of the acoustic stream, the comprehension of the spoken sentence (to which I would misapply, because it is convenient, Chomsky's corresponding term, language performance).

2. The complex action is not a rigid programme of particular muscular contractions and relaxations but an overall strategy, a schema of action at a very high level, perhaps taking the form of an 'image' of the intended action (an image of the achievement aimed at) which is a simultaneously-present patterning, presumably in the motor cortex, a unity which can be set in parallel to the unity of the meaning of a sentence, before it has been read out into a serial form as a collection of words in a particular order, and beyond that as a sequence of changes in the positions and movements of the articulatory organs—or one might set the 'image of action' in parallel to the unified coherent total comprehension of the complex visual scene, which is the product of the complex processes of decoding at the successive levels in the visual system of the brain of the crude input of light-energy activating the receptors of the retina;

3. The complex action is not a sequence of action-routines, muscular changes, carried through in isolation to reach the intended goal—it is a patterning superimposed on the continuing complex postural organisation of the body, the unceasing and continually varying background adjustment of the muscular system; the particular complex action, as executed, takes the form of a figure of action outlined against the general bodily background of the individual. Figure and Ground (as ideas developed by the Gestalt psychologists) are concepts relevant not only for the organisation of visual perception but also for the organisation of voluntary bodily action—and later this Chapter will go on to argue that Figure and Ground are concepts which also have their relevance for the construction and interpretation of language-forms, of sentences;

4. The complex action involves not simply a type but, as actually executed, a relation to the real environment; it involves a real source of the action, the actor, real bodily instruments of action as well as external instruments, a real physical and temporal framework

within which the action takes place and a real state of change in the environment, a real impact on the persons or things aimed at by the action. The syntax of the complex action has to deal with the way in which all these different elements in the total event which a particular complex action represents are ordered and related to one another;

5. the complex action is not only something executed by oneself but also the action as it is perceived to be executed by other individuals like oneself, or analogously by other animate creatures, or possibly, in a metaphorical way, by inanimate objects and forces. We may say: 'The wind blows' rather in the same way as we might say 'The man breathes'. We can comprehend the complex actions of others, analyse their syntax and meaning, simply because we are familiar with the structure and intent of our own actions. In speaking about action, we can translocate the subject of the action: we can say "I threw the cricket ball" or "He' (that specific man) threw the ball"—so that in setting out to analyse the syntax and semantics of our own complex action, we are at the same time giving ourselves an insight into the syntax and semantics of perceived actions of others. In fact, we can often in practice experience what one might describe . . . as 'motor sympathy'; we feel in ourselves the effort and difficulty involved in the tennis shot that has just been played, the physical strain of the athlete in the race;

6. Finally, a point implicit in most of what has already been said: the vital importance for the planning of action and for its effective execution (as well as for the understanding of the action of others) of context, the frame within which the action takes place, the experience immediately preceding the action and the circumstances expected to follow it. Complex action to be effective must be precisely adjusted to and regulated by the context, just as much as perception and language depend on the circumstances surrounding the particular visual scene or the framing (or comprehension) of the particular sentence. Context is not something minor and unimportant, but the extensive and complicated framework within which human behaviour, in all its forms, has to proceed.

The concept of the sentence

Preceding sections of this Chapter have discussed the concepts of the 'visual scene' and the 'complex action'—because the hypothesis being explored is that there must be some specific structural relation between the processes underlying vision and action and those underlying language. This section, concerned with the concept of the 'sentence- could be approached in varying ways, either by linking it directly to what has been said about the organisation of vision and action (the implicit syntax and semantics of the visual scene and the complex action) or by following a more conventional approach: starting by considering what present-day linguists and traditional grammarians have to say about the concept of the sentence and seeing how well or badly what they say can be fitted into the framework presented in this book, or finally, as a third approach, this section could consider the concept of the 'sentence' in a broad way, to avoid getting bogged down immediately either in the complicated detailed relationships with vision and action or in the marshland of much of what is said both in modern linguistics and in traditional grammar.

There are two preliminary remarks one can make: the first, not an entirely frivolous one, is that in attempting to discuss in this section 'the concept of the sentence', one is in fact unavoidably talking about the material that is actually being used in the section to describe the nature and construction of sentences—one is using an extensive collection of sentences, samples of actual sentences, in a continuous stream of discourse, to attempt to arrive at a view of the nature of 'the sentence'. This is a striking example of the self-reflexive property of language to which reference has been made on several occasions earlier. Secondly, in talking about 'the sentence', we have to some extent already assumed that we know how to recognise a sentence, what is a sentence and what is not a sentence; but there is a vital distinction to be drawn between a theoretical sentence (an isolated sentence where the material content is of no particular importance) which grammarians and philosophers take as the starting point for their theories and the actual sentence, the sentence as spoken or written in completely specific circumstances, against a fully determined background or context (both linguistic and experiential context); the distinction being drawn is analogous to that between the complex action as a theoretical programme, a sequence of movements, and the complex action as actually realised in a real material environment, or the distinction between the isolated sample visual scene and the real visual scene, perceived and interpreted as part of a continuing stream of perceptual and other experience. Where our true interest lies is not in the theoretical but in the actual, realised sentence, which gains its effect from the interpenetration of the syntactic and semantic features in fact present in the utterance; it is only for an actual sentence that one can explain how its form and content are functionally determined, not simply in a general way but by its use in completely specific circumstances. Whilst sample, theoretical, sentences may or may not appear to be meaningful, may or may not appear to be true (and a great deal of philosophical discussion has revolved round these issues), the actual sentence, in one way or another, is effective, alters the situation in which it is uttered. The purpose of the actual sentence is to have meaning and to be applicable to the real world.

In the light of these preliminary remarks, one can say something about the arrangement of the material in this section. First of all, there is a broad discussion of the English sentence (earlier in the Chapter the point was made that one needs first to get a satisfactory account of the functioning of syntax and semantics in one language, before introducing the greater complexities involved in extending any theory to the whole range of human language).

Secondly, it is important as a matter of exposition to attempt to keep separate from the broad discussion of the concept of the sentence the very many more detailed aspects of syntax and of the construction of the sentence—but this more detailed discussion is also necessary. There is some examination of what traditional grammar and more modern linguistics have to say about the issues, followed by consideration both of the types of sentence encountered and of questions relating to the construction and components of the sentence (including the linking together of one sentence to another in the continuous sequences of discourse).

What can be said in the broadest terms about the concept of the sentence can be modelled quite closely on what was said about the concept of the visual scene. The sentence, as heard, represents the unitary organisation of speech-sound within one pulse of the psychological present (where the psychological present may in fact extend over a period of several seconds) and it amounts to the extraction in this period from the continuous stimulation reaching the receptor-surface of the auditory apparatus (the basilar membrane) of a structuring of the acoustic information in terms of known speech-sound groupings (words and groups of words) relatable to the language-structure of the individual and to the purposes and actions of the individual. The sentence is thus, in the auditory field, very similar to the snapshots (frames in a film) constituted by visual perception, but in this case the sentence is a snapshot of the auditory world, the changing flux of acoustic energy on which structure has been imposed by the movements and activities of external objects, and of course primarily by the articulatory movements of the individual speaker. The 'sentence' in broad terms is something of an abstraction (though operationally a useful abstraction) similar in nature to the phoneme, or to the idealised visual shape, since the auditory stimulus is in fact a continuously varying, merging, stream of sound-energy, in which objective instrumental recording shows little that directly reflects the segmentation of phonemes, words and sentences that linguistics takes as its starting material. 'The sentence', as an abstract concept, is an idealised and generalised version of the integration which takes place at each stage in the processing of sensory inflow; a sentence is a high-level unit of organisation compared with the lower levels of integration of the word and the phoneme. The understanding of the sentence is essentially directed and purposeful analysis, parallel to comprehension of the single 'visual scene'.

Because this description of the sentence is modelled rather directly on what was said about the visual scene, it necessarily produces an account of the sentence far removed from traditional descriptions in linguistics (and of course it is an account of the sentence as heard and understood rather than the sentence as produced, since there seems no equivalent in the functioning of visual perception to what one treats as the production rather than the perception of language). But perhaps it is no bad thing to have such a different account of the sentence as one's starting point. In terms of linguistics, and for the simplification of discussion, the sentence can initially be thought of as a brief, simple string of words of subject-predicate form; but of course as has already been pointed out, there is no separate sentence in experience, in isolation, as there is no isolated visual scene. There is a super-unified overall scene, formed of perception, action, as well as language, and the real world; however, we can in practice only approach the total behavioural scene via the preliminary constructs of the sentence, the visual scene and the complex action, as segments rather arbitrarily detached from total individual experience.

It is instructive to look at what has traditionally and more recently been said about the concept of the sentence by others, to set it against the behavioural account given in the preceding paragraph. Linguisticians have often been rather cautious about defining precisely what they mean by the concept of the sentence. Crystal(8) refers to the hundreds of definitions of 'sentence' suggested since Plato, and himself treats the sentence as the maximal unit of grammatical analysis which is recognised by the linguist as being capable of accounting for the range of grammatical clauses and structures which turn up in a language. Sapir says rather grandly (but perhaps unclearly) that the sentence is the "outgrowth of historical and unreasoning psychological forces rather than of a logical synthesis of elements that have been clearly grasped in their individuality . . . and every language has its special method or methods for binding words into a larger unity"(9) but apart from implicitly defining the sentence as a 'larger unity', what he says does not throw much light on the subject. Bloomfield seems to present a very sketchy definition of the sentence as "an independent linguistic form, not included by virtue of any grammatical construction in any larger linguistic form"(10); he distinguishes between full sentences and minor sentences (such as 'Thank you') but this really begs the question about the external relations of the traditional sentence, and what should be treated as grammatical structure transcending the sentence. Lyons(11) says that the sentence is more abstract than the utterance: sentences as such do not occur—they are not bits of language behaviour or stretches of speech; they are theoretical constructs, postulated by the linguist in order to account for the grammatical structure of utterances, and he goes on to say "We will assume an intuitive knowledge of what is or what is not a sentence"(11). This seems rather unclear; how do we have 'intuitive knowledge' of a theoretical construct of linguists, which, rather circularly, is marked out by what the linguist requires in order to give a grammatical account of speech?

Lyons' approach, and indeed that of Crystal quoted earlier, suggests that the sentence ought to be treated as an ideal 'unit of discourse', discourse being the real flow of speech (but of course one can have ideal units which are also real in their operational contribution to a behavioural process, whether the phoneme or word schemas which Brain and others have referred to or the schemas for visual shapes and actions which also seem to have physiological and neurological reality as programs for comprehension or action). Chomsky(12), as a leading theoretician of the sentence, rather surprisingly, does not directly tackle the question of what a sentence is: he describes a grammar as the theory which deals with the mechanics of sentence construction (which establish a sound-meaning relation in the given language) but that still leaves obscure what a sentence is, how one tells whether this collection of words in fact is a distinct sentence (he refers at one point to the 'integrity' of the sentence); though he says that the connection between sound and meaning is not one at the level of words but at the level of the sentence, this does not provide even an indirect account of the 'sentence', since meaning can be found in word-groupings shorter than the traditional sentence. Some troubles of Chomsky indeed seem to indicate that the practical interpretation he gives to the 'sentence' by itself is not adequate; presuppositions which may affect the grammatical analysis (at the surface or deep level) of an individual sentence may in reality be derived from earlier sentences, earlier points in the discourse, quite apart from the non-linguistic context of utterance. (The linking elements between sentences cannot be adequately analysed with a single sentence in isolation; many function-word refer outside the single sentence and ambiguous sentences, of the kind which figure so prominently in Chomsky's account of divergent deep structures for similar surface structures, are prime examples of the dangers of seeking to analyse a sample theoretical sentence in isolation).

Others have approached the nature of the sentence rather more from the angle of psychology. Osgood(13), in an interesting discussion of "Where the sentence comes from", concludes that it comes from the non-linguistic cognitive system and that it is related to aspects of pre-linguistic perceptuo-motor behaviour—but saying where the sentence comes from is not exactly the same as saying what 'the sentence' is, though the whole argument of this book, in agreement with what Osgood says, is that the sentence and speech generally are directly related to the organisation of the perceptual and motor systems, and that 'linguistic patterning rests on extra-linguistic patterning'. Perhaps one of the more interesting early attempts to define the concept of the sentence was that of Wundt (quoted by Bever): "We can define the sentence as . . . the linguistic expression of the voluntary arrangement of a whole mental image in its components, set in logical relations to one another"(14), a union of psychological and logical elements. Though even this is pretty broad and unspecific (we still know little about mental images and voluntary organisation), it matches, from the point of view of sentence production what was said earlier in this section about sentence perception and comprehension—and what Wundt suggested seems to lead on quite naturally to the description of the organisation of the sentence as a typical product of central motor

answer, dependent and independent, preceding and succeeding, parataxis, novel or familiar.

The proposition is that the types of sentence available in a language, the specific forms they take and the interrelation of the elements going to compose the different types of sentence derive from the structuring required to represent in language the content and ordering of visual perception and action. Of the four categories of principle listed above, the derivation of types of sentence from the experience they relate to and the object with which the sentence is actually expressed directly reflect this view of the structuring of language; the basic structures of sentences are derived from the necessities involved in the perception of a visual scene (as reflected in the serial process of scanning from which the comprehension of the total scene is extracted) or from the ordering involved in the execution of a complex action (typically an action of the individual himself requiring interaction between him and some external object). The basic sentence types are structured to convey the content of an integrated perception or to convey an account of an integrated action and the ordering of words in each of these basic types reflects the ordering in the perception or action respectively. So one has, immediately, the subject/predicate/complement type of sentence, required typically for perception of a static scene or the actor/action/goal type of sentence representing the ordering of the typical action. Elaboration of the two basic types of sentence reflects the elaboration in real life of the circumstances of the action on the one hand and the detail of the perception reflected in the sentence on the other.

The other principles which have been identified above as a basis for the classification of types of sentence can in their turn be given an application, a realisation, in terms of the discussion in the immediately preceding sections of this Chapter of the concepts of the visual scene and the complex action. For example, the simplest types of sentences reflect the simplest types of perception and action. More complicated sentences (with sub-clauses, adjuncts of various kinds) reflect greater detail, specificity and complexity of action or perception. Compound or complex sentences reflect the compacting together of separate perceptions or separate actions, by the use of relative clauses, noun or verb phrases, expressions relating to internal perception and attitude or even to the second-stage of reporting, reference to sentences already heard or spoken. No doubt, as a complex action or a complicated scene could be divided up into sections, treated as a combination of different regions, so all that is said in compound or complex sentences could be spelt out at length in a succession of simple sentences or, at a minimum, instead of the involved clause-structure of a complex sentence, one could have a very long compound sentence, that is simple sentences joined by linking words. Complex sentences are thus in a way short-cut formulas, condensed sentences, rather as a number of distinct actions may be condensed into a complete complex action (such as playing the piano). Complex sentences offer an economy in time, in communication (which in practice may be very important) though at the expense of the greater decoding problems involved in understanding the complexity of form. So, the rules governing complex sentences are those by which a succession of simple sentences can most economically, and without losing precision, be combined into a shorter serial string of words (that is a shorter stretch of speech-time)—to match more rapidly the complicated perception or complex action to which the sentence refers.

The preceding paragraph was intended to illustrate how one could relate the third basis for classification of types of sentence, that is classification in terms of 'form' to the earlier discussion of the characteristics of the visual scene and the complex action. It would be possible to illustrate in a similar way the relation between the other three principles of type and the organisation of vision and action. But perhaps more important than this at the present stage in the discussion is the need to emphasise that though the two basic types of sentence-organisation are necessarily such because of the need to represent visual perception and action, sentences as encountered in reality involve combinations of these basic types, elaborations of them, and the introduction of related aspects of experience which make the total picture of sentence-structures in English considerably more complicated. Besides the two basic types, straightforward action and vision sentences, there are related types of sentence referring to internal perception as well as external perception (the use of words such as: 'I feel' 'I know' 'I think' 'I remember'); or to the internal planning of action ('I will' 'I intend' 'I am going to') or referring to the act of speech itself ('I tell you' 'I say' 'I hear') or constituting not simply an aim to communicate but to produce action, a change of attitude or of internal state in the person to whom the sentence is spoken ('I promise' 'I ask' 'I wish' &c). And, of course, as discussed at some length in Chapter IV, there are the additional possibilities and complexities introduced by the metaphorical use of language, the very important process of formation of a 'metaphoric sentence' structurally patterned on the more straightforward types of sentence just discussed.

Parallelisms of structure and process underlying visual scene, complex action and sentence

The preceding sections of this Chapter have dealt separately with the concepts of the visual scene, the complex action and the sentence, as part of the exploration of the central hypothesis (presented in Chapter II) that there is an essential interrelation and integration of the structures and functioning of language, visual perception and action. Though each section has concentrated on presenting a broad description either of the scene, the action or the sentence, of the complexities of construction and perception of each and of the different types of scene, action or sentence that in practice are encountered, there has been some effort, throughout each of the sections, to bear in mind and to bring out the points where there seem to be resemblances between the structures and processes of these three aspects of human behaviour. In the current part of this Chapter, the object will be first to recall briefly the broad ways in which the discussion so far, not only in this Chapter but also in Chapters III and IV, has given some more solid content to the original proposition of the interrelation between language, visual perception and action and secondly to examine, necessarily rather briefly, some of the lines on which the interrelation structurally between sentence, scene and action might be pursued in more detail, in the light of the results available on many distinct issues from current work in linguistics, and research into visual perception and voluntary bodily action.

First of all, a summary of some of the broad parallelisms which have been noted in this and earlier Chapters between the functioning of language, perception and action:

1. In Chapter II the evolutionary point was made that any animal to survive must be organised to adapt its behaviour as effectively as possible to the perceived world. The content of perception must be such as to serve the needs of action organisation and be as precisely and closely integrated with action-organisation as possible; in the same way language, to serve perception and action effectively, must, in its content and organisation, be such that it can as accurately

as possible provide the information needed and can be integrated as closely and precisely as possible with perception and action. Nothing in research in any of the three fields casts doubt on this general proposition;

2. In Chapters III, IV and V, a strictly hierarchical system of organisation has been postulated for the functioning of language, vision and action—derived initially from the familiar stage by stage approach in linguistics, with the progress from the first stage of phonetics, to the second stage of semantics and the third stage of syntax (which really is the stage at which the functioning of all three stages is integrated into the normal process of speech). Evidence has been given of specific parallelisms of organisation between speech, vision and action at each of the three Stages: the detailed equivalences between the elementary units of vision, speech and action in Chapter III, the parallel modes by which the elementary units are formed into complete forms, words, shapes, action-routines in Chapter IV, the natural relation between word-structure and word-meaning (in terms of the associated visual or action contour) illustrated in the Annex to Chapter IV; and in the same Chapter the extent to which the Primitive Vocabulary (and deriving from that eventually the full lexicon of a language) is structured by the source of the link between words and meanings in actual visual (or other perceptual) experience or in experience of action;

3. If one takes together the discussion of the formation of visual shapes, word and action-routines in Chapter IV and the discussion of the construction of visual scenes, sentences and complex actions in the present Chapter, there are several important physiological and neurological parallels which can be noted:

  a. for visual shapes. actions and words, contours seem to be of key importance, both as the expression of the construction of the forms from elementary units and as the instrument by which recognition of the shape, action or word is achieved;

  b. there seems to be the closest possible relation in the construction and recognition of contours, whether for shapes, actions or words, between the elements and order in which the elements are grouped and centrally controlled patterns of muscular movement. Central motor patterning seems to be the level at which the processes underlying the formation of visual shapes, words and action-routines are brought into contact with each other, and in fact integrated;

c. whilst developmentally, and in terms of apparent structure, visual shapes, words and actions are built up from several categories of elementary units, the evidence seems clear that as development proceeds, speed of recognition and repeated use call for and make possible short-cut methods, both for the formation of more complex word-groupings or actions or for the recognition of words, actions or visual shapes in more complex combinations. This involves the vital role of stored patterns or models of the whole structure of a word, a visual shape or an action-routine. For each of these aspects of human behaviour, speech, perception and action, there is a normal and useful progress from reliance on the elementary units to reliance on central stored patterns (in a kind of prolongation or extension of the hierarchical process demonstrated by Hubel and Wiesel's researches into the more complex combinations of visual experience dealt with integrally at higher and higher levels within the visual cortex);

d. for speech, vision and action, the great growth in complexity comes with the linking of individual words, visual shapes and action routines into extensive sequences and combinations, upon which a higher level ordering is imposed—and which Lashley described as the parallel syntaxes of vision, action and language. At this Stage, there is a sharp distinction for all three modes of behaviour between the problems of construction of the complex sequence (the sentence, the visual scene and the complex action) and the problems of decoding, that is the process of interpreting the acoustic or visual information into which the sentence spoken by another individual or the perceived visual world or the ordering and intent of the complex action initiated by another individual (or otherwise in the external environment) is converted. It seems probable that there are similar techniques, physiological and neurological, employed in the decoding, the solution of the problem of interpretation presented by immediate experience, in the different forms of vision, action and language

e. in the visual scene, complex action and sentence, there is an extraordinarily complicated interrelation of the semantic content and the syntactic ordering. For the real visual scene, the real complex action and the real sentence, there is the same overriding importance of the total context in which the scene is observed, the action is executed or the sentence is spoken or formed; the extraction of the meaningful content of the scene, action or sentence, from the context is closely analogous to the separation of scene into Figure and Ground as discussed by the Gestalt psychologists; the observing individual has to be find somewhere, somehow, in the overwhelming complexity of forms and relationships with which he is presented at any moment, the outline that really matters, that can be directly related to his own structure of perception, expectations and intentions for action, his own understanding of the meaning of what he hear or his own preparation to convert what he thinks into a communicable language-form;

f. the living fact of speech, action and vision is continuity; in reality the human individual's experience is unbroken, other than by deep coma or death. In reality, there are no distinct, separable, visual scenes, complex actions or sentences. They all form part of an unbroken stream of perception, action and speech (or thought about or in terms of speech). In a sense, then, visual scene, complex action and sentence are ideal units, the sentence a discourse-unit in some ways parallel to the phoneme as a speech-sound unit, and so on. But at the same time these units are operationally real; we store complex actions as plans or integrated intentions, we have an integrated pattern of meaning which by the speech processes we convert from its simultaneous form as a pattern into a serial string of words spread over time, and we convert the serial sequence in visual perception constituted by the eye-movements and fixations into an integrated, momentarily perceived, total scene. For speech, action and vision, there is as an experimental fact something one can describe as the 'psychological present', the time taken for processing detail and sequence into unity—and even though reality, external and internal, is continuous, nevertheless we need the possibility of discontinuity which the 'psychological present' represents (and which for action, vision and speech has a very intimate relation to the research done into the characteristics of Short Term Memory and the well-known limitations on the number of distinct items, distinct focuses of attention, that we can hold in mind at any one time);

g.   finally, amongst these broader points extracted from earlier discussion, there is the overriding one that quite apart from the underlying structural interrelation of language, visual perception and action, there is in real life no sharp division of our experience in any period into vision, action or language. Vision and action proceed together mutually modifying each other; language itself is action, can refer to action, can cause action and can be modified in its form from moment to moment by the train of visual perception. Even if, in evolutionary terms, the needs of action gave rise to the need to perfect perception and language developed to support and supplement both action and perception, the three now are co-operating aspects of human behaviour, three intersecting circles—where one might, quite helpfully, conceive of the central area which the three circles share as that part of the physiological and neurological processes, controlled by the cortex, and particularly the motor cortex, where the patterns of action, vision and speech come together and mutually determine each other. In this central area (or in some area of the brain closely related to it) one kind of action is enabled to regulate and be regulated by other types of action, one kind of perception (external perception or perception of internal state) can be scrutinised and interpreted by another more abstract form of perception (perception of perception) and language at a more abstract level acquires the ability not only to speak about the contents of action and perception but also about the character of language itself—language becomes self-reflexive as perception becomes self-reflexive.

The immediately preceding paragraphs have listed a number of the more striking parallelisms of structure and process underlying speech, visual perception and action as they emerge from the detailed examination in Chapters III, IV and V (so far) of each the three Stages in the hierarchical progress, Stage I—the elementary units, Stage II—the formation of words, shapes and action-routines from the elementary units and Stage III—the formation of sequences and combinations of words, shapes and action-routines into sentences, visual scenes and complex actions. Against the background of the basic evolutionary hypothesis in Chapter II on the relation of language, perception and action, these broad parallelisms suggest that it might be profitable to take the next, much more concrete, further step in the examination of the interrelation or speech, vision and action, namely (taking into account work in linguistics, and research into vision and voluntary action) to try to establish a listing or table of specific possibly equivalent aspects and then to see how far progress made in one sector, for example the study of scanning in vision, can be related to progress made in another sector, for example the study of the functioning of word-order in speech. Obviously a great mass of material could be introduced, and would be relevant, at this point in any extensive synoptic view of work in progress in three such active fields of scientific study as language, perception and voluntary action. Some limit must be placed on what can be discussed here and some not too complicated way found of setting out the possible equivalent aspects for treatment. What seems most straightforward is to provide a list or table, divided into groups which bring together aspects of theory or research from the fields of language, perception which may repay joint consideration. The table or list of possible equivalences for consideration is as follows:

TABLE OF ASPECTS AND PROCESSES UNDERLYING SPEECH, VISUAL PERCEPTION AND ACTION FOR EXAMINATION IN PARALLEL

1. Processing period Short-term memory and the limitation on the number of itemS which can be held in attention at any one time seem to be general aspects found in psychological research. In particular the standard finding is that no more than 7 items can be attended to at one time and this must have implications for the comprehension of the sentence, for the perception of the contents

within the framework of the present book, to attempt any comprehensive treatment in depth of these topics or even of any considerable selection of these topics. Nevertheless, it may be useful to illustrate the practical way in which the basic hypothesis on the relation of language, vision and action can be developed in specific fields of study (and can be related to work already in progress in specialised fields) and also as a preliminary to the discussion in the concluding section of this Chapter of the 'solution' of the visual scene and the sentence in general terms, to pick out a few topics from the list for comment—together with brief reference to some of the more interesting pointers or speculations to which other items in the list give rise.

Of the fourteen topics, there are four which seem to call for more extensive treatment here, that is No. 5, dealing with the parallels between word-order and scanning in vision, No. 8, dealing with the relation between parts-of-speech and parts-of-sentence on the one hand and the comparable aspects of the visual scene, No. 10, dealing with the relation between types of sentence and the material drawn from perception or action with which different types of sentence are concerned and No. 12, the parallel treatment of ambiguous sentences and ambiguous pictures, topics of central importance both in linguistics and in vision research. Probably rather little extra needs to be said about a number of the other topics, either because they have already received a good deal of attention in the course of earlier discussion (such as No. 2, hierarchical processing and feature-detection, No. 6, the significance of the Figure and Ground, or No. 15, metaphor, considered at some length in Chapter IV) or because they can be treated more relevantly later in this Chapter or in Chapter VII (dealing with broader philosophical issues (topics No. 1 and No. 4). Nevertheless, subject to the different degrees of attention or emphasis given to the different topics, the remaining material in this section of the present Chapter is arranged broadly in the order in which the topics appear in the Table on pages 116/18. For topics dealt with more briefly the comment is in note form and reference is made elsewhere to fuller discussion in the literature.

Processing period With this it is convenient to take the fourth topic, the unity or integrity of sentence, scene and complex action. The sentence and the scene (and the complex action plan) are psychological unities where the meaning of the whole depends on the meaning attached to the parts, and the meaning ascribed to the parts is determined by the meaning derived for the whole. Sentence, scene and action constitute or express unitary meanings—fragments which go to form or modify the total cognitive structure of the individual and the individual's moment-to-moment organisation for action or perception. The meanings which the sentence, the scene, or the complex action plan constitute have been described as partial states of organisation of the complete human organism. The formation or the expression of a particular unity of meaning depends on two closely related factors, the extent of the psychological present, within which the incoming information has to be formed into a unity, and the number of distinct items of information which can be focused on at one tine, the span of attention. Man's immediate memory capacity is limited to about seven concepts, plus or minus two or three in individual cases, but each concept can be quite complex (not just seven dots but seven objects, or possibly even seven theories); the processing problem is to identify within the available 'psychological present' the distinct items on which to focus and then to construct these parts into the whole. The operation in effect in each case is either the conversion of the serial (the information produced by scanning) into the simultaneous, which is the unitary meaning-pattern, or the reverse process of conversion of the simultaneous, the present meaning-pattern of the sentence or the action-plan, into the serial form of the string of words in the sentence or the sequence of action-routines going to form the complex action. One aspect of particular relevance to the typical structure of the sentence (discussed later) is the strong tendency for the string of words to be grouped round a small number of sentence-nuclei, often only two or three—and this simplicity of basic patterning may be related to the psychological factors referred to in this paragraph.

Hierarchical processing and feature-detection A great part of the discussion in earlier Chapters, in relation to speech, vision and action, has been concerned with these broad characteristics of the apparent functioning of the systems for constructing and perceiving complex forms. There seems no need to go over the ground again at this point though of course there are many aspects which are currently the subject of extensive research and there are other research topics which might be useful to test or explore the implications of the broad hypothesis presented in this book.

Deep structure and surface structure The terms 'deep structure' and 'surface structure' are those popularised by Chomsky(17). On his approach, the deep structure of a sentence is the abstract underlying form which pattern of saccades and fixations in scanning, the segmentation of the scanning process;

— the distinction of word-order between active and passive sentences can be taken as reflecting simply a difference in the choice of initial focal element in scanning—and the differences of ordering in interrogative sentences can be related to differences of scanning strategy in visual search;

— neither in scanning nor in word-order is there anything which requires attention to be paid to the items in a sequence only once, in a given order. It seems clear that in vision scanning is not straightforwardly serial but the eye may return to examine more closely an object already looked at, i.e. scanning may be a recursive process with an initial provisional interpretation from a first scanning confirmed or adjusted by a further sequence of fixations. It seems probable that in the decoding of the sentence, much the same procedure can operate, that is attention may concentrate first on certain elements of the sentence and may then be switched back to earlier points in the word-order for closer examination of detail—a process very similar to what in some recent Artificial Intelligence work has been described as interpretation-guided segmentation and parsing. Something like this provisional and recursive process is apparent in Karl Lashley's famous example of the problems involved in the serial interpretation of the spoken sentence: "Rapid righting with his uninjured hand saved from loss the contents of the capsized canoe"(21)—where the last two words required an instant revision of the interpretation of the whole preceding string of words.

Figure and Ground

A good deal has already been said in this Chapter and in earlier chapters about the relevance of the concepts of figure and ground as developed by the Gestalt psychologists—and which, one might say, seem to have some real physiological significance or equivalence in the processes of contour and contrast enhancement operating through lateral inhibition at every stage of the visual process, to intensify the perception of a straight line, a particular contour or shape or possibly even more complex groupings recognised as three-dimensional objects (related to the process by which stored schemas or models are developed). As certain contours are sharpened, other material necessarily sinks into a less clearly perceived background. Perception thus becomes organised in terms of focal objects, the detail of such objects, and the relations of focal objects, one with another and with the general framework of the scene, the background. A similar process of separation of figure from ground almost certainly underlies our ability to perceive and interpret significant sequences of action in the external environment. Much of this thinking can be applied to the organisation and comprehension of the sentence; language communicating a perception must reliably indicate the elements on which attention should be focused (the 'figures' against the general background of the sentence) and the relations between the focal elements as well as aspects of the focal elements. In the same way as, to quote Neisser: "The Gestalt psychologists had innumerable examples to prove that the figure as a whole, rather than its parts individually or additively, determines what we see" (perceptual constancies, visual grouping, apparent movement, colour relationships), so one can readily quote examples to show that it is the sentence as a whole which determines the values, both functional and semantic, to be given to the individual words in it. There can be remote effects of local variations as Karl Lashley's sentence quoted in the immediately preceding paragraph strikingly illustrated.

Semantic fields and selection restrictions

Chapter IV discussed at some length semantic fields and the questions raised in relation to the structuring of the lexicon. Perhaps nothing more on this needs to be said here—but a word on selection rules or restraints, an idea associated closely with the development of Chomsky's transformational generative grammar. The need for selection rules in transformational syntax seems to arise rather artificially from the pre-eminence given to syntactic rules and the practical difficulties then encountered in the grammatical analysis of sentences where the appropriateness of the structure depends on the meanings of the nouns and verbs appearing in the sentence. The proposition in transformational grammar that particular nouns impose selection restraints on the verbs with which they can be used can much more simply be dealt with in terms of the structuring of the lexicon, the semantic groupings into which words naturally fall (on the lines proposed in Chapter IV).

Parts-of-speech and parts-of-sentence

This is a very large topic and one of central importance. One's first simple view may be that, as the traditional grammar tells us, there are eight or nine parts of speech (the number varies from language to language and even for English some grammarians offer slightly different groupings) such as Noun, Verb, Adjective, Adverb, Preposition, Conjunction and so on and that in the lexicon each word can conveniently be assigned to one or other of the categories of parts-of-speech; similarly the traditional grammar tells us that there are several familiar parts of the sentence and, by parsing, one can determine to which category of parts-of-the-sentence any individual word belongs, such as Subject, Object, Verbal Predicate, Complement, Indirect Object (and of course there is a larger-scale categorisation of parts of the sentence into main clause and subsidiary clauses (of various types) and into groupings of words in phrases which have functions similar to those of individual words serving as Subject, Object &c). More modernly, the parts of the sentence may be somewhat differently described, as Actor, Action and Goal, Agent and Instrument, Head and Modifier as constituents of a phrase) and so on.

The important question, from the point of view adopted in this book on the relation between the structure of language and the structures of vision and action, is whether these traditional parts-of-speech and parts-of-sentence are purely formal and arbitrary classifications (just another aspect of what linguisticians generally describe as the arbitrariness of language) or whether they have some natural basis, some relation in fact to syntactic and semantic organisation of vision and action. Why should there be these parts of speech and these parts of sentence? Why should there be the classifications of noun and verb? Are the other parts of speech equally natural and necessary—or simply arbitrary features of a particular language? How universal in fact is the classification of parts of speech and parts of sentence as an indication of the natural basis of this aspect of grammar? To answer these questions, one would ideally like to have available a generally or universally agreed account by professional linguists of the definitive list of parts of speech and parts of sentence, which one could then match or contrast with the aspects of organisation found in the descriptions so far given in this book of the structure and processes underlying vision and action. The reality unfortunately is that the nature of parts of speech, the proper analysis of the sentence into parts, are the subject of fierce and so far inconclusive debate between linguists. Not only is there argument about what should or should not be treated as a part of speech and about what should or should not be categorised as a functional part of the sentence—but many linguists indeed would challenge the idea that one can think separately and usefully about two such broad classifications as parts-of-speech and parts-of-sentence. One's impression, after studying the accounts of a number of respected grammarians and linguists, is that there is an unresolved confusion between the classification of words in isolation (as segments of the lexicon) and classification of words as functioning in particular sentences—and that the confusion extends to the issue whether the categories used, in terms of meaning or in terms of sentence-function, have or have not any relation to the world of experience, to which language as actually used must relate.

A few quotations from discussion about parts-of-speech in the English language, will illustrate the situation. The traditional approach is to define a part of speech in terms of the class-meaning. So: 'a noun is the name of a person, place or thing' but is 'fire" a thing? Class meanings elude the linguist's power of definition'. 'It may be that our nonlinguistic world consists of objects, actions, qualities, manners and relations, but we would still have to determine the English parts of speech not by their correspondence with different aspects of the practical world but by their functions in syntax'. According to some grammarians, accordingly, the very definitions of Noun, Verb and similar word-classes must be formulated in terms of the positions where particular words can appear in sentence 'frames'. 'A noun can be the subject of a verb or the object of a verb or a preposition, an adjective can modify a noun and be modified by an adverb, a conjunction occurs between words of comparable classes &c &c (Yuen Ren Chao(22). But in fact in English, and in other languages, "the various parts of speech not merely grade into each other but to an astonishing degree are actually convertible into each other" (Sapir (23)); many words in English may in different sentences have different functional classifications, may serve as noun or verb or adjective; a verb form, the infinitive, may function in the same positions in a sentence-frame as a noun, so that function as a basis for the classification of parts of speech either collapses or becomes circular. The definition of parts-of-speech both in terms of categories of meaning of individual words and of the typical functions of individual words in a sentence seems, in the discussions of professional linguists, to have reached an impasse: so, some say "the form-classes of English words are largely arbitrary', there is nothing in the overt character of a word to settle that it is a noun, a verb or an adjective; at best, class-meanings of parts of speech may represent "vague situational features, undefinable in terms of linguistics" or "composites, the highest common factors of the grammatical meanings which accompany the forms'; though the parts of speech may have begun as semantic classes they have "now grown fuzzy and inconsistent through historical change . . . to the point where semantic attributes are only probabilistic in their association with form classes"(24). At worst, in the view of Sapir, who devoted a good deal of attention to the nature of the traditional parts of speech, "conventional classification of words into parts of speech is only a vague wavering approximation to a consistently worked out inventory of experience. A part of speech outside of the limitations of syntactic form is but a will o' the wisp. For this reason no logical scheme of the parts of speech—their number, nature and necessary confines—is of the slightest interest to the linguist"(23).

Even if for the moment one accepts this extremist view of Sapir about the status of the parts-of-speech classification, the question remains whether there is greater agreement on, or greater validity in the traditional and more modern classifications of the parts-of-sentence, the way in which a sentence is segmented, either in terms of the function of individual words or of particular phrases. A traditional list of parts-of-sentence would be Subject, Object, Indirect Object, Verbal Predicate, Complement or Attributive Predicate, and the simple sentence, which might have a two-nuclei or three-nuclei form, might be elaborated by the use of adjuncts (phrase groupings) or sub-clauses with similar roles to adjuncts, which might be attached to any of the basic parts of the sentence (subject or object adjuncts or clauses, adverbial or predicate adjuncts or clauses) or there may be 'free adjuncts', which are detached from and relate to or are set in opposition to the whole of the sentence. On the traditional view, these various parts of the sentence, and elaborations of them, tend to cluster round the two or three main nuclei of the sentence.

But some of the difficulties already encountered in determining and distinguishing the parts-of-speech in relation to individual words are found again in attempts to find a systematic basis for classifying particular word phrases or classes in a given sentence as belonging to one or other of the specified parts-of-sentence. There have been rather parallel, and almost equally unsatisfactory, approaches to the problem. Some would say that the character of a word, a phrase or a clause as a particular part of the sentence is to be determined by the characteristic slots in the sentence frame in which the word or words are found; others would say that there are intrinsic markers of words or phrases to indicate the part of the sentence that they constitute e.g.—less—s—ly are markers which show the surface-structure, the parts-of-sentence, in a sentence such as Chomsky's 'Colourless green ideas sleep furiously'—and, in rather a similar way, the sentence-structure can be indicated by function words, determining adjectives, prepositions, coordinating conjunctions and subordinating conjunctions and such words can, because their classification as parts of speech is known, go to determine the form-class of the phrase or clause in which they appear. On the other hand, there is a powerful school of thought which rejects such markers as indicators of syntactic structure, that is the parts into which a sentence ought properly to be divided (and so one has the 'deep structure' approach to syntax). Others point out that one can only determine the sentence-structure, the parts of the sentence, by a comprehension of the meaning and that 'normally it is possible to decide intuitively on the basis of the way in which the meaning of a sentence is organised where to draw the dividing line between constituents' (one needs to understand the actual meaning of the particular words in that particular sentence). But this is open to the same criticism of circularity as applied to the somewhat similar attempt to determine the part of speech to which a particular word belongs. If one has already interpreted the meaning of the particular sentence and of the individual words as used in it, to analyse the sentence then into parts-of-sentence based on the meaning seems a purely formal and rather pointless exercise.

At first sight, the discussion based on the views of linguists on the definition, the identification and reality of traditional parts-of-speech and parts-of-sentence leaves one with a rather desperate impression that grammatical analysis, perhaps the whole approach of linguistics, is founded on a quicksand; there is no solid ground from which one can start to compare the syntactic features of language and the organisational features of vision and action, as correspondingly complex behavioural processes. This rather confused picture of modern analysis contrasts with the splendid order of classical grammar, in Latin or Greek; in Latin parts of speech were marked off from each other structurally as well as in use. Nouns were declined and their role in the sentence defined by the varying suffixes; verbs were conjugated and marked by variations in form for their relation to other words in the sentence and for tense; prepositions and conjunctions were invariable in form but their role in the sentence was clear by the modifications of the nouns or verbs associated with them; adjectives were marked by their form and their role indicated by declension in agreement with the associated nouns; adverbs were marked generally as a form derived systematically from an adjectival form. And of course there are still living languages where the difficulties and ambiguities found in English are avoided because they have retained complex inflectional structures resembling those in Latin or Greek.

The situation is perhaps not so desperate as it seems. Though English and other languages may have parts-of-speech or parts-of-sentence which are difficult to identify or classify, and some languages may have a much smaller list of parts-of-speech than one finds in traditional grammar, there are universal or near-universal features which comparative study of a wide range of languages seems to demonstrate. Joseph Greenberg, in his work on language universals, includes amongst the list of likely universals:

1. All languages have sentences made of at least two kinds: nominals and verbals
2. All languages have adjectival expressions which modify nominals and adverbial expressions which modify verbals
3. All languages have devices for linking of nominals and of verbals (heaven and earth, sink or swim)
4. Many languages have 'dummy' elements (analogous to pronouns or demonstratives)—all languages have pronominal categories.

No language then wholly fails to distinguish between noun and verb and though in particular cases the distinction may be somewhat blurred, the near universality of these as categories suggests that they have a natural base. It is interesting, though not conclusive, that some of the earlier experiments in neurology on the effects of comprehension of speech and perception of visual objects in 'split-brain' cases (that is where for clinical reasons in human beings a complete division has had to be made between the right and left hemispheres of the brain) showed that whilst normally the left hemisphere (which in most individuals is specialised for language comprehension and production whilst the right hemisphere is more specialised for analysis of visual shapes and structures) could comprehend and use verbs as well as other parts of speech, the right hemisphere could comprehend nouns but not other parts or forms of speech; if this finding were to be fully confirmed, then noun and verb would be distinct categories in the most definite natural, physiological sense. The distinction between the noun, as a structure, and a verb as an expression of action would seem to be positively established.

As regards other parts of speech, the degree of universality is much more uncertain—though it must be remembered that what in one language may be conveyed through an isolable word, as a distinct part of speech, may in another be conveyed by a prefix or suffix; in a language with a theoretically complete case system for the noun, there would be no need for prepositions as distinct parts of speech, even though the language would, by a different device, convey exactly the same kind of information as is represented by the class of prepositions in a language such as English. Greenberg's study of universals also showed evidence for more uniformity in sentence-construction, the parts-of-sentence, than the earlier discussion might suggest. For the range of languages he examined, by far the dominant order, with the elements as Subject, Verb and Object, is that the Subject precedes the Object and there are systematic relations between other features of sentence-construction and the particular order of the three main elements that a language adopts.

What in the light of this discussion can one say about the relation between parts-of-speech and parts-of-sentence in language and parts-of-vision or parts-of-complex action in voluntary activity? As regards the parts-of-sentence, this is closely related to the issues already discussed fairly fully above—the relation between word-order and the system of scanning in visual perception (or the sequential analysis of a complex action). Subject Stative Verb and Attribute or Complement, or Actor Action and Goal as modes of analysis of the construction of sentences seem to have a clear natural relation to the processes of perception of a visual scene and the planning or execution of a complex action. The more important question for this section is whether one can have, for language, what might be called a 'neo-parts-of-speech' approach based on the relation between language, vision and action.

A common view (as represented in quotations earlier in this section) is that it is a mistake to suppose that our parts of speech system represents universal features of human expression; if such classes as objects, actions and qualities exist apart from our language, as realities either of physics or psychology, then of course they exist all over the world but it would still be true to say that many languages lack corresponding parts of speech'. But in the end any language to be effective must make possible the communication of the specific structure of experience, and particularly of visual perception and action. To say that the parts of speech identified by the classical grammarians only imperfectly correspond to the parts of speech, for example, in English, or that other languages do not have the same sets of parts of speech as are found in English and other languages, does not mean that the set of parts-of-speech, theoretically or actually, is an arbitrary, purposeless structure—any more than the fact that different languages use different phoneme-sets means that phonemes are arbitrary and purposeless forms. Maybe the analysis of words into parts of speech (or of sentences into distinct parts) by the grammarians was a provisional or defective exercise, based on too narrow a range of languages or on too imperfect an understanding of the way in which language functions—but underlying the parts-of-speech system, which forms only a part of the total communicative system of language, lies inevitably the structure of parts and relations of which human experience is composed. The set of parts-of-speech available to us indicates at least some of the aspects of the perceived scene, the complex action, that must be represented in language, even if other devices in this and other languages have to be used in combination to produce a precise and useful representation of the scene or action.

If one adopts a quite new approach, that is considers how one might categorise parts of speech in terms of what we know about the structure and processes of perception and voluntary action, then one could arrive at a much more securely based categorisation, which could be tested in physiological and psychological research, or used in the Artificial Intelligence approach to natural language processing. The identification of analogous parts of speech could proceed quite straightforwardly from analysis of the components of the visual scene: the focal elements, distinguishing and qualifying features of the focal elements, the spatial and other relationships of the focal elements in the scene, the distinction between primary and secondary focal elements, together with aspects of the scene referring to movement within the scene or movement of the scene as a whole, the linking of one scene to another, directions of movement, types of movement. In this way, one would quickly arrive at visual equivalents for nouns, adjectives, prepositions adverbs, verbs, and conjunctions—and in the aspects of familiarity, novelty or emphasis in the scene one would arrive at analogies of pronouns, demonstratives, determiners (the articles) and so on. On such an analysis, the parts of speech, matching parts-of-vision, would divide into the more important features, the static elements on which the eye focuses (the nouns), the pattern of change within the scene (the verbal aspect) and relational features between elements in the scene or action in progress (prepositions, adverbs, functional words more generally).

This set of equivalences between parts-of-speech and parts of a relatively simple visual scene could be developed to apply to more complex scenes, to combinations of action and perception, to sentences reflecting internal perception or more abstract experience. In much the same way as earlier the vital role of metaphor was described in extending the application of the primitive vocabulary and the structuring it reflected to remoter intellectual subject-matter, the parts-of-speech identified for the simple scene would still remain applicable by analogy, or metaphor. For example, whilst the simplest natural base for the Noun as a category is the figure, shape or object in visual perception, it would be extended metaphorically to cover units in internal perception (patterns on which focal attention would be directed) so that it would not be surprising that abstract concepts like civilisation or processes or events considered as a static pattern, should be treated as nouns, as 'things'.

The conclusion reached is that whilst there is a question whether the traditional parts of speech analysis, derived from Latin, was an adequate or experientially fully appropriate one for English and other modern languages, it remains the case that it is convenient to be able to approach sentences in terms of parts-of-speech (even if the classes are sometimes imprecise and sometimes it is difficult to say whether a word belongs to one class or another). The traditional set of parts of speech does reflect, even if imperfectly, real aspects of our experience of vision and action and, with some modification, one can easily construct a 'neo-parts-of-speech system' which can be correlated reasonably well with a parts-of-vision or parts-of-action analysis. How other languages in fact manage with fewer or different parts of speech is something which can more appropriately be considered in the comparative chapter, Chapter VI, but where they have fewer parts, they seem to achieve the economy by greater complexity in other aspects of their syntactic structures.

Syntactic system

It might seem superfluous to deal specifically at this point with questions relating to the syntactic system of a language (as set against the syntactic systems of visual perception or action). In a sense, the whole book has been concerned with syntactic issues—the ways in which parts and aspects of language are organised into meaningful wholes—and certainly a number of the individual topics listed in the Table on pages 116/118 are typical aspects of syntax: deep structure and surface structure, word-order, selection restraints, parts-of-speech and parts-of-sentence, types of sentence. Nevertheless. there are some broader questions about the syntactic system on which points can be made more conveniently here than elsewhere. There are after all now a number of competing accounts of syntactic organisation as a result of discontent with the application of traditional grammar to modern languages. One has had the development of the very powerful school of transformational generative grammarians; there have other important attempts at systematisation on a new basis such as Halliday's(25) systemic grammar and Fillmore's(25) case grammar approach; there has been a great deal of work done in computational linguistics in the development of programs for handling syntax as part of the Natural Language effort in AI.

In the prolonged campaign to find a satisfactory approach to syntactic structures, there have been the pessimists, such as Sapir: "form, form for form's sake is as natural to the life of language as the retention of outmoded conduct"(26) and others who have said that the mechanisms of grammatical speech are almost too complex to contemplate. There have been not so much the optimists as the hopeful, who think that there is a strong case for saying that the whole of language is a network of mutually defining structural relationships—between sounds, between morphemes, between words and between sentences. Saussure's concept of language as a system (rather like the system of rules of the game of chess) was perhaps the first approach of this kind. And there have also been the pragmatists, those searching for an approach to syntax which works, has a practical value (most notably those seeking to construct syntax programs for computers).

Despite the dissatisfaction with traditional grammar (and discussion earlier in this section has indicated some of its weaknesses), it still has its uses; it is still largely the basis on which languages are taught to foreign students, it provides a framework for comparative statement of the syntactic features of different languages and even the newer linguists, who criticise it most severely, still find themselves using terms and classifications drawn from classical grammar. In much the same way as we go on using the traditional alphabet (despite its imperfections for representing distinct speech-sounds), so traditional grammar still retains a value as a starting point, a point of reference from which new theory has in fact developed. As a heuristic device (which has been used already in this Chapter), one can ask such questions as: How orderly is traditional grammar? How intelligible is the system it presents? How universal are the features it identifies? How useful is it as a practical instrument of analysis? How natural (based in human experience) are the categories and relationships it provides? The different approaches of modern linguists are in effect attempts to answer questions of these kind—and one can evaluate their new systems by the same criteria as have been applied to depreciate the value of traditional syntax and grammar. Perhaps in the end one may find that what is needed is not so much some totally new system of syntax but a reinterpretation of traditional syntax combined with an effort to show how different languages use different combinations of syntactic features to achieve results isomorphic with those produced by the traditional syntactic system.

Each of the new systems has its merits and its critics. This is not the place to attempt to expound at length either the form of the new theories of syntax or the merits and weaknesses which others have seen in them. As regards transformational grammar, something has already been said in an earlier part of this section about the concept of 'deep structure' which is fundamental to it and about the usefulness of the idea of selection restraints as a way of incorporating semantic features in the syntactic system; a later part of this section discusses briefly two other fundamental terms in transformational grammar, competence and performance. The debate about transformational grammar continues but perhaps to the quotation from Luria earlier in this Chapter one can add George Lakoff's very general criticism of the assumptions on which transformational grammar was founded twenty years ago, assumptions which he now believes to be too limited or completely wrong-headed, namely "that language acquisition consists of constructing grammars on the basis of primarily linguistic data . . . that linguistic structure is independent of linguistic function . . . that phrase structure rules and transformations are the right kinds of devices for characterising linguistic rules"(27). At a minimum one might say that transformational generative grammar has not yet been developed into a system which gives an adequate, complete and operationally useful account of the syntactic functioning of language which one can rely on totally to supersede and make unnecessary the more traditional approach to syntax.

On the other hand, a good deal of practical value can be derived from two other new approaches to syntax, Fillmore's case frame approach and Halliday's functionally-based systemic grammar. Fillmore's approach is not in terms of the traditional concept of 'case' (inflections of the noun) but in terms of the types of judgments which human beings are capable of making about events going on around them; in his system the verb, the action element, is the central feature and he would say that the sentence in all languages can be reduced to a set of propositions, principally taking the form of a configuration of cases (in terms of semantic aspects of the real event or scene) grouped around the verb(28). The emphasis on the contact between syntactic structure and the real event is also one aspect of the more extensive and systematic account of syntax presented by Halliday. In his approach there are two key elements: first his view that the structure of language as a whole has been built up in such a way that it reflects the demands made on language and, the functions that it is required to serve and secondly his concept of the ordered hierarchical network which the grammar of a language constitutes, that is the analysis of the traditional categories of grammar into an assembly of features which are structurally related one to another; the network takes the form of a collection of systems, an arrangement of options, in simultaneous and hierarchical relationships. This opens the way to the idea of formation of a sentence as the outcome of a serial process of choosing between available options at each level for realising the particular function the sentence is intended to serve. In place of the unordered collection of categories and forms found in traditional grammar, one now has an operationally usable ordered structure of grammar, which empirically is found in the specific pattern of its structuring to be directly related to the functional capabilities of language. This is inevitably a very compressed account of the extensive and carefully formulated presentation by Halliday of his ideas. Perhaps one of the best indications of the practical usefulness of his system is that, in one of the most successful (though still limited) attempts in Artificial Intelligence to formulate a program for the interaction in computer operation of vision, action and language (Terry Winograd's(29) program by which a computer was able to analyse (and reply to) sentences spoken to it in ordinary language and, on the basis of its understanding of any sentence to execute particular changes in the simplified environment with which it was presented—the movement and arrangement of blocks of different colours and shapes on a table-surface), the very effective parsing component of the program, by which the computer extracted the meaning of the sentences spoken to it, was based on Halliday's systemic grammar. Since then, there has been a very considerable development of work in Artificial Intelligence in relation to natural language understanding, machine vision and the control of action. Apart from the contributions made by theoretical linguists and by work in AI, there is perhaps no need to recall here once again in any detail the influential views of Karl Lashley on syntax as a phenomenon of the greatest importance and generality in the functioning of all types of human behaviour, not only language but also vision and action; parallels derived from his approach have been used at many points in this and in previous chapters.

This brief discussion of the different approaches to syntactic system, by linguists, computer experts and even a neurologist, is intended to make it possible to see how far or how little there are points of contact between the views presented in this book on the natural basis of syntax (and of language generally) in the structures needed to parallel visual perception and voluntary activity as aspects of human and the traditional and more modern grammatical and syntactic theories of others. Earlier it has been suggested that 'deep structure' as a concept from transformational grammar can be reinterpreted to refer to the underlying physiological and neurological structuring of vision and action. Fillmore's approach to syntax in terms of the analysis of the structure of events in the real world is obviously fundamentally not far removed from the view in this book that the structure of action is reflected in the structuring and syntax of language. The combination in Halliday's theory of emphasis on grammar as a very specifically structured hierarchical system, the character of which is related to and largely determined by the functions which language has to serve, comes even closer to the hypothesis examined in this Chapter and in the book as a whole. Finally, one can say that even traditional grammar (certainly as evolved for the classical languages) constituted an attempt to establish a structural relation between language and the world of experience—and that traditional grammar represent the choice of one amongst a number of possible, naturally-based and isomorphic systems of coding for the conversion of the ordering of perception and action into the serial form which language must take.

Types of sentence

Earlier in the Chapter there was fairly extensive discussion of the bases on which sentences might be classified into different types and the relation of the types of sentence to the types of visual scene or action to which they referred. Whilst one can readily start from the two basic types of sentence, those related to perception of the visual scene and those related to complex action, in reality there is a very great range of types of sentence, deriving from elaboration of these basic types, the combination of the material that the sentence expresses of experience involving both perception and action, the introduction into the sentence of aspects of internal perception (what the speaker feels or intends &c), the modification of the type of sentence by the objective with which it is expressed (whether to describe, command, persuade, warn &c); and beyond the variation in the types of sentence actually encountered because of variations in the type of experience to which the sentences refer, there are variations of type due to formal changes, resulting from the combination of sentences, the compression of a sentence-meaning into a single clause or phrase (or possibly even into a single word) in the sentence, the reference in one sentence to other sentences, preceding or following, or to concurrent non-linguistic context; beyond all these, there are the complexities of sentence-type due to the fact that sentences can refer directly to other sentences, report what has been said or thought and even discuss the manner in which language has been used in a particular instance to express a particular content. One finds an immense range in the complexity of sentences from the simplest: 'The cat is white' 'The man hit the dog' to highly-involved sentences encountered in philosophical or scientific discourse, far removed from the easily identified structures of sentences patterned directly on vision or action. Complexity of the sentence may arise from the process of compacting into one sentence different categories of experience, or experience acquired at different points in time (remembered experience, expected experience) or more generally from the requirement that the sentence must be capable of reflecting the real complexity of human behaviour, human intellectual processes and of the external world. Though language cannot possibly reflect the total complex detail even of the simplest scene (the sentence must always to some extent be a skeleton representation), there must be forms of sentence, types of sentence, which make it possible to model the complexity of reality, the complexities of organisation not only in time and space but also in cognitive organisation of the individual.

Context

In this Chapter and earlier, there has already been a great deal of stress on the importance of context for the perception of the visual scene, the comprehension of the spoken sentence or indeed for the execution of the complex action (or the understanding of the complex action executed by another). The importance of context exists not only at the level of the sentence or scene but in relation to each word in the sentence or each word in the sentence or each element in the scene. Each word has associated with it certain other words, closely or remotely, and each perceptual shape or object has associated with it other shapes and objects, parts of objects, frames within which the object is usually found, sequences of events in which the object forms an element and so on. Much of the discussion of presuppositions (of sentences), of 'frames' in AI vision research, of semantic primitives and semantic fields, of 'conceptual dependency' and 'scripts' in Schank's(30) approach to knowledge-representation by computer, of the function of 'deixis' and demonstrative words, in fact forms part of the very broad subject of the relation between context and the particular event of experience or behaviour. No doubt, what would be useful, but cannot be attempted here, would be the drawing-together and comparison of the research and theoretical discussion of these different aspects of context; it is something of this kind that in fact is being attempted in the effort currently devoted in Artificial Intelligence to the construction of knowledge representation systems, knowledge representation languages, for use in computer programming. What so far has hampered progress in many aspects of computer program development, to simulate or replicate human abilities, has been precisely the lack of a rich enough context, available to the computer, for adapting its execution of the program in the kind of way that a human being automatically adapts his sentence or his action to the circumstances.

Ambiguous sentences and ambiguous pictures

The importance of the 'ambiguous picture' as a central topic for vision research has already been stressed, and the 'ambiguous sentence' has in recent years played an almost equally important role in modern linguistics. The dictionary definition of ambiguity is the property of having double or dubious meaning, something open to more than one interpretation. The question of the ambiguousness of the visual scene or of the sentence is very closely indeed related to the issue of the significance of context which has been discussed immediately above and also to the central problem dealt with in the concluding section of this chapter, that is how, as a general matter, the processes underlying language and visual perception operate to allow one to arrive at a single correct interpretation of the sentence or visual scene, precisely how one disambiguates the information presented in the visual stimuli to the retina or in the acoustic stimuli to the receptive surface of the ear.

Neisser(31) has drawn attention to the effective use made by the Gestalt psychologists of ambiguous pictures to illustrate the importance of the structure of the scene or figure as a whole in determining the meaning attached to particular parts or regions of the scene, and has pointed out that in modern linguistics ambiguous sentences have been given a similarly important role. To match the familiar ambiguous figures, the pattern which can be seen either as the outline of a vase or as the contours of two faces looking at one another, the Necker cube which at one moment appears to project out of the plane of the paper towards you and the next moment appears to recede away from you, the detailed drawing of a woman's head which can be interpreted at one moment as that of an old woman and at the next moment (with a shift of perception) as that of a young woman (originally published under the title 'My Wife and My Mother-in-law'). For striking illustrations of the range of ambiguous pictures see Attneave's article "Multistability in Perception"(32). One has a substantial collection of now very familiar ambiguous sentences (which have been the subject of much discussion by Chomsky and his followers) including such examples as: 'The police were ordered to stop drinking' 'Flying planes can be dangerous' 'They are eating apples' 'What disturbed John was being disregarded by everyone'.

Chomsky has argued forcefully that ambiguous sentences provide a particularly clear indication of the inadequacy of the surface structure of a sentence as a representation of deeper relations. His position is that surface structure of any type, any type of labelled bracketing of words in the sentence into constituent groups, any attempt to account for the structure of the sentence in terms of contiguity of parts or association between successive parts is bound to fail—as, he contends, is shown by the impossibility of satisfactory grammatical analysis of some of the typical sentences: 'Mary saw the boy walking to the railroad station', 'What disturbed John was being disregarded by everyone' or even such an apparently simple sentence as 'I had a book stolen'. In the case of such ambiguous sentences, he would say that whilst only a single surface structure (grammatical analysis) might be assigned, there must be differing deep structures related to the differing possible interpretations of the particular sentence. For example, in his view, for the very simple sentence quoted: 'I had a book stolen', there can be at least three divergent deep structures (divergent grammatical analysis at the deeper level).

In visual perception, ambiguity may exist in the perception of material or scenes varying very greatly in complexity and there is a complicated relation between competing interpretations of ambiguous scenes, the set of elementary visual illusions which have been identified and the underlying neurological and physiological processes of the visual apparatus by which coherence is introduced into a scene, through the operation of the visual constancies, the clues which are used to determine relative depth, size, orientation &c. At the simplest level, in the Muller-Lyer or arrow illusion, a line of a given length will appear shorter if at each end it is bounded by an angle resembling an arrow-head and longer if at each end the angle is an open one forming a Y-shape. The length of the line perceived thus depends on the context in which it is placed, in terms of the other lines to which it is joined at each end. At the next level, there may be ambiguity of contour in a two-dimensional drawing—the typical Vase/Faces ambiguous pattern; with more complex line-drawings, there may be three-dimensional ambiguity, for example, the interpretation of the Necker cube as projecting towards or away from the viewer; a still more elaborate example of the ambiguous picture (though still line-drawing) is the Wife/Mother-in-Law example (also referred to above); and there can be ambiguity at a higher level, involving contour, colour, depth, structural relationship, of which a remarkable illustration is given in Attneave's article, the reproduction in colour of a portion of Salvador Dali's painting entitled 'Slave Market with Apparition of the Invisible Bust of Voltaire'—where at one moment the picture can be seen as one of a group of men and women and at the next moment it can be seen as a painting, a typical portrait bust of Voltaire. Another important example of the interaction of visual illusions (based on the processes by which the visual constancies operate) and ambiguity in what is perceived is provided by the 'Ames' distorted room' illusion; in this three-dimensional real ambiguous structure, two persons who in fact are of the same height are shown standing in a room and one of the persons appears to be perhaps twice the height of the other (even though both also appear to be at the same distance from the observer); in fact the room is not a normal room; it is not rectangular but our visual apparatus automatically assumes that it is and adjusts its perception of the relative heights of the two persons in the scene so as to preserve the normal framework of perception, that is that a room of this kind is straightforwardly rectangular. Quite clearly then there are forms of ambiguity in visual perception at many different levels, from the simplest to the most complex scene—and the ambiguity derives basically from misinterpretation of the information provided to the visual apparatus, from lack of adequate information to achieve successful disambiguation and from the complexities of the unconscious processes of vision (which under the description of Figure and Ground have already been discussed and which normally operate to establish the coherence and integrity of the whole scene). There are still many unsolved problems in the explanation of the precise way in which visual illusions and ambiguities are caused—but the field of study could fairly be described as that of the functioning grammar or syntax of vision.

One can make the same kind of analysis of the different levels of ambiguity in the sentence. Ambiguity in the sentence may at its simplest level come from ambiguity of the individual words used, or from ambiguity in the clustering or grouping of words into phrases or clauses or from ambiguity in the function, within the sentence, served by a particular word, phrase or clause. Is the word or phrase a noun, verb, or adjective in its function? At the highest level of complexity, the ambiguity may derive from the overall structure of the sentence, from indecision between competing analyses of the grammatical organisation of the sentence. Individual words may introduce ambiguity into a sentence because, most obviously, a word spelt or pronounced in the same way has a wide range of meanings; Karl Lashley pointed out that, in the sentence he quoted to show how the appropriateness of the meaning of an individual word depends on the meaning attached to the whole sentence; the word 'right' as spoken has at least ten meanings and four spellings. In English, there is a considerable number of words pronounced the same (homophones) and also spelt the same (homographs); there is a larger number of words pronounced the same and spelt differently and there is in addition a number of words spelt the same but pronounced differently (which could cause ambiguity in written text but not in speech). Quite often, homophones do not in practice cause any real ambiguity because they are found in quite different verbal or real contexts or because they typically have different functions as parts of a sentence. That is, the theoretical ambiguity is eliminated by variation in typical context. (Some examples of homophones more likely to create ambiguity are HERE-HEAR RIGHT-WRITE NO-KNOW TWO-TOO-TO FOR-FOUR-FORE NEW—KNEW LIE-LIE ONE-WON LIGHT-LIGHT. On occasion, ambiguity may derive not from the individual word but from varying uses of a standard part of words, bound morphemes; for example a final S may represent a plural, the third person of the present tense or a possessive; IN may as part of a word indicate negation eg. INEFFECTIVE, or operation e.g. INFLECTIVE or position e.g. INCLUSIVE; DE may indicate reversal e.g. DEFROST or lack DEFICIENT or direction of attention e.g. DEBATE.

Perhaps an even more important source of ambiguity in English than homophony or homography is that the same word, spelt in the same way, with essentially the same central meaning, may have varying functions in a sentence depending upon its position in the word-order and the grouping of words it is associated with. The discussion earlier in this section of the Chapter of parts-of-speech has emphasised how easily in English the same word may serve as noun, verb, adjective, possibly adverb—or as preposition, adverb or conjunction. Bloomfield(33) pointed out that the simple word ONE could in fact in different sentences be found performing five completely different grammatical functions. Even what one normally would class quite straightforwardly as functional words, with closely restricted meanings and uses, can on occasion be found serving other grammatical functions (prepositions or adverbs serving as verbs or adjectives as, for example, THE IN THING, HE IS OUT, TO OUT HIM).

In addition to ambiguity deriving from the sound, spelling or function of individual words, there can also be an important type of ambiguity in the isolated sentence from the uncertain reference to be attached to words such as IT THIS HE where the intended reference may be derivable from the meaning or grammatical analysis of the isolated reference or more often from other context, linguistic or real. Another important source of ambiguity is the varying grammatical use of aspects of the verb, which structurally are identical. The most notable of these is the formation of the present participle and the gerund in the same way by the addition, normally, of ING to the verb stem:

EATING may serve as an adjective, EATING APPLES, or as a continuative form of the present tense, HE IS EATING or as a gerund (noun-form), EATING IS GOOD FOR YOU. A somewhat similar source of ambiguity arises from alternative uses of certain verbs as Transitive or Intransitive, TO FLY TO STOP TO MOVE and so on. All these different types of ambiguity can result in ambiguity of the sentence as a whole and ambiguity about the way in which a sentence should most appropriately be segmented.

So far in this section what has mainly been considered has been the types and sources of ambiguity both in the visual scene and in the sentence. The processes by which the ambiguities are resolved and the sentence or scene as a whole is disambiguated, given a coherent unique total meaning, are something which inevitably will form a central part of the concluding section of this Chapter, on the 'solution' of the sentence and the visual scene. At this stage, one might say that in principle every sentence and every scene is ambiguous until the whole string of words has been heard and the visual scanning process has been completed (regional scanning of a sentence or scene may not resolve the ambiguity as Lashley's sentence demonstrated, and as do Escher's ingenious drawings of scenes which are intelligible if one examines particular regions of the scene but impossible and incomprehensible if the total structure of the scene is considered). Where isolated sentences are ambiguous (as for the various examples used by Chomsky) one ought to examine how far the ambiguity is due to the ambiguity of individual words (of the types described) rather than to any problem of underlying divergent deep structures. A sentence such as: THEY ARE EATING APPLIES is ambiguous not because of any syntactic complexities but because of the inherent ambiguity., double or dubious meaning of two words in the sentence THEY and EATING—and the ambiguity exists precisely because sufficient context, linguistic or real, has not been provided to allow the ambiguity to be resolved. As an utterance in an actual situation THEY ARE EATING APPLES would not be ambiguous simply because the person hearing the sentence would know to whom THEY referred and would be able without difficulty to identify EATING as functioning as a continuative form of the verb rather than as an adjective. Most of the difficulties encountered with similar ambiguous sentences used in transformational grammar can be resolved in an equally straightforward way.

Successful interpretation of the visual scene or the sentence depends upon on the use of complex processes (with the available context) for step by step removal of the ambiguities which may be encountered at each level, from the individual word or bound morpheme meaning, its function as part of the sentence, the grouping of words into phrases, segmentation into clauses for the coherence of the overall structure of the sentence. Parallel processes are required for the extraction of the meaning of the visual scene—and though nothing has so far been said about it in this section, one could easily discuss in similar terms the problems of the ambiguity of action-organisation, both the preparation of a plan of complex action which can in its execution follow two or more distinct routes, depending on the circumstances, the context in which the action in fact takes place, and ambiguity from the point of the person who perceives the sequence of actions of another and seeks to draw conclusions about the overall intent and objective of the action (one could describe as an obvious example of the ambiguity of an uncompleted action-sequence the posture and movements of the opponent about to serve or return the ball, in a game such as tennis).

Metaphor (in language, vision and action)

The significance of metaphor in language, as a central and not a peripheral process, has already been very fully discussed in Chapter IV; there the point was made that metaphor, as a process by which the structure of a familiar perception is extended to apply to and allow one to organise one's understanding of much remoter material (the discussion of thought and feeling) is not in essence a purely linguistic stylistic device but a fundamental physiological and neurological one. Metaphor is a process operating on the structures of perception, the extraction from the perceived structure of a familiar concrete object or visual scene of ordering which can be applied, analogously and in parallel, to unities identified in thought, to the analysis of internal perception and mental processes. Chapter IV made it clear how the process of metaphorical transformation links together the two great blocks of the English lexicon, the block of words referring to concrete objects, events of external experience, and the abstract block of the lexicon, referring to the whole range of human intellectual operation and experience.

The point was also made that metaphor as a process can operate to transfer meaning from one structure to another not only at the word-level or the level of the phrase but also, perhaps most importantly, at the level of the sentence—and it is in this way that the concept of metaphor acquires direct and immediate importance for the discussion of the functioning of the sentence in this Chapter, and particularly for the concluding section of the Chapter which deals with the 'solution' of the sentence, in the sense of its interpretation and disambiguation to arrive at a single, total, unique, coherent meaning from a given string of words. The range of types of sentence which one has to tackle is immensely extended by the operation of metaphorical transformation and given the great development of human thought, knowledge, consciousness and self-consciousness, metaphor provides a very powerful way for tackling otherwise elusive things, by anchoring them however distantly or indirectly in the concrete base of experience from which language originated. Though at many points in this Chapter, the line taken has been in conflict with the views of Sapir (as one of the early great American linguists), on this issue of metaphor his approach exactly coincides with that suggested here: "No proposition, however abstract in its intent, is humanly possible without a tying on at one or more points to the concrete world of sense; such relational concepts must be expressed as moor the concrete concepts to each other and construct a fundamental form of proposition, where there can be no doubt as to the nature of the relations that obtain between the concrete concepts"(26). And one perhaps might add, as regards the significance of the metaphorical process for the sentence, that there is a very fundamental drive which impels the hearer of a sentence to search for some specific meaning, even if on the surface the concrete elements forming the sentence may seem completely incompatible; that is metaphorical interpretation is one way in which apparent and on the surface insoluble ambiguity or lack of clarity of meaning of a sentence can be resolved. Indeed, some of the 'impossible' sentences used in discussion of the relation of grammaticality and meaning in modern linguistics can, without too much effort, be interpreted metaphorically. More specifically, where sentences break selection rules (that is the association of inappropriate nouns and verbs or adjectives), a metaphorical solution can often be found.

One final point: on the view presented here metaphor is as much a basic process in perception as in language. But one can go further than this and plausibly recognise as equivalent to metaphor processes involved in the perception of movement and complex action. Michotte's work on the perception of causality in external events (1954 and 1962) remains of continuing and central interest in this connection. In his series of experiments, in which observers were asked to look at and then describe and interpret as events carefully programmed sequences of movement of a variety of inanimate objects (in fact moving dots and patches of colour, which the observers interpreted as solid moving objects), the very uniform result found was that, with certain spatial and timing patterns of movements, the observers interpreted what was seen as causal sequences, one object striking another and causing it to move, and so on. Miller and Johnson-Laird point out in their discussion of causation: "the perception

of one event as the cause of another is a psychological fact"(34) (regardless
of Hume's criticisms of the concept of cause). Margaret Boden(35) has
described the manner in which later experiment has developed from
Michotte's approach so that movement of simple forms (triangles, circles
and squares) is perceived by the observers as involving complex sequences
of causal behaviour, of exactly the same characters as one would attribute
to relations between human individuals. This obviously very interesting
topic is subject to continuing extensive experiment but the point to be
made in this section is that this perceived attribution of causation to the
interrelation of inanimate shapes or objects on the basis of sequences and
directions of movement could very well be described as the process of
metaphorical transformation operating in relation to action; the structure
of plan, intent, sequence of necessary movement, which we are aware of
in our own complex actions is transferred to apply to the interpretation of
the superficially similar structuring of the movements of external shapes
and objects. At the most extreme point, one might say that our concept of
causation as a force operating generally in the external world is precisely a
metaphorical transformation of the structure of our awareness of our own
voluntary activity.

Competence and Performance

These terms derive from Chomsky's approach to syntax. Perhaps the
question is whether they can have a useful application to the discussion of
language in this book and, more specifically, if they can be applied helpfully
in considering problems of language, is there any comparable interpretation
of them which one can make in considering what, on the hypothesis, are
parallel structuring aspects of vision? The distinction as made by Chomsky is
between the speaker-hearer's knowledge of his language (competence) and the
actual use of language in concrete situations (performance)—and the linguist
is concerned rather with discovering 'a mental reality underlying actual
behaviour'. Chomsky relates the distinction to some extent to the Saussurean
one of langue-parole but traces its origin more directly to Humboldt.

Chomsky(36) argues that a grammar in the traditional view is an account
of competence; it describes and attempts to account for the ability of a
speaker to understand an arbitrary sentence of his language and to produce
an appropriate sentence on a given occasion; ideally, the competence of the
speaker-hearer can be expressed as a system of rules that relate signals to

semantic interpretations of these signals; the problem for the grammarian is to discover this system of rules and the problem for linguistic theory is to discover general properties of any system of rules that may serve as a basis for a human language, that is to elaborate the general form of language that underlies each particular realisation, each particular natural language. Chomsky says that a primary interest in competence entails no disregard for the facts of performance and the problem of explaining these facts—performance provides evidence for the investigation of competence. But, Chomsky would argue, contributions to the understanding of performance have largely been by-products of grammars that represent competence and it is difficult to see how performance can be seriously studied except on the basis of an explicit theory of the competence that underlies it.

Whilst perhaps there is not much to criticise or challenge in the general account given above of Chomsky's initial approach to the distinction between competence and performance, there is rather more question about how useful in the fuller development of his theoretical approach the distinction has been. It would be disproportionate to attempt to deal at length with the practical consequences of the distinction for the course actually taken by transformational generative grammar; it may serve to refer to the searching examination of this and other aspects in Derwing's book(37). He points out that the notion of linguistic competence is central to Chomsky's conception of linguistics as a discipline (and some might even say that the emphasis on competence as against performance is a manifestation of Chomsky's preference for proceeding on the basis of intuitive, introspective evidence, essentially the linguist's own intuition—rather than on the basis of empirical evidence about actual speech). Derwing says that at different times Chomsky has put forward three distinct interpretations or justifications for the concept of competence:—competence as an idealised model of linguistic performance (abstracting away hesitations, distractions, shifts of attention), competence as a central component of an idealised performance model (that is: a reference essentially to generative grammar) and competence as an independent abstract entity remote from linguistic performance (a non-empirical axiomatisation of sentences and their structural descriptions where there is a difference of category, a difference of logical character, between competence and performance). If, as a mode of evading empirical disconfirmation, competence as a concept assumes this final form as mere 'formal and frozen abstraction', then generative grammar takes on the appearance of an arbitrary descriptive system of no inherent interest for the purposes of explaining how speakers comprehend sentences or how children acquire language—a theoretical approach "more vulnerable (in Warnock's phrase about metaphysical systems which Derwing quotes) to ennui than to disproof".

Where then does the above discussion leave the question of the useful application of the competence/performance distinction for the purposes of the view of language presented in this Chapter? Such psychological experiment as there has been has failed to establish any real link in speech processing between the transformational complexity postulated and actual difficulty of comprehension. The competence/performance distinction—in Chomskyan terms—is clearly open to severe theoretical attack, which on the face it seems in good part valid. The conclusion must be that the distinction (as Chomsky makes it) is doubtfully relevant for the central concern of this book, that is the effort to arrive at an understanding of the processes of sentence comprehension in parallel with the processes by which a visual scene is interpreted.

A more important distinction for present purposes may be between speech comprehension (depending on a joint decoding of the syntax and semantics of the word-string heard and which may require much wider 'competence' in the hearer than he would normally need for his own speech production) and speech production (reinterpreted as 'performance'). Using the terms competence and performance in this more straightforward way, with competence equalling the effective ability to understand speech and performance the practical use of speech by the individual, could be helpful and emphasise the different skills and experience involved in speech comprehension and speech production—as manifested for example in the difference between a child's ability to understand speech and produce speech. But competence and performance, in these new senses, would of course remain inextricably interlinked parts of one total language-system, which could be matched with the total system of visual perception and action-organisation.

But if competence and performance are reinterpreted in this way in relation to speech, how should such a distinction be applied to vision (or action)? After all, we have only to comprehend and not in any sense to produce the visual scene, though comprehension in itself may be a very active process with a considerable input from the knowledge-structure of the individual as well as from all the syntactic elements of visual perception. Can one say that performance in vision differs significantly between one individual and another—and if performance does differ between individuals (as it almost certainly does), does not this mean, in the new terms being used, that visual competence differs between individuals? Or could one maintain the distinction by treating competence as the generalised ability to comprehend visual input and performance as the individual manifestation of this generalised competence, in the particular real circumstances of the individual and the situation? But that would take one back close to Chomsky's original distinction between competence and performance. Another approach would be to draw a distinction between the competence for visual perception provided through the hierarchical system of vision, the operation of the visual constancies and the factors going generally to organise the perceived visual scene into a whole (the grammar and syntax of vision), and the performance involved in the use of these general processes to achieve decoding in any particular instance of the contents presented to the retina in the array of visual stimuli. Somewhat similar difficulties arise in considering how the distinction of competence and performance might be applied in the third field of human behaviour considered in this book, that is complex action, human voluntary activity. At first sight, the distinction applies most directly and obviously to action—and the distinction is in fact drawn directly from experience of action and applied only by metaphor to the analysis of language. Put most simply, competence would be 'knowing how, in principle, to construct a complex action' and performance 'being able to execute the action' in the concrete circumstances prevailing.

A closely related term with which Chomsky has made considerable play is the 'open-endedness' of language; the point is really a simple one, that language competence underlies the production of an essentially infinite number of sentences, and the crucial problem is how the language ability operates to comprehend and produce totally novel sentences, something he also describes as the 'creativity' of language; one of his main criticisms of current linguistics was for its failure to come to grips with this central issue which rules out any account of the understanding of language in terms of linguistic habit. It hardly seems necessary to discuss open-endedness or creativity and competence separately. Clearly language can be used and generally is used for referring to novel matters, for the speaker if not for the community as a whole—and language is pointless if it conveys to the hearer only what the hearer already knows. But Chomsky's stress on the creativity of language seems misplaced, or wrongly expressed. What is creative, what is open-ended in fact, is human behaviour of the individual and of humanity as a whole, or more generally what is open-ended is the continuing development of nature and society. The remarkable feature about language is not that it is intrinsically creative or open-ended but that it has resources and mechanisms which allow it to match, to continue mapping, the ever widening range of human experience, the ever more complex development of animate and inanimate nature. Once again, as in the central argument of this book language derived its structure and its functioning from the structures and functioning of perception and action, so language derives its ability to deal unceasingly with new material from its association with the open-ended processes of perception and action.

The 'solution' of the sentence in parallel with the 'solution' of the visual scene

With this section of the chapter one comes to the crux of the whole problem of the effective use of language. The discussion in earlier Chapters of the preceding hierarchical stages, the formation of the elementary units of speech, vision and action, the combination of the elements into words and visual shapes, together with the account given earlier in this Chapter of the concepts of the sentence, the scene and the complex action (with the broad parallelisms between them and with the fourteen more specific aspects of processes functioning in vision and language), have all been essential preparation for tackling the question that really matters, that is by what processes, conscious or unconscious, do we in fact manage to arrive at the unique meaning of a particular sentence, or to comprehend the unique content of a particular visual scene. At the beginning of the Chapter, in a preliminary discussion of this central problem, the point was made that we do not just want to parse a sentence but to find a correct solution; a distinction was drawn between a formal solution and finding such a solution for a particular real sentence spoken or heard on a particular real occasion in particular real circumstances—because to give a complete explanation and account of the total meaning of such a sentence would require us to know more than we ever possibly could about the minds and experience of the speaker and the hearer and the real state of the world to which the sentence related and was appropriate. What we can reasonably look for, in itself all we can look for but at the same time extremely worthwhile and important, is a general solution, specifying the steps and processes involved in extracting a specific meaning from any sentence (and in the same way all we can look for in relation to the visual scene is a general solution, an account of the processes by which the contents are extracted from the scene and formed into a coherent unity). The correctness and value of a general solution resides precisely in this, that it offers a reliable set of techniques for combining together the materials given in a real sentence, uttered in real circumstances, with a justified expectation that by using these techniques one can arrive at a specific meaning of that sentence which one must understand correctly if one is to communicate effectively and act appropriately in the real world in which one finds oneself. Exactly the same kind of importance attaches to the correct general solution of the visual scene: the techniques we have available for analysing given visual material must allow us to decide reliably, and quickly, whether, for example, the object approaching us is a tiger, a racing motor bicycle or whatever visual threats and conundrums we encounter in the cultures to which we belong.

'Solution' is not an altogether inappropriate word. Given a number of words, with a range of meanings and functions for each, and an order in which they are presented, the task is very much like what is dealt with in Artificial Intelligence as 'problem-solving', something analogous to the solution of complex simultaneous equations, or finding the unique correct answer to a chess problem or to a problem in logic or cryptarithmetic ; similar problems arise in solving jigsaw puzzles or breaking codes and ciphers. In the scientific world proper, the kind of problems encountered in determining the structure of enzymes or of chemical compounds and interactions or, more generally, in finding a theory to bring order into a particular array of experimental facts, raise difficulties and call for approaches in some ways parallel to those involved in tackling the problem of the sentence (and the problem of the visual scene). Some of these analogous problem-solving situations would involve too complex discussion and take one too far from the issues of language and vision with which this Chapter is concerned. At one stage, Roman Jakobson was much struck with the parallels that could be drawn between the structure and functioning of language and the new discoveries in molecular biology (the coding elements of DNA grouped and through a hierarchy of processes going to form eventually ever more complex tertiary and quaternary forms of proteins, enzymes and other biochemical materials). However, though the analogy between the language of molecular biology and the language of speech is a striking and interesting one, at this stage it does not help very specifically in allowing one to identify general techniques for the solution of the sentence.

The more mundane problems, such as the solving of a jigsaw, the breaking of a code or cipher or the solution of a number-puzzle (cryptarithmetic), come closer to techniques for tackling the sentence. It is possible to specify techniques, or computer programs, by which these problems can be tackled. All work by considering the range of possibilities, narrowing down the probabilities, using set sequences of processing, trying hypotheses and drawing provisional inferences. In the case of a number-puzzle for example one can set out precisely the steps which should be followed in a specific order to arrive at the correct solution, and in the case of a code or cipher one can at least describe the general approach to be adopted in looking for a solution. Amongst the possible analogies originally considered for adoption in this book in approaching the 'solution' of the sentence were those of the visual scene and the complex action—but in fact these now have become very much more than simply analogous approaches; the full behavioural integration of speech, vision and language should allow one to find a physiological and neurological basis for the solution of the sentence, not simply some theoretically suggestive ideas drawn from vision and action research. The relevant techniques and approaches, the clues and the patterns of organisation for comprehending how the sentence functions are derived from the discussion earlier in this Chapter of the apparently equivalent aspects and processes underlying speech, visual perception and action: the processing period for the sentence, the hierarchical organisation, the real deep structure underlying language, the unity or integrity of the sentence, the relation of word-order and visual scanning, the significance of Figure and Ground, the organisation of the semantic field, parts-of-speech and parts-of-sentence and the corresponding parts of the visual scene or complex action, the syntactic system of language, vision and action, the types of sentences and types of scenes, the importance of context, the key importance of the ambiguous sentence and the ambiguous scene in any approach to decoding, the role of metaphorical transformation and finally the reinterpretation to apply to vision as well as language of the concepts of competence and performance.

Put most concisely, the initial problem of the sentence (and of the visual scene) is ambiguity, indefiniteness of interpretation, and the solution is a process of disambiguation, general techniques for disambiguation applied to the specific materials of a particular sentence. Comprehension of the sentence and of the visual scene are processes which take time; the solution of the sentence has the form of a sequence of progressive disambiguation of the elements in the sentence or the scene, a progressive narrowing down of the meaning and function attached to each word in the sentence or to each element in the visual scene. As one author put it, 'we are constantly disambiguating sentences all the time when we use and listen to language; so much so that any grammatical theory must have as one of its primary goals the means of accounting for this facility. Meaning and grammatical analysis on this account turn out to be two sides of the same coin'. The argument here is that we progressively disambiguate the sentence and the scene as a result of processes operating in parallel (and interacting with each other); the interaction of semantic and syntactic devices and structures together on the serial order of the word-string (or in the scanning order of visual perception) restricts progressively the possible range of interpretations of individual words, morphemes, phrases or clauses (or, in the case of the visual scene of individual shapes, contour elements, object groupings and regional patterning).

In the preceding section, which considered the comparable significance for research of ambiguous sentences and ambiguous pictures, an attempt was made to set out in the case of the sentence the possible sources of ambiguity; there has to be decoding, disambiguation, at a succession of levels. In any stream of speech, there must be cues to establish the presence of particular phonemes, particular syllables and particular words: there has been separate research and discussion of the way in which this basic stage of speech-comprehension is successfully tackled. But assuming that the syllables and words present in the sentence have been identified, and assuming that the words identified are known (not meaningless or incomprehensible in themselves), the next stage in the processing of the sentence can proceed. At the word level, there are, as already indicated, a number of sources of ambiguity, semantic, functional, segmentation, as well as straightforward acoustic (or graphic) ambiguity. Not all sentences intrinsically are equally ambiguous; there are different degrees of probability of ambiguity (though, with an effort, ambiguous examples could be constructed for nearly all words in English, some of them would be highly improbable and the hearer would not usually take them into account as a possibility in seeking to comprehend a sentence). In practice, the hearer may rapidly reject obviously irrelevant meanings or functions of words in a sentence-cluster—and syntactic criteria can operate as short-cut rules for disambiguation to make unnecessary more elaborate investigations of the possible semantic ranges of words in the sentence. But every real sentence is potentially ambiguous because its function is to express something novel, in novel circumstances, and the general techniques for disambiguating word-strings have to be available to apply to any sentence.

Put most simply, the process of disambiguation for a sentence requires that for every word in the string it must be possible to say: what is the range of possible meanings of this word, which meanings may be relevant in these circumstances, which particular meaning in fact is the appropriate one, is the word to be associated with the immediately preceding or following word, does it form part of a particular phrase or clause, which out of the range of functions a word in its different meanings can have is likely to be relevant, which precise function (as noun, verb, adjective) does it in fact have; out of the roles the word can play in the sentence or clause (as subject, verb, object, adjunct, actor, action, goal &c), which role could it have and which role precisely does it have in the total sentence; and in disambiguating the individual word, one needs at the same time to perform a similar process for the word-group, the phrase, the clause and the sentence itself as a whole. What role in the sentence-structure does the phrase or clause play, how should the sentence be segmented, what basic kind of sentence is this (in terms of the type of material it relates to:—abstract, or concrete, perception or action) what functional type of sentence is this:—descriptive, interrogative, assertive, imperative, performative (promise, warn &c), hypothetical and conditional, simple, complex or compound, and so on.

The earlier discussion of the 'ambiguous sentence' identified as sources of ambiguity those related to individual words and others related to functions. To some extent in English, homophones may cause difficulty (but nothing on the scale of the complexity introduced by the massive number of homophones in Chinese) but more important sources of ambiguity are the use of words with the same central meaning but different functional roles (as noun, verb or adjective &c) and this can lead to ambiguities in the analysis of phrases and clauses and the segmentation of the sentence as a whole. Closely related to ambiguities of parts-of-speech are the ambiguities relating to parts-of-sentence, as already discussed, and involved here of course also is the ambiguity deriving from different uses of similar bound morphemes,

influenced by controlled manipulation of the perceptual context in which they are produced.

Primitive Vocabulary (and related lexical structure)

Chapter IV illustrated how each individual builds up a primitive vocabulary of words the meanings of which he derives directly from experience, an array of words referring to familiar things and shapes, movements and actions, qualities and relations—and pointed out that the words in such a list were not simply grouped in broad categories of this kind or as traditional parts of speech, but also in terms of the usual frameworks in which particular objects or qualities are found, the usual patterning of events in which different types of action, different things or different familiar relations are encountered. Beyond this, Chapter IV indicated how the underlying relation between speech, vision and action meant that there were natural clues, in the form of associated visual or action contours, to the meanings of words derived from their specific structures as combinations of speech-sounds. In considering the material which one brings to the process of disambiguating a sentence, the contents and structuring of the Primitive Vocabulary are obviously of critical importance. Words in the individual's Primitive Vocabulary are likely to be recognised more quickly than less familiar ones and there will be more experience of the functioning of such words in varying contexts, with more strongly associated frames, presuppositions &c. Not only does the Primitive Vocabulary serve as the basis for the structuring of the larger lexicon used by an individual (or available in a language) but it is possible that the structuring of the Primitive Vocabulary in fact provides a set of primitive sentence patterns, for example related to bodily organisation, order or action within a room or a house, in a street or in a landscape. To the extent that the progressive interpretation of the sentence proceeds in part through the formulation of hypotheses and the use of clues, the Primitive Vocabulary (in its content and structure) may give a higher probability to certain interpretations of a particular sentence than others and may itself generate hypotheses about the segmentation and meaning of the sentence or parts of it for further examination. For example, in segmentation of a sentence, one of the important questions is: which words should be taken to form part of a single cluster? a noun or verb phrase? One of the factors establishing a first hypothesis about the clustering of individual words would be the prior association of those words (or not) in the Primitive Vocabulary.

Semantic markers
(words or morphemes with narrow meaning or function)

In any cluster of words forming a sentence, any word which is known to have only one meaning, one function as a part of speech or one role as part of a sentence is an obvious starting point for disambiguation of the meanings, functions and roles of the remaining words in the sentence. Such words may not simply be relational words or what is often known as functional words but can equally well be verbs, nouns or adjectives with very sharply defined meanings. The presence of a word such as 'sun' 'god' 'purple' 'octopus' 'think' in a sentence makes as immediate and substantial a contribution to the process of disambiguation as do many so-called grammatical or functional words. Indeed, one might reasonably argue that there are no strictly grammatical words, that the distinction between function-words and content-words is an imprecise and often not very useful one, and that the key aspect of any word's usefulness in helping one to understand a sentence is, as has been said, how narrowly its accepted meaning, function or role is defined. Probably there is quite a long list of words used in English which give a precise or highly likely indication of their exact meaning, their form-class or role in the sentence whenever they occur. Such words, whether we class them as nouns, adjectives, verbs, prepositions, adverbs or conjunctions, are acquired early on, for the most part, as elements in the Primitive Vocabulary (even if for some, such as OF IF BUT it may be difficult to describe exactly the process by which a child acquires them so rapidly). One should note that the list of especially useful word-forms (for sentence-comprehension) includes some bound morphemes, familiar parts of other words which indicate function or role e.g.—TION for abstract nouns,—ESS and—ISM for other noun-forms,—IOUS and—FUL for adjectival forms, and so on. Though bound morphemes of these kinds may not always be infallible markers of the parts of speech to which the word of which they form part belong, they are generally reliable semantic and sentence-markers.

As regards what are usually classed as function-words (some of which may on occasion have different functions in a sentence or be replaced by phrases which are not function-words but in fact operate in the sentence in the same way as a function-word would), it is normally said that there are only 100 or 200 of these in English and that they play crucial roles in delineating the structure of a sentence (along with some bound morphemes). It is certainly the case that some of the so-called function words do operate in this way; in the concrete sentence (but not so clearly in the abstract or metaphorical sentence) relational prepositions of spatial or temporal position give a pretty clear indication of the category and the relation within the sentence of the word or phrase with which they are associated; the relational prepositions, used for concrete reference, in fact constitute a system within which to a good extent they define each other's area of application (as might occur in an actual visual scene or in the ordering of real objects), but even so quite often it is not automatically clear whether a function-word is being used as preposition or adverb (even though the core of its meaning is known). Time-words often point to action-sentences and space-words to sentences relating to perception but the distinction is not clearcut (particularly since a number of words relating to time are derived, by metaphor, from equivalent words relating to spatial organisation).

In practice, words which operate most reliably as indicators of sentence-structure, associated part-of-speech or part-of sentence, are words such as : A THE NOT IS OR AND IF BUT I ME WHICH WHEN HAS DOES OF IN ON TO FROM BECAUSE SINCE YET TOGETHER AGAIN SOON (&c &c) plus words where the kind of meaning or role is fixed but the precise reference has to be identified such as: HE SHE THEY YOU THIS THAT THERE HERE THAN THING plus a range of common words used regularly with the same meaning, functions or roles: VERY MUCH MORE SAME DIFFERENT OTHER and so on. If to words such as the above which give a certain or nearly certain indication of their meaning, function or role in the sentence, one adds words where there is a high probability that the word will have a particular narrow meaning, a particular use as noun, verb or other part of speech or a particular role in the sentence, then one quickly arrives at a very much longer list or semantic markers. The material, for many sentences, provided in this way as the starting point for disambiguation is extensive and, used with the techniques of progressive disambiguation described somewhat earlier, allows very frequently a rapid solution to be found for particular sentences. What this means is that the semantic aspects of the particular words in a sentence play a key role in directly determining the associated syntactic organisation—the exact reverse of what in traditional grammar, and indeed in some more modern systems is believed to be the primary role of syntax as the key to sentence-comprehension.

Sentence-pattern and sentence-type

The operational techniques required in the 'solution' of a sentence are procedures for examining the words of the sentence in one order or another, for setting up hypotheses about the meaning, role or function of a particular word or group of words and for drawing inferences, once a particular word or phrase has been reliably categorised, about the likely functions or roles in the sentence of other words or phrases. So far the material resources which are brought into play for these operational techniques have been listed as the particular words in the order in which they appear, the suprasegmental features of the sentence (punctuation, intonation &c), context (near and remote), the content and structure of the Primitive Vocabulary and its relation to the larger lexicon, and the availability of semantic markers (words or morphemes with narrow meaning or precise function or role which can serve as starting points for disambiguation). But there is another category of material resource which we bring to the solution of a sentence, one which is of comparable importance to those already listed, namely, our familiarity both with the structuring derived from action and perception underlying the natural patterning of sentences (the Subject Stative Verb Complement pattern and the Actor Action Goal Object pattern) and also our familiarity with standard forms of sentences used for different purposes, questions, assertions, conditional statements, commands, promises, &c.

The earlier discussion of types of sentences brought out clearly what a wide range of types of sentence is possible, varying with the experience to which the sentence relates, the extent to which internal experience as well as external experience of the speaker is involved, the function or purpose which utterance of the sentence is intended to serve, and the extent to which a sentence may be self-reflexive (refer to what has already been said by the speaker or someone else). Beyond the range of types of sentence derived from variations in content, there is a whole further category of types of sentences derived from variations in the form in which any particular material is presented in a sentence, ranging from the simplest (perhaps ultimately the single word 'holophrastic' sentence) to the most complex, not simply in terms of the length of the sentence but of the clause and sub-clause structure, the expansion of sentence-parts (Subject or Object) into extensive phrases or clauses in their own right, all of which may be combined with an intricate intellectual relationship of the different parts of the sentence-structure (such as one would find in much philosophical or scientific discussion). To solve a sentence, to disambiguate, we have to be prepared to tackle difficulties of this much greater order; in terms of the material resources we bring to the task, where our understanding of the framework of the subject-matter to which the sentence refers is adequate, we obviously have available one of the major disambiguating resources already discussed, that is context. But for complex sentences (even about reasonably familiar subject-matter) we must also have in our armoury a familiarity with the ways in which sentence-structure can be developed from its simplest form to one of great intricacy. Our store of knowledge of the organisation of complex sentences very probably will have started from the simplest structures, associated with our acquisition of the Primitive Vocabulary, and developed in step with the growing complexity of our experience (perceptual, of action, and intellectual), so that as we move from the Primitive Lexicon to the full lexicon, we also move from a set of simple sentence-patterns to a range of complex sentence-patterns (nevertheless in the last resort elaborated from the simple base).

The extent to which in finding the solution of any sentence we in fact need the full range of techniques of disambiguation and of the material resources available for use in disambiguation obviously depends on the content and the form of the particular sentence. At the formally simplest level, a sentence may consist of one word, the child's holophrasis; by saying simply HAT, a child may mean any one of a number of things and the interpretation of this primitive sentence depends wholly on the fullness of context available. There can of course be much more sophisticated one-word sentences: a cry of HERESY! for example, but again the interpretation depends wholly on the available context. At the opposite extreme, the interpretation of a single word in a complex sentence may depend on the successful disambiguation of the whole of the rest of the sentence (the word RIGHT in Karl Lashley's illustrative sentence). In the more difficult sentences, not only is an early hypothesis about the context, the subject-matter of the sentence, necessary, but also an early hypothesis about the sentence-structure, the formal type of sentence. Often it will be possible to draw a clue to the sentence-type from the presence of semantic markers (in the sense discussed in the immediately preceding section)—most simply when the sentence starts with an interrogative word—or semantic markers may indicate, provisionally, clause or sentence structure (the use of IF OR BECAUSE SINCE AND WHICH and so on). Semantic markers in fact may establish a plausible hypothesis that in form the sentence is compound or complex, that the clause-divisions occur at these points, and that the interrelation in the complex sentence of the clauses is likely to be of a particular type. For example, where a sentence starts with IF, the immediate hypothesis is that there are at least two clauses, the clause expressing the condition and the clause expressing the result or implication.

Once progress has been made, provisionally, in disambiguating the type of sentence, the broad sentence-structure or the probable segmentation and interrelation of clauses, further stages of disambiguation can proceed, on the basis of hypotheses about the likely pattern of a clause (a two-nucleus or three-nucleus form), the identification of words as parts-of-speech or parts-of-sentence (or parts of a particular clause) and semantic markers can often also be used to identify probable adjunct phrases. At the same time, hypotheses are made, derived from context and from the meaning-ranges of the words used in the sentence about the type of experience to which the sentence relates, action, perception, internal perception, intellectual operation, which will assist in disambiguating individual words where some variation of meaning is possible in different contexts.

There is one other aspect to the problem of the 'solution' of more complex sentences which should be mentioned here. In one sense, any sentence used to describe an actual visual scene or a complex action, or indeed to explain a train of thought is a skeleton representation of the always much richer reality—one cannot say everything at one time in one sentence—but the more complex the scene perceived, the more complex the action or the train of thought, the greater the incentive to construct the descriptive sentence in such a way as to bring in as much as possible of the relevant detail and relationships. There are formal devices by which this compression can be achieved. Information of a kind which can be conveyed by an independent sentence can also be conveyed by a sub-group of words within a more complex sentence, either as a subordinate clause, as a phrase or even by the use of a single complex word. The content of previous sentences can be systematically converted into subordinate parts of the new sentence—so that any complex sentence may in fact constitute a condensation of many previous or possible sentences. And these subordinate forms, in a complex sentence, may themselves be of any of the types to which an independent sentence may belong, in terms of subject-matter (action, perception, internal perception, reported speech) or in terms of function (questioning, informing, persuading, warning commanding &c). To disambiguate a very complex sentence of this kind, one has to identify the distinct elements going to form it (where potentially independent sentences have been replaced by clauses, phrases or single words) and to see how the complex sentence, with all its elaboration, has been developed both from the range of material it expresses and from the skeleton simple sentence-structures from which all sentences must start (as they match the basic patterning of organisation of perception of a simple visual scene or the planning or execution of an action-sequence). Finally, one must note that a most important device for compressing together diverse experience, bringing remote experiences close together and establishing order in experience is the introduction of the structure of time (joining past remembered experience, present perception and expected future experience, linking one point in a serial sequence of action to the next, the beginning to the end)—and that all the complexities of organisation of human behaviour which result from the interpenetration of spatial organisation and temporal organisation have to be describable in language, in the words, the word-functions and the sentence-structures; the disambiguation of the sentence has to provide for the additional layer of complication provided, in brief, by tense and time-related words. The disambiguation of the sentence in terms of tense is perhaps one of the least of the problems; there are generally straightforward semantic markers for past, present and future tenses and for more complex tense forms. The real problem with tense is much more the complexity of the underlying real material which the sentence reflects and the mysteries of the relations of Time and Space are not something which can be tackled in this Chapter.

The relevance of this approach to the 'solution' of the sentence to the 'solution' of the visual scene

There are a few preliminary points: first of all, much less is known about the semantics and syntax of the visual process than is known about the semantics and syntax of language (however deficient one may find much of this linguistic knowledge in practical experience). The construction and the analysis of sentences are, in a sense, overt processes, which have long been categorised and discussed; the construction of visual scenes and the decoding of visual stimulation are processes which for us proceed unconsciously and automatically, and what has been discovered about these processes has been the result of painstaking and extremely complex experimental work over many years. There is no question therefore in this Chapter or this book of claiming in any way to make a definitive or substantive contribution to the solution of the physiological and neurological problems which the functioning of the visual apparatus still presents. At most, what is said about the disambiguation of the sentence and the functioning of language may, it is hoped, be suggestive, in so far as vision and language are both extremely complex systems which have a necessarily close relation in human behaviour. Secondly, if some features of what is said about the 'solution' of the sentence appear relevant for considering problems of vision (and particularly of how we come to perceive the integral visual scene), this is only to be expected simply because the discussion of the functioning of language has already at many points drawn clues and analogies from what is known about vision (and from work that has taken place in the field of artificial intelligence on machine-vision). It would be improper, and indeed impracticable, to attempt any discussion of the 'solution' of the visual scene at the length or in the depth applied to discussion in the earlier part of this section about the disambiguation of the sentence. What can be said more briefly is that for the disambiguation of the visual scene, the same distinction can be drawn between the operational techniques employed and the material resources made available to assist in the process. As in the case of the sentence, the objective is to find a method by which all the elements in the scene can be accommodated with each other so as to make the whole scene comprehensible, graspable, as a single perceptual unity. A full understanding of an actual visual scene is as difficult to achieve by rule as a full comprehension of a real sentence (one uttered in real circumstances) so that once again one is concerned with the general approach to the perception of a single scene. The fundamental difficulty to be tackled is the same as that in the case of the sentence, the unavoidable ambiguity of individual elements in the scene, of relationships and of the structure of the scene—and the range of ambiguities in vision is perhaps even greater than the range of ambiguities possible in language. What is suggested is that a rather similar process of disambiguation must be used for comprehending the scene as is used for comprehending the sentence. The disambiguation must be carried through successively from the simplest elements in the scene to the most complex structures and relationships; at the simplest, any straight line falling on the retina at a particular orientation may represent a more of less infinite family of lines (varying in distance and position in three-dimensional space) so the task of disambiguation is not a simple one. The operation of disambiguation of the elements in a scene may well be comparable to the serial process (using cues, hypotheses, inferences and alterations in scanning-pattern) which it has been suggested is used in seeking to interpret a sentence. Familiar elements are used to help disambiguate more obscure elements and to provide a source for hypotheses about the local and regional relation of elements in the scene; the scanning pattern in many respects resembles one of visual search.

In parallel to the material resources employed in the 'solution' of the sentence (by way of the operational techniques described), there must certainly be equivalent familiar patterns, stores of information about structure, which can be called upon to assist in interpretation of the scene. Comparably to the information provided in the sentence by the specific word-order of the sentence, is the ordering of the elements in the scene identified by scanning; context plays as important a role in perception as it does in sentence-comprehension (including the context of the perceiver's own bodily position and state as well as context associated with particular familiar elements in the scene. In parallel to the resource provided by the content and structuring of the Primitive Vocabulary, in vision one no doubt has a store of visual schemas and an awareness of the relationships in which different objects and qualities stand to one another, the frameworks within which shapes, objects and qualities are found and so on. Differing contexts and the differing familiarity of particular visual schemas will tend to alter the probabilities for the way in which any scene will be interpreted. In vision, there may well be key features (which aid rapid disambiguation) comparable to the semantic markers described for the interpretation of the sentence, though these may take the form of standard expectations about positional relationships within the scene as well as particularly frequent and familiar qualities or objects.

Finally one asks what equivalent might there be in visual processing to the syntactic complexities of types and structures of sentence found in language, reflecting normally equally complex perceptual or intellectual experience. What are the inherent structures or processes in the operation of the visual apparatus which organise parts or regions of the scene into a complex whole? At this point one enters the fiercely debated field of general theories of visual perception, the views of James Gibson that all the structure and content of the perceived scene is derived from patterning of the visual stimuli, the not unrelated views of others such as Uttal that the structure of the scene is extracted by a process of autocorrelation, the contentions of those who believe that perception is based on a template-matching system or on construction using a feature-detection process (of innate origin). In these theories are involved all the enigmas associated with the operation of the visual constancies, the perception of depth, of movement, of invariant shape or size, the distinction of figure and ground. Someone has commented that whilst there is no single and accepted formal theory of perception, there is a plethora of informal theories 'but they come in a distressing variety of shapes and sizes'. Whether in fact these are competing theories or in the end complementary but partial views of the total complexity of the visual system remains to be seen. What seems clear is that whether the information in the visual scene is extracted purely from the structuring of the stimuli or whether perception depends upon the use of pre-existing schemas and other innate features, in one way or another the visual process must have evolved under the constraints imposed by the structure of the real world. If there is a large internal component in normal vision, then this is because it must have evolved in this way to serve as an instrument for reliable perception. As Konrad Lorenz has put it more definitively: "our cognitive apparatus is itself an objective reality which has acquired its present form through contact with and adaptation to equally real things In the outer world . . . our modes of thought and perception are functions of a neurosensory organisation that has evolved in the service of survival"(38). In the same way, one might say, our faculty of language has acquired its form from its necessary adaptation to the real world to which language relates and it also is a function of neurosensory organisation evolved in the service of survival. At the beginning and at the end there is the link between language and perception and, beyond these, the link with human action, the totality of human behaviour.

CHAPTER VI

Comparative Application
of the Hypothesis

Chapters III, IV and V have examined, respectively in relation to speech-sounds, words and sentences, the application of the initial hypothesis that the structures of language are interrelated with and ultimately derived from those underlying visual perception and action. Though the discussion of the hierarchical processes involved in visual perception and the organisation of voluntary action has been necessarily completely general i.e. relating to the general physiological and neurological functioning of vision and action, the specific parallels with language at each level, speech-sound, word and sentence, have so far been confined to one language only, the English language. However, the basic hypotheses, that language is natural and not arbitrary in its origin, that children learn a specific language as a result of a process analogous to imprinting (as investigated in the behaviour of birds and animals), and that the sound-structures of words (more particularly those acquired as part of an individual's Primitive Vocabulary) are directly related to specific contours, either visual contours or action contours, and so carry with them a natural indication of the percept, action or quality to which they refer, in principle apply to all languages and to any specific language. Similarly, the hypotheses presented in chapter V on the relation between the organisation of the sentence and that of the visual scene and the complex action are also to be applied to the examination of sentences in other languages.

Though it is often the case in modern linguistics that theories are developed solely in terms of one language and little attempt is made to give them a wider application, it obviously would be unsatisfactory in the present instance not to seek to apply such a fundamental hypothesis to a wider range of languages: English, it may be said, is in many ways an unusual language, in the massive size of its vocabulary, in the extent to which its formal grammatical structure has been eroded and in its reliance on word-order as the main syntactic device. At the end of chapter II, the point was specifically made that a hypothesis of this kind should not be too narrowly based in term of the languages in relation to which it was developed. Accordingly, this chapter contains a fairly full discussion of the comparative application of the ideas in the earlier chapters—but the caveat must be repeated that no author can claim to know, in the depth required, many languages and very few can claim to know any second language with the fullness and intimacy of knowledge that an individual has of his mother tongue. Unavoidably then, what is said in this chapter about the phonetic, lexical and syntactic characters of other languages relies heavily on the work of those who have devoted themselves to the particular languages referred to and on the expertise of those rather few linguists who in modern times have applied themselves to the problems of comparative linguistics (unfortunately most of the extensive work of the 19th century comparativists was concentrated very narrowly on detailed examination of the forms and sounds of words—and they said little that bears directly on the issues that are nowadays the centre of attention in linguistics).

The lay-out of this chapter follows that of the earlier parts of the book. First of all, there is some comment on the general aspects of comparative linguistics as they relate to the hypothesis considered here, and then, in separate sections, the comparative application (in terms of other languages) of what has been said in the previous chapters about speech-sounds, word-forms and the problems of the sentence. The issues to be tackled are easily seen: different languages use different sets of phonemes, there are wide differences in the word-shapes found in the lexicons of different languages, and indeed in the range of percepts and concepts provided for, there is a great range of syntactic differences not only in the broad structures of languages but also in the multitudinous detail found even in languages which belong to the same general type (in traditional terms, inflexional, agglutinative, isolating and polysynthetic language types).

There are differences in word-order, parts-of-speech, sentence-structure, the number and nature of verb tenses and in many other respects. These obvious surface differences between languages are what have led so generally to the conviction discussed at length in chapter I, that language as a whole must be an arbitrary system, inexplicable other than as a result of chance development in different societies. Chapter I set out the powerful arguments, despite the appearances, for the view that language cannot be arbitrary and must be related to other major aspects of human behavioural organisation. The objective of this chapter is to suggest how the fundamental hypothesis can be maintained, despite the apparent obstacles presented by the diversity of existing languages.

If one asks what are the implications of the findings of comparative linguistics as a science for the kind of hypothesis advanced in this book, one faces immediately the handicap that there really is no 'modern' science of comparative linguistics. Traditionally, comparative linguistics concentrated almost wholly on the classical languages (with some extension to cover Sanskrit and the Semitic languages) and was concerned with the very fine detail of changes in sound and form within and between a limited number of related languages, especially in the Indo-European group. There has been later work on similar lines, for example, studying the phonetic structure and vocabulary of remote languages (American Indian, New Guinea and Australian, African) but, as Gleason commented not so long ago, "comparative linguistics has been characterised in recent years by rather scant discussion of theoretical and methodological questions"(1). Others similarly have noted that "there is at present no unified theory of diachronic syntax beyond the general notion of rule change within generative grammars" and that, "ultimately, comparative linguistics, so far as morphology and syntax are concerned, will have to be completely overhauled and perhaps largely scrapped, so that a fresh start can be made . . . The panchronic view of language has so far not emerged." Greenberg(2) has made a most useful and systematic attempt to identify the universal features of language and reference is made later to some of his suggested universals but beyond that there is very little of general relevance that can be drawn from the literature. Typically, there are generalities such as: language must be an immensely ancient heritage of the human race since no idiom at present known to us gives any impression of language in a primitive state; every human community, even the most culturally backward, is found to have a completely formed, complex language often with full inflectional forms (comparable to those of classical and modern languages) with definite patterns of forming words and joining them into phrases and sentences; there is no evidence of languages which are in vocabulary or syntax inadequate to the intellectual and cultural level actually reached; every language has been judged to be quite sufficient to meet old and new needs of the people who use it. But beyond this kind of generality (in some respects open to question) comparative linguistics does not take us very far; languages are compared in vocabulary and type, resemblances noted as derived from various sources (historic connections, inheritance and borrowing, analytic artefacts, modelling of syntax on classical forms, possible language universals and mere chance). Despite the detailed work done, the relationships of most individual languages and language groups remain a matter more of debate than of established fact—and Whitney's conclusion many years ago (when traditional comparative linguistics was in full flower) remains still true today: "The evidence of language can never guide us to any positive conclusion respecting the specific unity or diversity of human races"(3).

In the absence of any well-developed theory and even of much validated evidence from the science of comparative linguistics, the question is how most usefully one could approach the problem tackled in this chapter, that is, the comparative application of the hypothesis on the universal underlying structure of language and languages. Apart from the more detailed consideration of speech-sounds, the lexicon and syntax in the succeeding sections of the chapter, it may be worthwhile to start from three unchallenged observations:

1. Children learn extremely rapidly to understand and speak their native language (regardless of its type or complexity) and appear to acquire the lexicon and the syntax of the particular language equally easily. Why should this be possible for all languages without exception?

2. Despite great differences in syntax, word-formation and in every aspect of language (including differences of the experience which language is used to refer to in different cultures), every human language is intertranslatable. How is this possible? (if differing language systems are all equally arbitrary, it is difficult to see how the necessary equations for translation could be established)

3. There are no systematically primitive languages and, for their own purposes, all languages are, on the accepted view, equally effective. How again if languages have been independently and arbitrarily developed is this possible and by what criteria should one assess the adequacy and effectiveness of any particular language?

Taking the questions in the reverse order, one might say in answer to the third that, on the hypothesis put forward in chapter II, the character of language in general, and of any particular language, has been determined by the function it developed to serve; language developed as a vehicle for communicating the content of perception (and perception became perfected as an adjunct to effective voluntary action of the human and the animal). Language has been perfected as a system of communication in each community because in every community the same survival pressure has operated; human communities failing to develop an effective medium of communication will have been unlikely to survive in competition with communities having the use of language. In evolutionary terms, one might list as the minimum universal properties of any effective language (as a vehicle for communicating the content of perception and as an adjunct to voluntary action):

1. Any language must be capable of representing accurately, in the words it has available and the grammatical structures it uses, the ordinary external visual scene, and particularly the aspects of movement, change, action and novelty in it;

2. Any language must use such coding and timing as to produce a very high probability of rapid and successful interpretation of a spoken string of words by the person to whom it is addressed;

3. Any devices available for reducing the time taken to transduce perception into language and to interpret language back into equivalent perception must be used;

4. Any language must make sufficient provision for avoiding confusion in hearing between speech-sounds, to allow recognition of speech-sounds of a given category when spoken in different ways by different individuals (dialect, accent, voice-pitch, loudness and softness) and to enable speech-sounds to be clearly distinguished from other accompanying non-speech sound;

5. Any language must have procedures for linking without ambiguity a specification of the detail or qualities perceived to the object identified;
6. Any language must have procedures for identifying without the slightest ambiguity the actor, the action and the creature or thing being acted upon;
7. Any language must have clear procedures for asking and answering questions quickly;
8. Any language must have procedures for marking off the already known from the new, for conveying the relative importance of elements in the word string;
9. Most importantly, any language to be effective for survival must have speech-sounds, words and grammatical formations which are the common possession of a substantial number of individuals in a community, and must have procedures for forming new words and combinations of words to cope with new categories of experience.

This list of what one might describe as practical language universals can be contrasted with the formal language universals of the kind identified by Greenberg and can also be used in examining the functioning of individual languages which have very different principles of word-order, morphology and syntax.

As regards the first universally true observation about language, that all children learn their particular language equally rapidly despite differences in structure and apparent complexity between languages, the only conclusion can be that all languages are, in some sense, equally learnable (which seems inconsistent with any assumption that languages are arbitrary, conventional structures); chapter I sets out the surprising regularities in children's acquisition of language (based on observation of children learning other languages, as well as of children learning English). The evidence seem to point clearly towards the operation of some special process for acquiring language analogous to the process by which birds of different species learn especially rapidly the song appropriate to their species. The foundation of imprinting can only be a genetic predisposition to acquire with particular ease a specific pattern of behaviour, appropriate to the actual environment in which the infant creature finds itself at birth; in the human case, this implies a genetic predisposition to learn some language, and the predisposition must obviously be a multipotential one because it enables an infant to acquire any one of the many different world languages. A child must be neurologically and physiologically prepared to hear and distinguish speech-sounds within a limited range, to be able to distinguish combinations of speech-sounds (forming words) and to relate particular sound-structures to particular percepts (the meanings of the words) as well as to identify and acquire the syntactic and grammatical structures and procedures in use in the community into which he is born.

If, as seems the case, there is a genetic pretuning to acquire language, it seems inescapable that it extends to pretuning for the acquisition of words as well as pretuning for the acquisition of syntax; in studies of English-speaking and other children, the evidence is that children learn individual words and their meanings earlier and more readily than they learn grammatical forms; but there are clear signs that the acquisition of grammatical forms takes place in accordance with a maturational programme (the evidence of Roger Brown's work quoted in chapter I). In the case of children whose mother tongue is an inflectional one, almost all studies of child language have noted that inflections emerge suddenly, generally a few months after the beginning of two-word utterances.

Genetic pretuning to acquire any one of a range of languages would explain some curious observations; Jespersen(4) describes the case of an Icelandic girl who began early to converse with her twin brother in a language entirely unintelligible to her parents (and when the twin brother died the parents decided that their only course was to learn the child's individual language); clearly in this case, there could be no question of a language being learnt by imitation by the child—rather the language was a joint natural creation of the twin children. The second intriguing observation (made in studies of aphasia) is that lexical and syntactic functions can, to a large extent, be disrupted independently, especially in speech production (which would seem to be in accord with the evidence for separate neurological maturation for the acquisition of words and of grammatical forms by children); the third observation is that innovation in grammar and lexicon is surprisingly rare (Saussure refers to the stability of language); Meillet(5) noted that when changes took place, for example in the pronunciation of the French L-sound, these tended to occur uniformly in a given region in a given generation of children. Though not conclusive, these observations suggest the operation of natural and not conventional factors (an even more curious parallel illustration of the stability resulting from imprinting is given by

Thorpe(6) in relation to bird-song: apparently 100 years after migrating from Europe the New Zealand chaffinch still sings much the same song as its distant relations remaining in Europe).

Besides the established fact that children learn their mother tongue equally rapidly, whatever form it takes, and that every community, however apparently primitive culturally, has developed a complex fully-formed language of its own, there is the third unchallenged fact in comparative linguistics, that every human language is inter-translatable; interpreters can be found to convert the stream of speech-sounds produced by the speaker of one particular language into an equivalent but different stream of speech-sounds comprehensible by the speaker of any other language. To say that translation is universally possible is of course not to say that it is easy (it obviously calls for special skills and knowledge) nor to say that perfect translation is always, or perhaps ever, possible; the more concrete the subject-matter, the more nearly perfect the translation that can be achieved. The greater the difference between the cultural or other experience of those communicating, the more difficult it is to achieve perfect translation—but this is a difficulty due not to the divergence of language-structures but to the divergence of perceptual and intellectual experience. Two scientists or two chess-players speaking different languages may be better able to communicate with each other, by way of a translation, than two people speaking the same language, one of whom is a scientist or chess-player and the other is not. In a sense, every conversation in one language involves a process equivalent to translation—the translation by the hearer, in terms of his own experience and understanding, of the perception, feeling or thought converted into a sentence or stream of sentences by the person speaking to him; one should not confuse difficulty of translation in a particular case due to differences in culture or experience (which could apply between people speaking the same language) with difficulties of translation due to differences in structure and the functioning of two language-systems as such.

That translation should universally be possible between human languages is not really surprising. To recall once again the view of Malinowski and Halliday, the structure of each language has been built up in a such a way that it reflects the demands that are made on language and the functions that it is required to serve. The functions all languages were originally developed to serve were the same: the communication of the content of perception and consequently improvement of the effectiveness of voluntary action of the individuals communicating with each other. Languages in this sense then are different patterns produced by identical general principles (for example meeting the minimum requirements for effective communication listed a few paragraphs earlier). Roman Jakobson has said that what he describes as 'interlingual code-switching' can be and is practised "just because languages are isomorphic: common principles underlie their structure"(7); and Yuen Ren Chao has made the point closely related to what has already been said above that translation is easier "where there is close isomorphism of vocabulary because of isomorphism of culture". He gives a useful description of what he means by isomorphism in this context:

"Two things are isomorphs of each other when they share certain structural properties, such as that from those of one certain inferences can be made about the properties of the other. A map of the world is an isomorph of the earth . . . a structural formula of a chemical compound is an isomorph of the structure of the molecule. Members of the same species . . . are close isomorphs of one another"(8). The central question of comparative linguistics is: if, as Jakobson says, every language is isomorphic with every other language (because the interconversion of the codes by translation is possible), how does one arrive at a clear idea of the universal principles of structure and functioning of language which constitute the isomorphism?

The argument in this book is that the structure of language is isomorphic in an even more fundamental way with the structure and functioning of visual perception and action; and the earlier chapters of the book have attempted to substantiate in detail the nature of this isomorphism for one language, namely the English language. One is on firmer ground in looking for the structural relations between language, vision and action in one language first, because the structure and principles of operation of this one language, English, are much better known and much less contentious (even if there are difficulties) than what has so far been established universally about the structure and principles of operation of language generally. A satisfactory account of the relation of language, perception and action in one language can be the starting point for identifying the universal principles of language, which constitute the isomorphism between languages to which Jakobson referred.

In examining the comparative application to other languages of the central hypothesis in this book, one can proceed in two ways. One can either repeat for each language (or at least for each major language) the kind of study of the relation between speech-sounds, words and sentences on the one hand and the structures of vision and action on the other hand which has already been undertaken for English (obviously a massive task to be undertaken only by experts in the different languages) or one can accept Jakobson's principle that all languages are isomorphic so that if the structural relation between language, vision and action can be demonstrated for English, then by accepted procedures what has been established for English can be converted to apply to other languages i.e. an isomorphism between language, vision and action established for one language is potentially a universal isomorphism. So, whilst in principle the relation between any specific language and the structure of vision and action could be established independently (because each language is a direct transduction of vision and action), to establish the relation for one language is to establish it for all. To put the conclusion most succinctly and strikingly: The isomorphism for any one language between the structures underlying speech, vision and action is at the same time the isomorphism, in the universal context, underlying the structures of all languages and making possible translation between all languages.

Now the reader may say that this seems all very well as an argument of great generality but in the earlier chapters of this book the structural relation between speech-sounds, word-forms and sentence-structures in the English language has been spelt out in considerable detail in terms of the elementary units, of vision and action, the processes by which visual shapes and action-routines are constructed and the syntactic and semantic processes underlying the perception of the visual scene and the planning and execution of a complex action. The relationship proposed has been between the detailed aspects of English lexicon and English syntax on the one hand and detailed aspects of vision and action-organisation on the other hand. For other languages, the fact remains that the details of their lexicon and syntax differ at very many points from the detailed features of English lexicon and syntax. How then can the detailed processes of vision and of action-organisation be set as isomorphic with both the specific features of the English language and the different specific features of other languages? The critic may go on to say that many languages use very much the same set of speech-sounds as English; if the relation proposed in chapter III between speech-sounds, visual units and action-units holds, why should other languages form different words for the same percepts (if the sound-structure of the word and the visual contour or action contour of the object referred to are related)? If, as they do, syntaxes differ widely between languages, and on the hypothesis presented the syntax of speech is correlated with the syntax of perception and action, does this mean that the speakers of other languages in some sense are less effective in converting their perception into speech (because the syntax is less directly integrated with the process of visual perception) or is the suggestion that there is some difference actually in their mode of perception, which results in a matching difference in the syntax of their language? The unchallenged view is that the physiological capabilities of other communities or other races in terms of visual perception and coordination of voluntary action are no different and anatomically their articulatory equipment for speech is the same. Are you suggesting, the reader may ask, that there are neurophysiological differences (affecting speech perception or action-organisation) between members of different communities speaking different languages? And if so what evidence is there for any such differences?

The dilemma presented is essentially the same as that discussed in chapter I where convincing reasons were presented for thinking that language cannot be arbitrary or artificial but at the same time the diversity of languages made it difficult to see how languages could be natural. In the present chapter, for the reason. given by Roman Jakobson and the other arguments presented, all languages must be isomorphic, that is share common underlying principle., but the surface features (of lexicon and of syntax) differ greatly between languages and seem to offer no clue to the kind of universal principles which make possible 'inter-lingual code-switching'. Where the structure and functioning of a particular language (in a sentence of the language) differ from the functioning of an English sentence, this may represent either a less direct transduction (or encoding) of the same processes of perception and action-organisation (for example, if the natural sentence order is Subject Verb Object and the particular language uses the order Subject Object Verb), or an equally direct transduction (or encoding) from different processes of perception and action organisation of speakers of the other particular language. If the transduction is less direct, then it implies that the language less directly and precisely represents the process of perception, so that the language would be less practically effective and thus a language-community for some reason has preserved uneconomical modes of speech. This seems generally improbable (though there are of course instances where out of date functionless grammatical forms have been preserved, as a result of deliberate political, cultural or academic pressure).

Assuming then that current modern spoken languages (disregarding more artificial written forms of some languages) are in fact equally effective media of communication and that their structures are related to the structures underlying visual perception and action organisation, the issue has to be faced head on whether differences in language structure imply or involve differences in perceptual processing or other neurological differences between those speaking different languages. It does not follow of course that differences in the processes by which in a particular individual or in members of a particular community perception takes place or a complex action is planned mean that the outcome, the comprehension of the visual scene or the execution of the complex action, differs in any way: there are equally valid alternative ways of doing things and there is no reason why there should not be equally valid (neutral in terms of effectiveness) ways of scanning a visual scene or indeed describing, in a sentence, a particular event or pattern (as Osgood's experiments referred to in chapter V clearly indicated).

At the most obvious level, there can be neurophysiological differences between individuals speaking the same language and between members of different language-communities in scanning a visual scene, performing a complex action or expressing in language a particular sentence-meaning, simply because the different ways of doing these things involve the use of different groupings of muscles, different timing and sequences of action and different central programming. The answer then to the question whether people speaking different languages must, to some extent, (on the hypothesis that language, perception and action are integrated) perceive differently or organise action differently is Yes. But the differences are only in the underlying processes of action and perception and not in the overt effective outcome, the comprehension of the visual scene or the actual execution of the complex action concerned.

Applied to the hypothesis being considered in this book, this conclusion means that there can be differing syntaxes between different languages because there can be different, equally valid, organisations of the processes underlying perception and action. In parallel to the general isomorphism of languages (demonstrated by their inter-translatability) there is both syntactic isomorphism (in the sense that different use can be made of the available coding resources in different languages) and perceptual isomorphism (in the sense that effective vision can be organised in a variety of ways)—and there is no reason why one form of syntax (of language or of perception) should not be as natural as any other: man is a versatile animal and can select from a range of possible natural patterns of behaviour. The same arguments which lead to the conclusion that there can be different but equally natural forms of syntax can be used to support the view that there can be different but equally natural words (structures of elementary speech-sounds) in different languages which indicate by the associated visual or action contour the percept, quality or action to which the word relates. This latter aspect is developed more fully in a later section of this chapter.

The evidence and argument in support of the contention that the processes underlying perception and action can differ between members of different speech-communities take two form. First of all, one can argue the point generally in term of other categories of human behaviour, Secondly, one can draw on evidence from experimental psychology and from research into vision for widespread differences between subjects in their approaches to problem solving and in their perceptual capabilities—and one can also draw on the evidence of differences of perception between communities (and possibly also between races) in some widely-applied tests, for example differences in perception of certain standard visual illusions.

Perhaps there is no need to labour the general argument in terms of other types of human behaviour. The argument is one from analogy. As between communities, there are many instances of behaviour which is similar in its effect or outcome but different in the processes by which it is achieved. Using natural materials and natural processing methods, communities have different processes of cookery which must in the end produce the same physiological effect, namely material which can be digested by the human body and incorporated in it (curiously, but appositely, Wittgenstein in Zettel asked himself: "Why don't I call cookery rules arbitrary and why am I disposed to call the rules of grammar arbitrary? Because 'cookery' is defined by its end whereas 'speaking' is not"(9)—but why Wittgenstein should have thought that speech is not quite as fully defined by its end (the effective communication of experience) as cookery is defined by the satisfaction of the consumer's physicochemical requirements for food, is left completely obscure). Similarly, different communities using natural materials and different processes produce equally effective houses and buildings, using similar materials but different processes produce effective clothing, and so on. The same materials and different but equally natural (alternative) human processes can be used in many ways to produce the same products or effects.

However, besides this kind of general argument, there is a good deal of much more specific experimental evidence of differences between individuals, communities and races in the processes underlying perception and other aspects of behaviour. Yarbus(10), a great Russian authority on the functioning of the eye and particularly on eye-movements, goes so far as to say, on the basis of his extensive study of scanning patterns, that people who think differently also, to some extent, see differently. Noton and Stark's(11) researches into visual scanning patterns showed very clearly that the scanpaths of different subjects for any given pattern were markedly different i.e. the underlying process of perception may vary from individual to individual. The manner in which a figure is scanned will determine the choice of interpretation ultimately given to the figure and inversely the interpretation of a pattern can in the first instance determine the nature of the eye-movements and then, in turn, can influence the field effects of the sensory input (that is the comprehension of the organisation of the whole visual scene).

An important source-book on the extent to which the processes underlying perception may differ is Davidoff's "Differences in Visual Perception"(12); he refers to the enormous variety of differences in visual perception that are known to exist, the large differences found between individuals belonging to different cultures in their perception of standard visual illusions (such as the Muller-Lyer or arrow illusion) and the racial differences that have been observed to operate in other perceptual tasks. It seems highly probable that there is a relation between the manner in which illusions are perceived and the fundamental processing properties of the eye, the mechanisms by which the visual constancies operate and to the extent that different individuals or members of different communities or cultures perceive standard illusions in different ways, they must be using different perceptual processes, a different perceptual syntax, but the difference of syntax only becomes apparent as a result of the use of the very special and unusual 'probe' into perceptual processes that presentation of the illusions constitutes; for all ordinary purposes, the fact that the individuals concerned were using different underlying perceptual processes would not become manifest.

Much of the discussion in the collection of papers published under the title "Formal Theories of Visual Perception"(13) bears on the same issues and supports the same sort of conclusions, particularly Simon's article on the induction and representation of sequential patterns. The close relation between the problem presented by perception, language and cognition generally emerge very clearly. The goals of universal linguistics are describable in term very similar to those used by Simon in referring to the goals of research in cognitive psychology and perception: "the central goal of cognitive psychology is to discover and describe the invariant structures and processes of the human information processing system" but difficulties derive from the ample evidence of individual differences between subjects in performing cognitive tasks: "the information processing system is adaptive; it does not behave in any unvarying, inflexible way . . . a closely related difficulty . . . is that many, if not most, cognitive tasks can be performed in a wide variety of different ways, using different programs . . . a small set of formalisms has been shown to be sufficient to describe the ways in which human subjects encode patterned sequences of digits or letters . . . However, there are usually a number of different ways of representing any particular pattern, and the actual encoding will vary as a function of the subject's previous experience and the strategy he adopts for performing a particular task".(14)

If throughout the above quotations, one substitutes for the reference to cognitive psychology a reference to universal linguistics and for the reference to differences between individual human subjects a reference to differences between human speech-communities, one gets a fairly accurate presentation of the problem faced in determining the uniformities of structure, the invariants underlying all human languages. No one can doubt that language, perception and cognition are inextricably related in the human brain and the evidence of individual variation in underlying perceptual and cognitive processes suggests that there must be ample natural sources of variation to explain the differing form which world languages take, both in syntax and in lexicon.

The question one is left with is not how is it that languages differ but rather how is it that members of a language-community deny themselves the great possibilities of natural individual variation available to them. For the infant learning its mother tongue, the answer is straightforward: out of the range of natural language forms for which it is genetically pretuned, it selects those which it first experiences in the community into which it is born and with this selection of language goes a bias towards the underlying the associated underlying structure of perception. The selection by the community as a whole of its language, that is of the particular syntax, lexicon and principles of word-formation, together with the underlying processes of perception and action-organisation associated with this syntax and this lexicon, obviously never was a once-and-for-all choice; it represents the long term result of genetic causes, influencing perception, action and language, which have been pooled as a result of the manner in which the imprinting procedure operates for each new infant member of the community. Biases of genetic origin, affecting a substantial part of the language-community, have become systematised and reinforced by the special nature of language as interactive human behaviour. The material from which the language-community has made its selection has been natural, because directly related to processes underlying visual perception and action, but the particular selection made has been the product of the historical development of the gene-pool which the community constitutes, and of the experience which historically the community has undergone i.e. the changing environment within which the pooled genetic character of the community has had to be expressed.

This account of the development of the genetic base of differing natural languages accords closely with modern study of genetics, both of the individual organism and of the population. For the individual, genes do not determine 'characters' but the reactions of the organism to its environment (Dobzhansky(15)); the genetic messages require the interpretation that is provided by the 'initial' environmental conditions and any behaviour must be based on the raw material provided by the inherited constitution (Berry(16)). Most obviously, for example, Berry instances the different type of body fat (depending on diet) produced by a rabbit with a specific genetic constitution; Sayre(17) similarly refers to the different manner of growth of a type of seaweed depending on differences in acidity, warmth etc. The processes by which the genes of an organism establish the neurological structures responsible for its characteristic behaviour patterns (as distinct from overt differences in form) are less well understood (Sayre); there is however no reason in principle why the cortical patterning, equipping the organism prenatally to cope with the environment, should not be established by genetic procedures.

Much the same is the case for the genetic base of social aspects of behaviour. Berry strongly makes the point that geneticists in future must study not the isolated organism but conceive of their subject as extending to population natural history. Social behaviour, like all forms of biological response, is a set of devices for tracking changes in the environment (Wilson(18)); in different species, the structure of the brain has been biased in special ways to exploit opportunities in the environment; Wilson refers, by way of example, to the behaviour of birds (evolution of bird-song incorporating a learning element to allow the individual bird to find quickly its niche in the environment), to social insects (he instances the behaviour of wasps), but extends the same approach to the biasing of the structure of the human brain. The human individual is equipped prenatally to cope with the human social environment and this is apparent in three major respects: the development of consciousness and the cognitive function itself (directly associated with the genetically programmed growth of the cortex see Monod); the development of the directedness of learning, the relative ease with which certain associations are made and acts are learned (the brain, says Wilson, is not a tabula rasa but more like an exposed negative waiting to be developed) and the development of the language capacity; Monod argues that the capacity for language, which now forms a central part of human nature, must have its source in the structure of the genome, that is expressed in the "radically different language of the genetic code"(19).

Variation between languages and the stability of languages can be explained in term closely related to modern genetic studies. For virtually every species, genetic variation between individuals is the normal situation (including genetic variation relating to the development of neurological structures underlying language). The possible permutations of the raw genetic material are enormous (Berry(20)). Consciousness and language are however major elements of human organisation which facilitate adaptation to the social environment and the coordination of group activity (Sayre(21)). Different groups may thus easily develop different languages but the balance between stability and change in a language exactly parallels the balance between phylogenetic inertia and micro-evolution (changes in gene frequency) as discussed by Wilson in his sociobiology.

At the speech-sound level: application to other languages

This section considers the manner in which the ideas presented in chapter III on the inter-relation between speech sounds and units of vision and action might be applied to other languages. Chapter III dealt with the structural relation between the elementary units of speech (identified as the phoneme-set in the English language), the elementary units of vision (taken to be the lines, angles, curves, corners etc. indicated by Hubel and Wiesel's research into the relation between retinal input and response in the cells of the visual cortex) and the elementary units of bodily action in the human being (the structuring of the movements of the different parts of the human body most obviously manifested in movements of the arm and hand and in expressive facial movement). The chapter argued the case for there being a direct physiological and neurological matching of these different kinds of unit and presented, with due qualifications, a precise table of equivalences between the three categories of elementary unit.

The hypothesis put forward has been that in every language there is some specific relation between the speech-sounds of the language and the elementary units of vision and action-organisation parallel to that proposed in the table of equivalences for English speech-sounds. Where other languages have the same, or broadly the same, set of phonemes as English, the question is whether the relation between the speech-sounds of these languages and the elementary units of vision and action is the same as for English; where other languages have a markedly different selection of speech-sounds, or have speech-sounds not used in English, the question is how then can one or should one establish a systematic relation between the speech-sound set and the elementary units of vision and action.

The first part of this chapter has argued the case for thinking that between members of different language-communities, there is the possibility of variation in the underlying processes of visual perception and action organisation in parallel with variation in the lexical and syntactic structures of the different languages, and this contention implies that where another language uses a different selection of elementary speech-sounds or completely different sounds (from English) as part of its phoneme-set, these differences in speech can be paralleled by differences in the system of underlying visual or action elements (i.e. by neurophysiological differences, analogous to the differences observed between members of different communities in certain aspects of visual perception, for example, the extent to which they see at all or see to the same degree some of the standard visual illusions such as the Muller-Lyer arrow illusion).

Unfortunately, it is not possible, on any conceivable scale on which this book might be framed, to undertake as detailed a presentation, even for other major languages, of the postulated underlying relation between the processes of speech, vision and action nor, apart from the massiveness of the task, could this author, or any single author perhaps, claim the depth of knowledge needed to undertake such a task definitively. What this section does is to consider first, drawing heavily on the work of linguists specialising in phonetics, the degree of difference and similarity between the phoneme-sets of different languages, secondly some of the theories that have been advanced to explain both the differences and the similarities, including particularly the genetic theory associated with the names of Darlington and Brosnahan, and thirdly the kinds of variation there may be, between different languages or groups of languages, in the underlying systematic equivalences between the sets of speech-sounds, visual units and units of action-organisation. What the section in effect attempts to provide is a plausible basis for further research, by those expert in other languages, into the possible natural relation between speech, vision and action at the elementary level.

Chapter III discussed in broad term the extent to which phonemes could justifiably be treated as natural units of speech-sound and concluded that the evidence drawn from research into the ability of infants (and some animals) to discriminate phonemically and from the work of Liberman and his associates in the acoustic analysis of speech-sound seemed sufficient to allow one to treat phonemes as real neurological or physiological elements. Accordingly, the phoneme-sets of different languages are taken as the starting-point in this section. The assumption is that the phonemes used are natural and not arbitrary and that the sets of phonemes in particular languages, the selections made in different languages, are, in some sense, natural and not a matter of chance, though it remains for consideration what the basis may be in any language for the system of phonemes adopted.

Catford in his Fundamental Problems in Phonetics (1977) starts by emphasising the difficulty of listing 'phonetic universals' and attempts to explore in some detail the major physical parameters useful in the description of human sounds. There are as many unanswered questions about phonetic universals as there are unanswered questions about linguistic universals generally (as the discussion in the earlier part of the present chapter demonstrated). The first major obstacle faced by what one might describe as 'comparative phonetics' is simply lack of knowledge in the academic community of the range of speech-sounds in many world languages; one estimate is that out of perhaps something like 5000 distinct world languages, we possess full and reliable descriptions of the sounds for no more than a score or so, and moderately good information for perhaps a few hundred more. For those languages for which there is a reasonably adequate knowledge of the system of speech-sounds used, the picture that emerges is a curious mixture of resemblances between languages in the sounds and their frequency of use on the one hand and of differences in the number of distinct sounds and their mode of articulation on the other hand.

In comparative phonetics, questions one would like to have answered are: why should the number of phonemes in any language be what it is and why should the language have that particular selection of phonemes? why should the community select certain articulations in preference to others or use certain phonemes in their phoneme-set much more frequently than others? Though several languages (according to Hockett(23)) appear to have the same number of phonemes, no two of such languages so far express these phonemes in the same phonetic way; the extraordinary diversity of phonetic forms in the complements of phonemes in various languages is, Hockett says, one of the most striking results of linguistic research: why should this be so? The phonemes of one community may be the allophones or free variations (that is, not affecting the meaning of words) of another community; even when the communities thus share in practice the use of the same speech-sounds. Simply in term of the number of distinct phonemes, there is a wide, but not unlimited, range of variation between languages; in some languages, e.g. Hawaiian and similar Pacific languages, the number is very small, as few as a dozen, whilst other languages have very much larger numbers of phonemes, though none is known to have an inventory of as many as one hundred phonemes (Yuen Ren Chao(24)). How many distinct phonemes does a language need? What advantages and disadvantages flow from having a relatively large set of phonemes?

Some of the similarities between the phoneme-sets of most languages are as intriguing and unexplained as the differences. Hockett estimates that the use of human language at present employs only about one-tenth of one percent of the bandwidth of acoustic frequencies available. The number of physically distinct speech sounds which can be made even in one language is said to be indefinitely large, and there would be no end to the refinements of phonetic transcription if one attempted to record every unique sound (allowing for the different accents, tones of voice, pitch, different sound-combinations etc.). But in fact all languages are found to have a surprisingly small inventory of sounds which they treat as distinctive, that is as phonemes. Against the thousands of potentially distinguishable speech-sounds, the typical range for the number of phonemes is between 20 and 60, and not in the hundreds (Zipf(25)), with an average of 25 to 30 (matching in number rather closely the 26 letters of the Roman alphabet). If one adds together the differing phonemes found in the wider range of languages, the number is really not very large; the more usable and familiar international phonetic alphabet comprises about 50 symbols and a dozen diacritica (marks to indicate variants) and this limited number of symbols is able to record all the vowels and consonants that are needed to distinguish meanings in any known language. Even if one takes account of refinements which some phoneticians have felt it necessary to record, the total number of symbols is not greatly increased. Why, one might ask, do all human languages make use of what in reality is such a restricted range of sound-symbols to construct the words they use?

Equally striking similarities are apparent if one looks at the different types of speech-sound found in the phoneme-sets of most languages and the frequency with which they are used. Some sounds are much used in forming words; others are rare, either in term of the languages in which they are found or in their use in a particular language where the phoneme does form part of the set. Jakobson(26) points out that in word-formation there are languages lacking syllables with initial vowels and/or syllables with final consonants but there are no languages devoid of syllables with initial consonants or syllables with final vowels. There are languages devoid of fricatives but none deprived of stops; there are no languages with an opposition of stops proper and affricates (e.g. /t/ /ts/) but without fricatives (e.g. /s/). There are no languages with rounded front vowels but without rounded back vowels.

The different categories of phonemes: stops and continuants, voice and voicelessness, are natural variables found in all human speech. Phonemes are, on Jakobson's scheme of distinctive features, formed from not more than a dozen distinct articulatory features; a few phonemes (/s/ /t/ /m/) are found in a great number of languages; a few phonemes (/gb/ /kp/) are found very rarely, but generally there is a similar frequency of use of similar phonemes in different languages (for 17 languages studied the order of frequency of use was /t/ /k/ /d/ /p/ /b/ /g/ among the consonants). The use of consonants tends to vary much less than the use of vowels and intonation. Despite the difference at first sight between the phoneme sets of different languages, the practical difficulties of learning the speech-sounds in a new language are much less since any given language (speaking generally) has only a few dozen phonemes and probably at least half of these are nearly enough equivalent to the phonemes of the learner's own language.

One of the most intriguing and suggestive similarities observed phonetically between languages is what Brosnahan (in his interesting study The Sounds of Language(27)) describes as the striking areal rather than linguistic distribution of a number of sound features throughout the world, that is, distinctive speech-sounds are found being used in limited geographical areas by people whose communities speak languages which otherwise do not, in terms of language descent or type, appear to be related. Often, the distinctive sounds are rare or non-existent outside the particular defined area. One important and prominent example of this, quoted by Brosnahan, is the presence in languages spoken in India of retroflex sounds, that is, consonants formed with the tip of the tongue raised and bent backward towards the palate; these sounds in Indian languages belonging to the Indo-European group are practically unknown in other Indo-European languages but frequent and in fact general in languages belonging to the Dravidian and Munda groups (that is other languages spoken in India completely unrelated to Indo-European). Brosnahan examines in some detail the strange geographical distribution in European languages of the /th/ sound, the presence or absence of which seems quite unrelated to language-family but rather to a peripheral geographical distribution.

Elsewhere, for example in the Pacific, there is a very narrow set of phonemes, typical of languages in the area; interestingly the Japanese phonetic system historically was of a simple type, originally only 11 consonants and 5 vowels, with a complete absence of the /l/ phoneme (where Pacific languages may correspondingly completely lack the /r/ phoneme). Where Japanese will hear /l/ sounds as /r/, the Hawaiian will hear /r/ sounds as /l/ so that, as Yuen Ren Chao(28) points out, in Hawaiian MERRY CHRISTMAS is pronounced as MELI KALIMAKI (Hawaiian also lacks the /s/ phoneme). Another peculiarity confined to a limited geographical area is found in the very large number of distinct languages in the Caucasus; these languages

"in the areas where Gaulish was spoken, the pronunciation has acquired characteristics recalling those that one observes"(32) in surviving languages of the group to which Gaulish originally belonged. In sum, the effects of general anatomy and physiology in determining modes of articulation have superimposed upon them genetically-derived specific features. If this is so, then there is a direct transition to the kind of theory developed by Darlington and Brosnahan on the genetic basis of the selection and distribution of speech-sounds.

Darlington's hypothesis, as a geneticist, was that the speech-sounds, the phoneme-sets, of particular language communities are primarily determined by the characteristics of the speakers themselves, that is, by the genetically determined physical characteristics, over the period of development of a language, of the members of the continuing language-community. Differences for specific articulations and combinations of articulations derive on a least effort principle (following Zipf) from average differences in the structure, organisation and functioning of the vocal apparatus from co-unity to community, such average differences in their turn resulting from differences in each community's total genetic inheritance and the total environment in which this inheritance has developed. On this view, all biological variations in the anatomy of the vocal tract and in articulatory motor co-ordination, leave their effect upon the acoustics of an individual's speech-sounds, and anatomic and physiological peculiarities are spread through the genetic mechanism; in the final analysis this theory holds that genes control vocal preferences of a community in much the same way as they determine the average physical characteristics of a community, in terms of hair, eye or skin-colouring.(33)

A biological or genetic model of language would at the same time explain the slow processes of language change, either as a normal evolutionary improvement in efficiency or as a result of drift in the physical composition of particular co-unities. A genetic model would also explain the kind of phenomena noted by Meillet, the reappearance of old phonetic habits in a new language, for example one imposed on a community by conquest or absorption in a larger community, as well as the oddities noted above in the geographical distribution of certain speech-sounds, tonality, click-phonemes, the retroflex speech-sounds of the Indian sub-continent, the distribution of the dental fricative (as described in detail by Brosnahan). With a genetic base for the particular features of a language, similarities in limited geographical areas between unrelated languages might well extend (as they do) to syntactic and lexical features (which otherwise have traditionally been explained as the result of diffusion or borrowing). Even as great a sceptic as Whitney) about the reliability of the inferences to be drawn from comparative linguistics concluded that "upon the whole, in the light of our present knowledge, we are justified in regarding the boundaries of Indo-European speech as approximately coinciding with those of a race; the tie of language represents a tie of blood"(34).

Whether or not Whitney's conclusion re presents too great a leap (and it probably does), Darlington's genetic theory seems plausible and helpful in explaining a good part of the enigmas of comparative phonetics. However, though it has not been examined or refuted in any detail, it has not generally appealed to professional linguists. A typical comment (by Anderson in Structural Aspects of Language Change is that "this view of language change has not won many adherents since it was first proposed almost three decades ago. It lacks cogency, especially with regard to the fundamental premise that there are anatomical differences relating to speech activity which are the result of the genetic make-up of mating groups. Much more work is needed to demonstrate the soundness of the hypothesis but such endeavours are still in their infancy and should not be ignored as an aspect of language change"(35). Similarly, Lord commented that anatomical change as a theory of sound change "is entirely discredited . . . The powerful objection to all hypotheses which posit a mutation in the vocal organs or a modification of the cerebral centres is the simple fact that young children of immigrants or refugee children learn the language of adoption with no trace of imperfection"(36.

In the absence of any other at all satisfactory theory of comparative phonetics (work in the generative context on diachronic phonology has been sketchy), rejection of the Darlington/Brosnahan theory seems unjustified and unduly hasty. The criticisms are partly the expression of a misunderstanding of the purport of the theory and partly the result of ignoring the very specific evidence about differences in the gross anatomy of the vocal tract assembled by Brosnahan. A genetic theory is not simply or primarily a theory of language change but a theory of the present phonological system of a language (as reflecting the average genetically determined articulatory preferences of the members of a language community). A great deal has been learnt (for example, from the work of Liberman and others) about the complex central coding of phonemes; a genetic theory is just as likely to be effective through the effects on the neurophysiological processes underlying the production and comprehension of language as through effects on the overt anatomy of the vocal organs. For any individual speech-act, involving changes in the shape and movement of the many different parts of the vocal organs, the extent and sequencing of movement of something like 100 muscles must be co-ordinated centrally, with individual muscular events (contraction or relaxation) occurring at a rate of several hundred events every second (Lenneberg(37)); given this order of complexity, it would be surprising if there were not systematic genetic differences between populations, at least equal in importance to the obvious differences in the conformation of the vocal organs.

These obvious differences are much more significant than is usually realised; the tongue in different races may vary greatly in length (between Japanese and negroes the extreme range in length was from 55 millimetres in Japanese to 123 millimetres in negroes i.e. the tongues of the negroes in this particular study were more than twice as long as those of the Japanese); the comment has been made that one can hardly avoid thinking that the unusual shortness of Japanese tongues must be relevant to peculiarities of the Japanese phoneme-system, for example, the absence of the /l/ phoneme. Brosnahan quotes other significant differences between races; the musculature controlling the shaping of the lips is quite different in most Australian aborigines and in many Africans from the corresponding musculature in Europeans and Chinese; there are equally large differences in the muscles controlling the larynx and those influencing the tension of the vocal cords; for example, (possibly related to the possession of the unusual click-phonemes) the form of muscle controlling the vocal cords in Hottentots is not found at all amongst Europeans. At the most obvious level, there are great differences between races in the external conformation of important parts of the vocal apparatus: the lips of Africans compared with those of Europeans or Chinese, or the great differences in the shape of the nose between different races. All these must have some effect on the ease or difficulty of articulating sounds which require the use of these particular parts of the vocal apparatus.

In the light of this discussion, it seems right to conclude that it is highly probable that the selection of speech-sounds in different languages, the frequency with which individual sounds are used to form words and the restrictions on the combination of individual sounds have been substantially influenced by genetic factors over the period of development of any particular language and that these factors have operated to alter the articulatory preferences of any particular speech-community both through direct effects on the vocal apparatus and probably as much or more by effects on the underlying neurophysiology of speech-processes. The fact that children of a different race may be able to learn as their mother language a language different from that of their race is in no way a conclusive argument against the genetic basis of articulation; the argument has been that genetic factors influence preferences in the use of speech sounds within a community, not rigidly determine which speech sounds can be produced, and that children's capacity to learn language by an imprinting process is a multipotential one, making it possible for them to learn easily any one of a range of naturally-structured languages (though whether a European child brought up amongst Hottentots could successfully make use of the click-phonemes without having the muscles that Hottentots apparently need to produce them is an intriguing speculation).

The final part of this section of the chapter is intended to consider in outline, if not in detail, in the light of the diversity of phoneme systems between languages and the conclusion that there is a substantial genetic element in the articulatory patterns of different languages, how the hypothesis developed in chapter III (that there is a systematic equivalence between the elementary units of speech, vision and action-organisation in English) could be applied to other major languages. As was made clear at the beginning of this section of the chapter, it would be out of the question to attempt in this book to propose parallel tables of equivalences between sound-elements, vision-elements and action-elements (similar to those suggested for English) even for selected major languages, not simply because of the scale of the task but because the preparation of a table of correspondences is something which could only be done by those with a perfect knowledge of the sounds and vocabulary of the other languages. What this section attempts to do is at the least to provide a plausible basis for further research into the possible equivalences between sounds, vision and action elements in other languages, on the assumption that there may be (on a hypothesis similar to that put forward by Darlington and Brosnahan) parallel genetic effects in different language communities on their speech-sound preferences and the associated underlying processes of visual perception or action-organisation.

Starting from the set of phonemes in English, and the five categories into which they were grouped in chapter III, one needs to consider for a selection of other languages how far their phoneme-sets diverge from the English phoneme-set, what important sounds are lacking or are found as additional in these other languages, and to what extent the phoneme-sets they have could be put in correspondence with the categories of chapter III either directly or by some straightforward general adjustment, or whether the phoneme-sets are so different that no obvious way of establishing a relation between them and the five categories in the English table of equivalences can be proposed. World languages can be divided (on conventional lines) into those which appear to belong to the same major family as English (that is, the Indo-European languages) and other important language groups: Semitic—Hamitic, Malayo-Polynesian, Sino-Tibetan, Altaic (Turkic), Bantu and other African languages (including Hausa), Finno-Ugrian etc. Some of the classifications of particular languages and even the demarcations of language families are highly debatable; the better-defined groups are Indo-European, Semitic, Bantu and Malay-Polynesian. Beyond these one can for interest consider some individual languages, with often unique features such as Japanese, Hungarian, Finnish, Korean, Turkish, Hausa, Australian aboriginal languages, American Indian languages (still far from well-categorised), Khoin (the 'click' languages) and last but by no means least Chinese with its many special peculiarities of which the most important for the purposes of the present section is its use of phonemic tone.

To make the discussion more concrete, the notes which follow indicate for a few languages representing the major language families and for some of the 'deviant' languages mentioned above, the extent to which their phoneme-sets appear to diverge from the English phoneme-set and how far the divergences would allow or make it impossible to look for some systematic relation between the table of equivalences given for English in chapter III and the phonemes of the other particular language. There is one preliminary remark to be made, which applies to all the languages dealt with below, namely that whilst generally particular consonantal phonemes common to a number of languages are pronounced similarly (or with relatively unimportant variations), there is much greater diversity in the pronunciation of vowel sounds, even though the sounds in different languages are broadly categorised by reference to the standard set of vowels A E I O U. This detailed variation in the pronunciation of vowels is of course something found not only between languages but very much within a particular language-community (in terms of accent or dialect); indeed the range of pronunciation of individual vowels in English is probably at least as wide (if not wider) than the range of variations in vowel-pronunciation between different languages; certainly it must be so if one takes into account vowel pronunciation by English-speakers in other countries, American, Australian, Caribbean, African and so on.

The notes for individual languages are as follows. Comparisons are with the English phoneme-set and relate to the five categories of phonemes set out in chapter III which were;

    I. B C D F G H
    II. A E I O U AA EE II OO UU plus diphthongs
    III. ZH V CH J P T TH Y
    IV. S SH W X Z
    V. L M N R

The notes refer to the sounds in the language and not to the letters in the alphabets ('?' indicates the speculative inclusion of a phoneme in one of the five categories):

French:

Consonants: lacks CH TH Tþ' W H J

Vowels: has some not used in English (eg. in 'rue' 'oeil') but major difference is the range of nasal vowels

Comparison with chapter III categories:

    I.   lacks TH H
    II. add nasal vowels and special vowel sounds
    III. lacks CH J TH'
    IV. no change
    V. no change

German:

Consonants: lacks J W TH TH' adds TS and KH (as in 'buch')

Vowels: lacks OI (as in 'boy') adds umlauted vowels
(some resembling French vowels)

Comparison with chapter III categories:

    I.   lacks TH
    II. adds umlauted vowels
    III. lacks ZH CH J TH' but ? adds KH TS SHP SHT
    IV. lacks W
    V. io change

Russian:

Consonants: lacks H (replaced by KH) J W TH TH' W adds TS SHCH

Vowels: lacks short A EE O (as in 'pot' or 'toe') short
U (as in 'cut' or 'put')

Comparison with chapter III categories:

    I.   lacks H (KH) TH
    II. lacks vowels as indicated
    III. lacks J TH' adds ? SHCH ? KH
    IV. lacks W
    V. no change

Japanese:

Consonants: lacks TH TH' V X ZH (as in 'pleasure') L (but confused with R)

Vowels: simpler set of vowels A as in French 'chat'

Comparison with chapter III categories:

    I.   lacks TH
    II. simpler vowels as indicated
    III. lacks ZH V TH' adds ?TS
    IV. lacks X?
    V. lacks L (confused with R)

Malay:

Consonants: lacks V X (H often omitted at beginnings of words) adds some Arabic sounds: KH TL GH

Vowels: vowel sounds mostly closer to Italian; has some but not all English diphthongs

Comparison with chapter III categories:

    I.   H often omitted
    II. purer vowel sounds as indicated
    III. lacks V adds ? Arabic KH ?GH ?TL
    IV. lacks X
    V.   no change

Swahili:

Consonants: has TH TH' (from Arabic often replaced by S Z) adds KH GH from Arabic but often as H G R often replaced by L

Vowels: minor differences from English (but fewer variants)

Comparison with chapter III categories:

    I.   some difficulty with TH
    II. as indicated close to English vowels
    III. some difficulty with TH'
    IV. lacks X
    V.   R tends to be replaced by L

Turkish:

Consonants: lacks TH TH'
Vowels: simpler set but includes some French vowel sounds e.g. for U

Comparison with chapter III categories:

    I.   lacks TH

II. vowels as indicated
III. lacks TH'
IV. W very rare
V. no change

Arabic:

Consonants: 24 including a number of special guttural sounds and glottal stop—Arabic has TH
Vowels: 3 vowel qualities covering a very wide range of sounds

Comparison with chapter III categories:

I. no change (though TH quality somewhat different)
II. vowels combine some near-English sounds and some near-French
III. lacks V CH J P adds ? GH Glottal stop
IV. no change
V. no change

Hungarian:

Consonants: lacks W X TH TH'

Vowels: near English vowels plus French or German U

Comparison with chapter III categories:

I. lacks TH
II. vowels as indicated
III. lacks TH'
IV. lacks W X
V. no change

Finnish:

Consonants: lacks B F G J TH TH' W? SH CH ZH Z

Vowels: mostly as in English but with a total of 16 diphthongs

Comparison with chapter III categories:

    I.   lacks B F G TH
    II. vowels as indicated
    III. lacks ZH CH J TH'
    IV. lacks SH W? Z
    V. no change

Korean:

Consonants: lacks F V X Z ZH TH TH' adds more aspirate versions of K X CH P

Vowels: mostly as in English (though fewer) with some U sounds as in French

Comparison with chapter III categories:

    I.   lacks F TH
    II. vowels as indicated
    III. lacks ZH V TH'
    IV. lacks X Z adds ? SS
    V. R and L interchangeable

Samoan:

Consonants: lacks B C D G H J R W X Y Z CH SH ZH TH TH' adds glottal stop

Vowels: vowels and diphthongs broadly like English

Comparison with Chapter III categories:

    I.   lacks B C D G H TH
    II. vowels as indicated close to English
    III. lacks ZH CH J TH' adds ? glottal stop
    IV. lacks SH W Z
    V. L and R to an extent interchangeable

Australian aborigine:

Consonants: most languages lacks F H K P S T V X Y Z CH SH ZH TH TH'

Vowels: for great majority of aborigine languages only 3 vowels A I U

Comparison with chapter III categories:

    I.   lacks K F H TH
    II. only 3 vowels as indicated
    III. lacks ZH V CH P T TH' Y
    IV. lacks S SH X Z
    V. no change (several variants of L N R)

Khoin ('click' languages): spoken in South Western Africa and Tanzania (Bushman, Hottentot, Hatsa, Sandawe)

Consonants: special implosive click consonants, 7 in Bushman, 4 in Hottentot and Hatsa, 3 in Sandawe

Eskimo: One of over 1000 original American Indian languages. Eskimo is a group of dialects forming the northernmost branch of the Amerindian languages. Small but distinctive sound system (21 basic sounds); satisfactory alphabet only recently in course of preparation

HAUSA (tonal African language):

Consonants: lacks V X adds glottal catch and glottalised B D K TS (sometimes produced implosively); glottal K has click-like quality; F often sounds more like P; R sounds like L; also lacks TH TH' X ZH

Vowels: near to English vowels but more nearly pure vowels

Tones: three phonemic tones (one rare)

Comparison with chapter III categories:

    I.   lacks TH

    II. vowels as indicated
    III. lacks ZH V TH'
    IV. lacks X
    V.   R and L interchange

(not clear where glottalised consonants and tones might be fitted into chapter III categories)

Chinese (tonal language):

Consonants: (initials) lacks V ZH X TH TH' (R) adds TS variant SH

Vowels: (finals) lacks A (in 'pat') E (in 'set') I (in 'sit') O (in 'pot') U (in 'cut') U (in 'pull') OI (in 'boy') (except in combination in some instances with N W or Y sounds) adds nasal vowels and French U

Tones: four phonemic tones in Peking (more elsewhere in China)

Comparison with chapter III categories:

    I.   lacks TH
    II. vowels as indicated
    III. lacks ZH V TH'
    IV. lacks X
    V.   very unusual and varying pronunciation of R; otherwise no change

(not clear where phonemic tones or variant consonants might fit into chapter III categories)

The information provided above for 13 languages (or in one or two cases for groups of languages) allows one to form some idea of the divergence between the phoneme-set in English (and the categories into which the English speech-sounds were grouped in chapter III) and the phoneme-sets in other languages. Quite obviously, the tonal languages included (Chinese and Hausa) cannot be readily fitted into a table of equivalences of the kind provided in chapter III between speech-elements, visual elements and action-elements; the research would have to be undertaken by those with a perfect knowledge of the spoken tonal language. As regards consonants, most other languages lack the English voiced and unvoiced TH (marked as TH and TH') which is a rare peculiarity, but apart from this, for French, German, Russian, Japanese, Malay, Swahili, Turkish, Arabic and Hungarian, the number of consonants lacking is quite small (as compared with the English set); the most frequent additional consonantal sounds are the gutturals of Arabic (which are found in some languages influenced by Arabic); several of the languages lack W or V (and in some the sounds interchange) and the pronunciation of R and L tends to be very special in many languages, with, in non-European languages, either R or L lacking from the phoneme-set or R and L being interchangeable or not clearly distinguished. Some languages (already generally recognised as deviant and not easily classifiable in terms of vocabulary or syntax with other languages) lack a large number of the consonants found in English; this is so for Finnish, Korean, Samoan and the Australian aborigine languages.

Apart from these latter languages which obviously have very different phoneme-sets, it is perhaps not irrelevant to note that some of the consonantal features in which the main group of languages diverge from the English consonantal set are ones which are not unknown as dialectal or accentual (class or regional) variations in English; for example, one finds the glottal stop in Glaswegian and Cockney; the pronunciation of R often varies (sometimes is replaced by V); at one time in English V and W were interchangeable; the inability to pronounce TH is common among Irish residents; H is often dropped at the beginning of words; one finds regionally quite often a hissing S (resembling the SS or IS in some other languages); the ZH sound (the rarest phoneme in English) is often replaced by J (for example, in the word 'garage'); the KH sound in German, Russian and other languages flourishes in Scotland as in 'loch' One might fairly conclude that, apart from the Arabic guttural sounds, there is nothing in the consonantal phoneme-sets of the main group of languages described above (French, German, Russian, Japanese, Malay, Swahili, Turkish, Arabic, Hungarian) which is really unfamiliar to spoken English (though the English TH is certainly difficult and unfamiliar to speakers of most other languages). The 'deviant' individual languages and the tonal languages are a different matter (though the Chinese consonant-set as such diverges no more from English than does that of French or German). As regards vowels, there is much greater variation between languages but it has already been pointed out that there is as great or greater variation in the pronunciation of vowels in English, regionally and accentually, and between English-speakers resident in different countries. Nevertheless, though some languages lack some of the central English vowels and others add peculiarities such as the French nasal vowels and the German umlauted vowels, every language has a vowel structure which can be related to the central set of A E I O U (with the exception of Australian aboriginal languages with their extraordinarily restricted set of only three vowels, A I U).

The purpose of this extensive discussion has been to consider how °
plausible it would be to think that similar tables of equivalence (between speech-sounds, visual units and units of action-organisation) could be formulated for other languages on the lines proposed in chapter III for the English language. The conclusion reached is that there seems nothing in the evidence offered of similarities and divergences between the languages considered which requires us to believe that the systematic relation of sound, action and vision at the elementary level is a peculiarity of English or of any single group of languages. A first hypothesis might be that for a central group of languages (the Indo-European languages, the Malayo-Polynesian group, Japanese, and possibly the Dravidian group), a very similar set of equivalences to those proposed for English might apply (with minor modifications for example to deal with the nasalised vowels in French and the introduction of a few extra consonantal sounds in other languages); for some other language groups, notably the Semitic and Bantu, it seems likely that a table of equivalences could be devised by way of a systematic general change in the English table of equivalences (reflecting general differences in articulation e.g. the guttural character of Arabic) and there is evidence for thinking that the same sort of approach might enable one to construct tables of equivalences for some of the 'deviant' languages: Finnish, Korean, Hungarian (as well as the most deviant of all, Basque). To this generally optimistic conclusion, there is one major qualification: Chinese (and other tonal languages) do not appear to fit the pattern; no doubt in time it may prove possible to relate the phonemic system in tonal languages to the phonemic system in non-tonal languages but cross-linguistic study of phonetic symbolism has shown that whilst for many languages (including Japanese), in linguistic experiments the subjects have been able to guess better than chance the meaning of words in a language unknown to them, this has not been the case for experiments where the unknown language was Chinese (some of the evidence on cross-linguistic sound symbolism is referred to at more length in the next section of this chapter).

At the word level: application to other languages

This section considers how far the ideas put forward in chapter IV can be applied to other languages. That chapter was divided into two main parts: the first dealt with the relation between language and perception in terms of the words found in the lexicons of any language. The central idea was that a child's Primitive Vocabulary is built up from the most familiar objects, actions, qualities and relations that it encounters, that this vocabulary has a strongly concrete base, in terms of the sensory modalities used in perceiving the objects etc. for which words are acquired and that the essential characteristic of the vocabulary is that it comprises words which a child learns only by direct experience and not by explanation. The significance of the Primitive Vocabulary is not only as a stage in a child's development of language but as a core on which or round which the fuller lexicon of the adult is gradually constructed; the structure of the full lexicon can be traced back to the natural framework in which elements in the Primitive Vocabulary were acquired and for a language, the total lexicon gains its coherence from its relation with the Primitive Vocabulary (from which it is developed by well-known processes of extension, composition etc. together with, in the case of a particular language, the borrowing of words from other languages, which words in their turn have been derived from the parallel Primitive Vocabularies in the other languages). Part I of chapter IV laid particular stress on the importance, in the full lexical and syntactic development of a language, of the process of metaphorical extension or transformation, the use of words or word-groups or sentences. to apply to a more abstract range of perceptual or intellectual material which has some parallelism of structure with the originally concrete words.

Except for the selection of some 500 specific English words for inclusion in the illustrative Primitive Vocabulary, 1 the discussion and line of argument in part 1 of chapter IV are expressed in wholly general terms and no particular adaptation is needed to apply the views and suggestions to languages other than English. The content of the Primitive Vocabulary, the percepts and actions etc. included, is likely to be much the same for children belonging to different language-communities which culturally are not far removed from English cultural patterns. One could translate the list of English words into parallel vocabularies for other languages but there would be little point in doing so; the preparation of an illustrative Primitive Vocabulary for French, German, Japanese or Chinese would be much better undertaken by a member of these language-communities. One would expect to find in such parallel vocabularies much the same structuring in terms of the sensory modalities from which the words selected were derived, with the same broad classification into shapes and objects, actions and movements, qualities and relations; in some languages, the vocabularies would include particles or bound morphemes which in England are represented by isolated words but chapter IV recognised that perhaps the English illustrative vocabulary ought to include some similar elements e.g. UN—RE—NESS and so on. The distinction between content-words and function-words or between words and grammatical forms is not a sharp or necessarily a useful one, even in English; the intermixture of the semantic and the syntactic is a good deal greater in a number of other languages than it is in English. Whilst for an isolating typically monosyllabic language like Chinese, a Primitive Vocabulary would comprise a collection of distinct words with no particular grammatical classification, in the case of inflected languages it would be a matter of practical detail how far a child normally acquires one or several inflected forms of a word as part of its primitive vocabulary. At the other extreme, with polysynthetic languages like Eskimo and other Amerindian languages (where the sentence is indistinguishable from a single polysyllabic word), it would be for investigation by linguists expert in Eskimo what specific pattern of acquisition of word-sounds Eskimo children normally have. What seems unavoidable is that whatever the type of language in its adult form, children will learn simpler and more concrete elements first, and the idea of a Primitive Vocabulary (as described in chapter IV) should be applicable

Nor is there any reason to think that the discussion in chapter IV of the manner in which the full adult lexicon and eventually the total lexicon for a language is built up from the Primitive Vocabulary, needs much adjustment for application to other languages. For most languages, the total lexicon and possibly also the typical adult lexicon are a good deal smaller than the English adult or total lexicon, and the gap to be filled between the Primitive Vocabulary and the fuller lexicons is smaller. Historically, in most languages, there has been a great growth in the number of words in the lexicon; against the several thousands of meaning-elements (lexemes) in English in the epoch of Beowulf, there are the hundreds of thousands (or getting on for a million) words in the present day total English lexicon. English and German are amongst the languages with the largest vocabularies, in the case of German no doubt to a good extent because of the freedom in formation of new words by composition and in the case of English because of the unusual profusion of near-synonyms (often borrowed words with slightly different shades of meaning from the native words).

More generally, the size of the total lexicon of a language is related to the stage of cultural development, particularly as a result of the rapid growth in the number of nouns as the material and intellectual culture becomes elaborated. Differences in the size or composition of the lexicons between languages, besides reflecting cultural factors (and indeed typological factors), may exist for other reasons, for example, because some concepts which we think essential are ignored in other languages and some distinctions we think unnecessary are expressed. One can draw illustrations of this from two extreme ends of the intellectual spectrum; Firth pointed out that "whole shelves of German philosophy when 'translated' into English are just nonsense (and certainly the Germans and the French have philosophical terms for which we have no precise equivalents) and, at the other extreme, less developed cultures often have a multitude of words for an object or action for which we have only one: Zulus have many words for different kinds of cows but no single word cow; tribes in Brazil similarly have many words for parrots but no word parrot'; Eskimos are said to have many words for snow; Mohicans have (or had) many words for cutting things but no word 'cut'"(38).

Most of the different ways described in chapter IV in which the use of the words in the Primitive Vocabulary can be widened, new words can be formed from it and other words added to it to create the adult lexicon and eventually the total lexicon of English, apply similarly to other languages. There may be difference in the facility for forming compound words (as already mentioned for German, in contrast with French), other languages may have more homogeneous sources and borrow very much less readily than English: Chinese historically has adopted extremely few foreign words (whilst Japanese and Korean have drawn a very substantial part of their vocabulary from Chinese). But, according to Greenberg, all languages have devices for converting verbals and sentences into adjectivals; all languages have devices for converting some or all verbals into nominals and many languages have devices for converting at least some nominals into verbals i.e. the flexibility one finds in English in creating new nouns, verbs or adjectives is available to a marked degree in most other languages. Certainly, the most important form which extension of the lexicon takes, that is the development of metaphorical forms and uses, is as prominent in other languages, even culturally relatively undeveloped languages, as in English.

So far in this section comment has related to the comparative application of Part I of chapter IV and the conclusion has been that the ideas contained in it raise no particular problems. The propositions, or hypotheses, advanced are supported by the same arguments and have the same validity for other languages. For much of Part II of the chapter, which dealt with the natural origin of individual words in the extended Primitive Vocabulary the same, surprisingly, is the case; this part of that chapter discussed, in parallel, the construction of visual forms (from elementary visual units), the construction of action-routines (from the elementary units of action identified in chapter III) and the construction of word-forms from elementary speech-sounds (phonemes). The earlier part of the present chapter has presented evidence on the degree to which neurophysiologically the processes underlying visual perception and action organisation may be similar or different between members of different language-communities; the immediately preceding section has brought out the extent of the similarities and differences in the sound-complements (phoneme-sets) of a wide range of languages.

Taken together, the evidence and arguments go to show that for other languages it ought to be possible to construct tables of equivalences between the elementary units of speech, vision and action more or less closely related to the table of equivalences proposed for English at the end of chapter III. The major conclusion reached at the end of chapter IV, as regards the formation of visual shapes, action-routines and speech-forms (words) was the overriding importance in all three cases of the central coordination neurally of the complex sequences of movements involved in seeing, in moving parts of the body in action and in movements of the articulatory apparatus in speech. The formulation of neural patterns (in the motor cortex) to initiate and execute the three forms of complex action that visual perception, bodily movement and speech-production constitute, provided a possible (and a probable) basis for the detailed interrelation between the structures of visual shapes, action-routines and word-forms which was the central hypothesis of chapter IV; and thus a basis for a natural relation between sounds going to form a word and the meaning of the word (the percept, action or quality to which it refers).

As a proposition, this is argued in relation to language generally and not in relation to English specifically. But the test of the validity of the proposition, the plausibility of assuming this particular neurophysiological basis for the relation between the sound and meaning of individual words, can only be in terms of particular individual languages, and particular individual words. As a problem in the comparative application of the hypothesis, the key section in chapter IV is the Annex. This was intended as a practical demonstration for specific words drawn from the illustrative Primitive Vocabulary of the manner in which their appropriateness, their naturalness, can be derived from the relation between their sound-structures and the visual contours, the contours of action and other features of perception and action necessarily associated with the particular speech-sounds used and the order in which those sounds are arranged in the individual word. The Annex did not set out to explain or justify in detail the way in which the combination of particular speech-sounds in a word gives rise to a particular visual or action contour; what the Annex did explain was how the words in the illustrative Primitive Vocabulary can be classified in terms of the visual and action contours associated with them and secondly it set out for a substantial selection of English words (drawn from the Primitive Vocabulary) the character of the particular visual or action contour associated with the particular word (the natural bond between the sound of the word and its meaning).

A full comparative application of the approach illustrated for English in the Annex to chapter IV would require construction of similar Primitive Vocabularies for other major languages (and indeed for some of the 'deviant' languages discussed in the preceding section), the determination for these languages of the appropriate table of equivalences for each language between sound-elements, visual elements and action-elements, the investigation of any special rules for combining the sound-elements in these languages into word-forms and finally how far the meaning of each word did or did not match the visual or action contour theoretically associated with it (as a result of the combination of the particular sound elements in the word) This is obviously something which can only be done by someone with a perfect knowledge of the particular language and who has been sufficiently convinced of the plausibility of the general hypothesis presented in this book on the structural interrelation of the processes underlying language, visual perception and action. This section presents evidence to show the plausibility of assuming a natural relation between the sound and the meaning of particular words (in English and other languages) and, for some of the English words listed in the Annex, examines the extent to which in a few other major languages there seem to be parallel relations between sound and meaning.

If, as is argued in this book, there can be a natural relation between the sound and meaning of words (particularly those words which form the Primitive Vocabulary in a language), and this natural relation takes the form of a correspondence between the sound-structure of the word and the structure of an associated visual contour or action, then one would expect every language to make use of this great convenience for the formation of words; where onomatopoeia, in the limited sense, is possible, that is, for sounds and creatures or objects which make a characteristic sound, every language creates onomatopoeic words. Henry Sweet(39) commented that the most primitive and indispensable words of language are just those which could not possibly have originated from imitation but Jespersen's view was that there must clearly be other forms of natural association of sound and sense (besides the limited number of sound-imitative words) but these other associations were arrived at "by devious and circuitous ways, which to a great extent evade enquiry and make a detailed exposition impossible"(40). The claim made in chapters III and IV is to have identified or at least plausibly suggested the 'devious and circuitous ways' by which sound and meaning are linked (through the relation between speech, vision and action) and to have explained how these ways operate in relation to English.

But one is faced with the standard objection, frequently quoted already: Why then should there be different words for the same percepts in different languages? The answer is that words for the same percepts may be different between different languages for several reasons: first, because the sound-elements available to speakers of another language may be different from those available to English-speakers so that the words which can be formed must differ; secondly, because even though the visual or action contours associated with a percept in another language may be the same as in English, the equivalences between the underlying speech elements, visual elements and action elements may be different (due to genetic variation neurophysiologically or in overt anatomy) so that again the word formed in parallel with a particular visual contour is bound to be different; thirdly, because even if the underlying relation of sounds, vision elements and action elements in another language is the same, there are alternative ways of putting the same pieces together: if, for example, one draws a simple visual contour, say the letter T, it is just as effective to draw the upright or the crosspiece first, and there could similarly be two or more equally valid sequences of action in forming the sound-equivalent of a visual contour. Fourthly, even though the associated visual contour for a word may be the same as in English, in the other language the contour may be divided up into a different set of parts, just as, with a jigsaw, one can produce exactly the same picture even though the puzzle is cut up into differently shaped parts; similarly, the associated speech-sounds related to the differing parts of the visual contour would be different and the final word-form would also be different. Fifthly, in other cultures, either the normal visual association with a particular word may be different e.g. the visual contour associated with 'tree' 'house' or 'chair' (in Africa or Japan e.g. a round African hut compared with a rectangular European house) or there may be different preferred clues to the meaning of a word e.g. an animal may be distinguished by the noise it makes rather than by its physical shape. Sixthly, as speech-sounds (on Jakobson's view) form a coherent system where the availability and use of each sound is influenced by the remainder of the set, so it is likely that in any language words also form a coherent system so that if in the language a particular word has been formed for a given percept, then that word is no longer available for use to refer to a different percept, for example, if in French 'sais' has already been formed to mean 'know', then the same sounds cannot be used to mean 'speak' (as in English 'say' which has exactly the same sound elements as the French word). It is obvious that Bloomfield's knockdown argument against a natural origin of language, that words must be arbitrary because, in the example he gives, the word for a horse is 'horse' in English, 'cheval' in French, 'pferd' in German and 'misatim' in Cree Indian, is by no means conclusive; there are many plausible reasons why differences may exist and each of these words, in the different languages, may have an equally natural relation with the meaning of the word, the percept to which it refers.

However, beyond this kind of explanation of differences between languages, there is a great deal of other evidence which makes it plausible to believe that a natural relation does exist and is recognised between the sound and meaning of words in other languages as well as in English. This evidence can be classified as:

1. Evidence of sound symbolism in English and in other languages, that is, the recognition that some words seem peculiarly appropriate for their meanings;
2. Evidence of cross-linguistic sound symbolism, experimental evidence that speakers of one language can guess the meaning of words in other languages unknown to them with an accuracy greater than can be explained as the result of chance;
3. Evidence of resemblances between the words used for particular percepts in a wide variety of unrelated languages to an extent that again cannot reasonably be treated as the result of mere coincidence;
4. Evidence that with other languages, as well as in English, there is a systematic resemblance and relation between words which refer to related percepts or otherwise have related meanings or aspects of meaning (where the resemblance between the words is not, according to authoritative judgment, due to accepted etymological links);
5. Evidence from studies on children's use of language of the extent to which children automatically believe in a natural relation between words and what they mean.

It would unduly lengthen this chapter to attempt to set out this evidence in full (in any case much of it has already been presented elsewhere) but it may be useful to give some indication, in relation to each category, of the kind of evidence that is available.

Sound symbolism or expressivism (the phenomenon that words are felt to be naturally appropriate to their meaning) is as well-established a fact for other languages as it is for English. This is as true for major European languages such as French, German and Spanish as it is for remoter languages. Linguists, even those like Sapir(23) and Firth who proclaim the arbitrariness of language, recognise that particular feelings of appropriateness are associated with particular words. Sauvageot, in his interesting study of French vocabulary, generally follows a theoretical line based on that of Saussure (the arbitrariness of the sign) but stresses the great importance in French of onomatopoeia and expressive words(41); systematic evidence for the reality of phonetic symbolism in French has been presented by Peterfalvi(42). Writing about Spanish, Garcia de Diego says: "all words in varying degrees have a sensory or emotive value"(43). Other authorities strongly support the reality of sound-symbolism: Jespersen "There is no denying that there are words which we feel instinctively to be adequate to express the ideas they stand for"; Roger Brown "the evidence is that speakers of a given language have similar notions of the semantic implications of various phonetic sequences . . . there is a less obvious phonetic symbolism where the referent is not acoustic"(44); Jakobson: "Sound symbolism is an undeniably objective reality, based on relationship between different sensory modalities, particularly between the sensations of sight and hearing"(45).

There seems no need to labour the point. Unlimited examples could be provided from different languages demonstrating the existence of sound-symbolism. Humboldt many years ago quoted words like 'wolke' 'wirren' and 'wunsch' as expressing the vacillating, wavering motion referred to; Jespersen(46) referred to Hilmer's work (170 pages of word-lists of expressive words in German); Firth(48) gives examples of a large number of expressive words in Norwegian, Swedish and Dutch (as well as in English). In many examples, the syllables in a word apparently correspond to the number of distinct elements in the sound, object or action, for example, Roger Brown(49) refers to 'ongololo' meaning 'centipede' in Samoan and to Wissemann's study which found that students chose invented words which in length were related to the number of distinct divisions in the patterns of artificial sound-sequences which Wissemann asked them to name; all the students followed similar principles in deciding what would be appropriate names to choose. A similar example is given by Garcia de Diego for Spanish: "in the word 'pimpim' (used for the wagtail) we have not an acoustic representation of its song but an acoustic expression which translates a visual impression of the rapidity of movement characteristic of the bird"(43).

Sound symbolism has been less studied for remoter languages but seems to be as much or more of a reality in them. Manchu, for example, is said to have been absolutely full of imitative formations. There are many examples of sound symbolism in African languages; in Ewe, high-tone words indicate small things and low-tone words large things; in certain Sudanese languages high-tone words are used to express long distances or high speed, and low tone words to express proximity and slowness. These examples are of particular interest as showing that sound symbolism is a reality also for tonal languages. In Chinese, it is not irrelevant, in considering visual contour as a foundation for the natural feeling of words, that many of the Chinese classifiers (words indicating the category to which an object belongs) are based on shape; there are, for example, classifying particles which indicate long, flat and round objects, containers, pairs and sets (curiously similar to classifiers used in some American Indian languages).

Cross-linguistic sound symbolism

There has been as much, if not more, research into the extent to which cross-linguistic sound symbolism is a reality i.e. that speakers of one language can appreciate the expressive force of words in another language (possibly one not at all known to them). There seems no doubt that sound-symbolism does extend across languages but it is unsettled how far this is universally true or whether there are some languages or groups of languages for which the expressiveness of individual words in the languages cannot be appreciated by members of other language-communities. Certainly, experiment has shown cross-linguistic symbolism between a number of completely unrelated languages but experiments involving Chinese (and other tonal languages) have been unsuccessful or unconvincing when those persons taking part in the experiments had a non-tonal language as their native tongue. It would not be surprising if speakers of non-tonal languages should find more difficulty in observing the sound-appropriateness of words in tonal languages or if speakers of tonal languages similarly found more difficulty in judging the phonetic appropriateness of words from non-tonal languages. The evidence otherwise seems to point strongly towards the universal reality of cross-linguistic sound symbolism.

Though it is not practicable to repeat here a full account of the very many experiments into cross-linguistic symbolism, the sequence of experiments has developed consistently towards greater and greater rigour. At first experimental subjects were asked simply to say whether a selection of words drawn from various foreign languages sounded appropriate or not to their meanings; though the result was that the subjects were able to judge the appropriateness of the words, the experiment was not conclusive because it might have been biased by the selection of words by the experimenter. At the next stage, the experiment took the form (devised by Tsuru(50)) of presenting 36 pairs of opposite words in Japanese (meaning 'hot-cold' and so on) to subjects with no knowledge of Japanese and asking them to match the Japanese words with the corresponding English words; the words were successfully matched more frequently than could result purely from chance and this finding suggested that the form or the sound of the

Japanese word must give some clue to the meaning. It was then argued that the Japanese experimenter might by his selection of pairs of opposite words have unconsciously biased the result; to eliminate unconscious bias in a new series of experiments the pairs of opposite words in Japanese were translated into Hungarian and Polish; the subjects taking part in these new experiments did not, of course, speak or know Hungarian, Polish or Japanese but again the result was that the foreign words were matched with the corresponding English words more frequently than, statistically, could be explained as resulting from pure chance. The same sort of experiment was repeated with Czech, Hindi, Croatian and Hebrew and in each case added to the cumulative evidence for the existence of cross-linguistic symbolism between non-tonal languages. Experiment on somewhat different lines (Ertel Dorst(51)) found evidence for expressive sound symbolism between languages for 25 languages.

Resemblance between unrelated words or the same percepts in different languages

If one examines the words in a large number of languages for a range of commonly encountered objects, actions or qualities (parts of the body, colours, simple actions, air, water, earth, pronouns, demonstratives), one finds that resemblances of sound and meaning spread across many languages, related and unrelated, including languages which geographically and in terms of language family are extremely remote from each other. The resemblances go beyond anything that can plausibly be explained as the result of chance or coincidence. Linguists have often noted the extent of these surprising resemblances, quoting particularly notorious examples such as 'have' in English and 'habere" in Latin (which etymologists say are unrelated to each other), 'path' and 'bad' in English and 'path' and 'bad' in Persian (also said to be unrelated), 'fire' and 'feuer' in English and German which are said to be unrelated to 'feu' in French, 'day' and 'dies' in Latin (not related), 'whole' and 'holos' in Greek (meaning 'whole' but unrelated to the English word.

Comparative linguists have reacted to these resemblances in two opposed ways: a very few (Trombetti, Swadesh) have argued that the extensive resemblances between distant languages in vocabulary can only be explained by assuming that all or nearly all languages, at some great distance in time, were related to a single parent language (Swadesh built up his procedure

of glottochronology on the basis that the degree of resemblance between
the words in different languages could be used to calculate how many
centuries or thousands of years earlier the different languages developed
from a common base). Other linguists dismiss any idea that all languages
are related. Typically, Whitney says: "There are no two languages (where
one cannot find) a goodly number of these false analogies of both form
and meaning, seeming indications of relationships which a little historical
knowledge at once shows to be delusive . . . It is only necessary to cast out of
sight the general probabilities against a genetic connection of the languages
we are comparing . . . and we may find a goodly portion of the vocabulary
of each hidden in that of the other . . . no single item of vocabulary is worth
anything until there are found kindred facts to support it"(52).

Over the centuries there has been a very great deal of effort put into
looking for resemblances between particular languages (to suggest that
Indo-European languages are related to Hebrew, or Basque to Georgian
or to any number of other languages) and also some effort, though on a
smaller scale, to support the contention that all languages are related and
derive from one primeval language. Comparative linguists have not been
convinced because, like Whitney, they argue that similarity of vocabulary
by itself proves nothing about the family relation of languages. On the
other hand, whether or not the resemblances indicate relationship, the fact
remains that the resemblances do really exist and call for some explanation.
A more scientific approach to the problem is to prepare a list of English
words referring to a range of ordinary objects, actions, qualities and
relations (chosen on the basis that they are words most unlikely to have
been borrowed into English and that for the most part they are likely to be
acquired by children from direct experience rather than by explanation and
instruction) and then to set this list of words in parallel with the equivalent
words in an extensive range of other languages (including languages totally
unrelated to English as well as related languages). One can then examine
what degree of resemblance is in fact found, how far the resemblance is
confined to related languages and how far it extends to unrelated languages
and whether the words in the other languages listed for a particular object
etc. resemble one another even if they do not resemble the word found in
English. In an earlier work, the author carried out an examination of this
kind for a list of 40 objects, actions, qualities and grammatical elements
translated into 23 languages (including languages from all the main
language-groups other than Amerindian). The extent of resemblances

found between the different languages was striking for many of the items included in the list.

A few examples using words included in the list illustrate this:

crab: out of 23 words for 'crab', 14 began with K or C or had K as a prominent sound in the word; for the remainder of the words in the list (that is referring to objects etc. other than 'crab') K as an initial sound or as a prominent sound was rare; interesting similarities between some individual unrelated languages for 'crab' were Korean 'ke', Swahili 'kaa', Japanese 'kani', Telegu 'kappu', Latin 'cancer' Malayan 'kepiting'.

cut: out of 23 words for 'cut', 15 began with K (or C) or had K as a prominent sound ('cut' was the only other word out of the list of 40 to have K (or hard C) as an initial sound). Interesting similarities between unrelated languages were Arabic 'kata', Chinese 'ko', Telegu 'koyu', Japanese 'kiru', Greek 'keiro', Hebrew 'karat', Spanish 'cortar'.

lick: 14 of the words began with L or had L as a prominent sound. Interesting similarities: Hebrew 'likek', Basque 'milikatu', Greek 'likhmadzo', Hungarian 'legyoz', Latin 'lingo' or 'lambo', Swahili 'lamba' (one Amerindian language has as its word for 'lick' the word 'lambi').

name: 12 of the words began with N whilst a further 8 out of the 23 had N or M as a prominent sound. Interesting similarities: German 'name' Japanese 'namae', Turkish 'nam', Malay 'nama', Finnish 'nimi' (an Amerindian language has 'mami' and Chinese has 'ming').

same: Interesting resemblances: Finnish 'sama', Malay 'sama', Arabic 'sawa', Telegu 'sawa', Lozi 'swana', and Russian 'samyi'.

This is only a very small sample of resemblances drawn from the much fuller study but it may be enough to show the basis for the general conclusion reached that in the case of many, and perhaps most, of the common words examined, there were resemblances between words drawn from remote languages which it is highly unlikely could be explained away as the mere result of chance or coincidence. They certainly could not be explained in terms of accepted views of the family relationships between languages.

Similar exercises were carried out to establish the degree of resemblance across languages for other common categories of words: pronouns, demonstratives and the names of colours. The results were equally striking. The comparisons were made for a larger number of languages, 70 in the case of the study of pronouns and demonstratives. A few examples follow of the resemblances found:

I the pronoun: Out of 70 words in the list, all except 11 could be arranged in two large groups within each of which there was a substantial resemblance between the words found in the different languages. Interesting similarities in the two groups: English 'I', Nubian 'ai', Dutch 'ik', Hittite 'uk', Javanese 'aku', Basque 'nik" Arawak 'nuka', Irish 'me', Georgian 'me', Yoruba 'emi', Swahili 'nimi', Finnish 'mina', Zulu 'mina', Khoin 'am" Sanskrit 'aham', Korean 'na', Malayan 'nan', Arabic 'ana', Hebrew 'ani" Hausa 'ma'.
you singular: 57 out of the 70 words in the list could be grouped with other words which they resembled more or less closely; only 9 words for this pronoun appeared completely isolated. Interesting similarities: Albanian 'ti', Welsh 'ti', Hungarian 'te', Russian 'tyi', Arawak 'tiwa', Mongolian 'ta', Hebrew 'ata', Japanese 'anta', Aranda (Australian aborigine) 'unta'

Equally striking similarities were found for other pronouns and for demonstratives. A similar exercise on an even larger scale (using about 90 languages) showed striking resemblances between the words used for different colours in different unrelated languages (though the degree of resemblance was less than the really remarkable degree of resemblance for pronouns and demonstratives where there is a clearly established tendency for a very limited range of sounds to be used for the specific set of meanings classed as pronouns and demonstratives).

From all this, there is clear evidence of a universal tendency for certain meanings to be associated with certain speech-sounds as formed into words. Chance cannot be an adequate explanation for the extent of resemblance nor can borrowing (because the words included in the exercise are common ones which no community would be expected to borrow from elsewhere). Accepted relationships between languages, as determined by classical comparative linguistics, also provide no explanation The evidence is however completely consistent with the hypothesis in this book that there is a natural relation between the sound and the meaning of words, particularly for words in the Primitive Vocabulary, derived from the processes underlying visual perception and action-organisation.

Systematic resemblance within a language between words with related meanings

Many words, in English and other languages, which are similar in the sounds going to form them, derive their similarity from etymologically standard processes of word-formation and word-development. This is true of the conjugation and declension of words in inflected languages, of the formation of comparatives or plurals in English and other languages, of the composition of new words by the addition of prefixes or suffixes and so on. This kind of resemblance between words, in a systematic way, is at the same time taken for granted and fully natural. The more interesting kind of systematic resemblance is where words have sounds and meanings which resemble one another but etymologically the words are judged not to be related or derived from one another by any standard process of composition, prefixing etc. This is a phenomenon which has been observed in English and other languages and has been commented on, as an unexplained curiosity, by a number of linguists and others. Tylor, the anthropologist, remarked on the way in which "words, whilst preserving so to speak the same skeleton, may be made to follow the variation of sound, of force, of duration, an imitative group will show;—CRICK CREAK CRACK CRUSH CRUNCH CRAUNCH SCRUNCH SCRAUNCH . . . "(53). Firth, whilst disbelieving in sound symbolism, assembled large collections of symbolic words and emphasised the systematic way they may be related to each other, quite separately from any etymological links: "We are appreciably affected by initial and final phone groups not ordinarily recognised as having any function. Consider the following English words: SLACK SLOUCH SLUDGE SLIME SLOSH SLASH SLOPPY SLUG SLUGGARD SLATTERN SLUT SLANG SLY SLITHER SLOW SLOTH SLEEPY SLEET SLIP SLIPSHOD SLOPE SLIT SLAY SLEEK SLANT SLOVENLY SLAB SLAP SLOUGH SLUM SLUMP SLOBBER SLAVER SLUR SLOG SLATE . . . A group of words such as the above has a cumulative suggestive value that cannot be overlooked in any consideration of our habits of speech. All the above words are in varying degrees pejorative"(54).

In English, there are many similar groupings of words where there is some underlying resemblance of meaning related to the surface resemblance of the sounds forming the words. Bloomfield(55) quoted a number of these: examples are such groups as: FIRE FLAME FLARE FLASH FLICKER POINT POKE PIKE PEG PEAK PIERCE PRICK PROD PROBE PRONG HIT HACK HEW HATCHET HASH THROW THRUST THRASH THWACK THWART THUMP THROTTLE SWEEP SWAY SWING SWIRL SWERVE SWOOP SWISH SWITCH SWAT SWIPE SWAB WAG WAGGLE WEAVE WOBBLE WANDER WONDER WADDLE WAVER WAVE. The felt resemblances between these sets of words is apparent and must derive from symbolism in the sounds used though not necessarily just from the initial letters of the words since one can easily find examples of other words with the same initial letters but belonging to completely different categories of meaning; the resemblance seems to derive from the whole structure of the words in each group.

It would be possible to present evidence of very similar groups of words, with an underlying relation between sound and meaning, but not etymologically connected, drawn from other languages but this is something perhaps done better by experts in the other languages who are better placed to Judge the feeling tone associated with particular sound-groups or words. What is perhaps of the greatest immediate interest and relevance is that in the case of some groupings of words in other languages (which seem to have related underlying aspects of meaning), these groupings can on occasion be matched with parallel expressive groupings of words in English. It may be enough to give two examples of this, matching groups of English words with, respectively, Malay and French:

Malay	English	French
KELEPOK	CLAP	CLAQUER
KUKU	CLAW	GRIFFE
KEPITAN	CLASP	AGRAFER
KEPITING	CRAB	CRABE
KETAM	CLAMP	CRAMPON
KERKAH	CRUNCH	CROQUER
KUMPUL	CLUSTER	GRAPPE
GENGGAMAN	GRASP	AGRIPPER
GILING	GRIND	GRINCER
KERTIK	CLICK	CLIQUETER
KERINCH1NG	CLATTER	CLAQUER
GERGAU	SCRATCH	GRATTER
KISUT	CRINKLE	GRIGNER
MENGGERUTU	GRUMBLE	GROGNER

These are only a selection from fuller comparative lists of English, Malay and French words. They show that Malay forms imitative and expressive words through the use of sound-sequences quite similar to those familiar in English and that one can extract parallel groupings of words in Malay and English, in terms of sound and meaning. Similarly, there seems to be some parallelism in sound and meaning between English and French for words beginning with CL GL GR—though the correspondence is not exact; words starting with GR in French may start with CR or with CL in English.

It would be burdensome to quote the much more extensive material available for these and other languages but it seems clear that there are parallelisms between languages in their formation of words which are grouped together by an underlying aspect of meaning. There may be direct resemblance in this respect between one language and another as is the case for the Malay and English words given above and for many of the French and English words listed.

Children's use of language

One type of evidence for accepting as plausible the idea that there is a natural relation between sound and meaning for many words is that systematic study of children's views about the origin of words shows that until they are brought, by instruction, to think otherwise; children uniformly say, when asked, that words are derived directly from the objects to which they relate. Piaget and his assistants have over many years questioned children of different ages about their understanding of words and the relation of words to things; they found that children of the same ages gave the same sort of answers to questions about the nature of words. Piaget refers to the 'well-known' theories of Sully, Compayre and many others "according to which it is maintained with much justice that to a child's eye every object seems to possess a necessary and absolute name, that is to say, one which is a part of the object's very nature"(56). Piaget believes that children's ideas of this kind are simply evidence of their lack of insight and understanding until, as they grow older, they come to accept the orthodox view that words are arbitrary and conventional and have no natural relation with their meaning. Before they reach this stage, the children questioned by Piaget and his helpers firmly believed that words share the nature of the things they name as well as of the voice producing them; words for them are a part of material reality; the children believe that they are not taught words for common things but the words originate of themselves within the child itself; for children, words, seeing, thinking and action are all intermingled and directly related to the objects the child sees or acts upon. Piaget says that children go on taking this sort of view until they have had several years of formal schooling and reach the age of about eleven. Because Piaget himself starts from the orthodox position that words are conventional and arbitrary, he attaches no weight to the surprising uniformity with which children, until they have been taught otherwise, believe that there is a natural link between word and meaning.

Taken together the five categories of evidence discussed above for the existence of some underlying relation between sound and meaning in other languages as well as in English very much go to strengthen the plausibility of the central hypothesis in this book, that there is a natural relation and it is based on the interrelation of the underlying structures and processes of visual perception, action-organisation and speech; in the light of the evidence, it should be worthwhile to examine for other languages whether one can determine for specific words the particular visual or action contour associated with the sound-structure of the word (on similar lines to the exploratory examination of this for a number of words selected from the English Primitive Vocabulary as set out in the Annex to chapter IV. At the beginning of this section, the point was made that such an examination for other languages could only in practice be undertaken by someone with a perfect knowledge of the particular language; accordingly, no attempt is made in this chapter to develop in detail any parallel for languages other than English to the material contained in the Annex to chapter IV. However, at the end of the present chapter, there is a brief note showing in parallel a selection of the English words dealt with in the Annex and the equivalent words in several other languages (so that one can form a preliminary view whether at first sight there may be some similar natural relation between sound and meaning for these words in the other languages).

At the sentence-level: application to other languages

This section considers how far the discussion of the relation between the sentence, the visual scene and the complex action and the detailed processes which may be involved in the correct but general 'solution' of a sentence (that is the decoding of the serial string of words formed by a sentence) can be applied comparatively to languages other than English of different language-types and with many differences in the specific features of their syntax and grammar. Chapter V was divided into a number of distinct sections: first, consideration of the correspondence of the concepts of the visual scene, the complex action and the sentence and the broad parallelisms of structure and process underlying them; secondly, a listing and discussion of specific possibly-equivalent aspects of these structures and processes (for example, word-order and visual scanning, parts of speech and parts of the visual scene, ambiguous scenes and ambiguous sentences); and thirdly and most importantly, examination of the techniques and available material resources for the 'solution' (decoding) of the sentence and the parallel decoding of the visual scene. The opening general part of the present chapter on the problems of comparative linguistics and the application to other languages of the basic hypotheses advanced in this book has, in fact, already dealt with a number of the major issues which arise at the sentence-level in relation to other languages: the implications to be drawn for differences of syntax and sentence-formation from the rapidity with which children learn any language as their mother tongue (regardless of differences of type or in apparent grammatical complexity); from the fact that there are no syntactically primitive languages and all appear to be equally effective instruments of communication within the limits of the culture and, finally, from the fact that all languages are intertranslatable, that there can be, in Jabobson's terms, 'interlingual code-switching' because of an underlying isomorphism between languages.

The conclusions drawn from these universally accepted observations about languages were that every language has to be equally effective because language, as a means of communication, plays a vital role in supplementing perception and allowing any single human community to act effectively (all languages must have certain minimum properties defined by the requirements of communication so that underlying the specific syntactic features of a language, there are what one might term practical language universals); that children can learn any language as their mother tongue equally easily because their imprinting to learn language is multi-potential: they are neurologically and physiologically prepared to acquire any of a range of possible natural syntactical and grammatical systems and they actually acquire the one they find in the community into which they are born; and that the intertranslatability of all languages is the result not only of the fact that all languages have to serve the same range of functions but also that all languages derive their structure and processes from the structures and processes underlying vision and action. This radical isomorphism explains the uniformity of the principles underlying syntax in all languages and the possibility of converting sentences created on one set of syntactic principles into sentences using a quite different set of surface-syntax rules. General and specific experimental evidence was presented for the fact of variation between individuals, communities and races in the neurological and physiological processes used in visual perception, cognition and action-organisation i.e. different detailed procedures to achieve the same effective result in the perception of a visual scene, the planning or execution of a complex action or the expression of a specific meaning by its conversion into a string of words. Genetic differences (in the gene-pool of a community over a long period of time) would tend to lead to preferences for one out of a number of possible systems of organisation of vision, speech and action, that is, to the expression of the isomorphism of the syntax of speech, vision and action in different, equally natural ways; such differences between communities would be consolidated by the mechanism of children's acquisition of language through an imprinting process combined with the very special interactive character of language as a part of human behaviour.

In terms of the present section, that is the application at the sentence-level to other languages of the hypotheses developed earlier in the book, the starting-point (justified by the general discussion summarised above) is that there can be different equally natural and effective syntaxes and modes of sentence-formation between different languages because there can be different equally valid organisations of the processes underlying perception and action. The issue to be tackled in this section accordingly is how far the description or the detailed methods by which sentences are constructed and decoded (comprehended) in English can be applied to the formation and decoding of sentences constructed in accordance with the completely different syntactic and grammatical rules of other language-types or, where languages are of the same type as English, in accordance with syntaxes differing in the detail of their rules (for example, in their use of word-order in the sentence). This section starts not only from the general discussion of the sentence in chapter V and the broad conclusions about the relation between the syntaxes of different languages reached in the opening part of the present chapter but also from the conclusions reached in the two previous sections of the chapter: the comparative application of the hypotheses at the speech-sound level and at the word-level: that in all languages one can find evidence of a felt relation between the sound and meaning of words (sound symbolism and the expressive use of language) and in all languages there is, certainly for words in their primitive vocabularies (those words learnt by experience and not by explanation), a direct natural relation between the sound-structure of the words and the contours (action or visual) of the percept, action, quality or relation to which any particular word refers.

Before one can contrast and explain differences in sentence-formation between languages, ideally it would be useful to refer to an authoritative systematic account by comparative linguists of the major different types of syntax found in world languages, the ways in which the different languages treat important aspects of sentence-formation: word-order, sentence-segmentation into clauses and phrases, parts-of-speech, the functional arrangement of sentences (in terms of Subject-Predicate or Actor-action and so on), the different forms of sentence used for distinct functions (questions, statements, reports, commands, conditional propositions etc.) and the way in which in different languages sentences refer to linguistic or other familiar context. In fact (as was pointed out earlier) no such systematic account by comparative linguists exists; one work on comparative linguistics put the position very clearly: "Sections devoted to syntax will almost always be the Cinderella. There seems so little left to say or classify. Syntactic semantics, including the meaning and function of grammatical categories, parts of the sentence, idiom and so forth, plays hardly any part at all in what are otherwise nearly always works of considerable scholarship, thorough-going down to the last detail". It is astonishing that whilst in recent years so much attention has been concentrated on syntactic structure, the surface and deep features of sentence-formation in one language (the work of Chomsky's school in relation to English), so little attempt has been made to study the universal features of syntax and sentence-formation by the comparative method.

The basic problem can be expressed as follows: Why should collections of words, in other languages as well as in English, put together in particular ways produce a definite coherent total meaning? The starting-point for each language is the same: a string of words (or possibly of fragmentary morphemes) arranged in a particular serial order, the surface-structure of the sentence. To determine the differences in sentence-construction and sentence-solution (decoding) as between English and other languages and the general applicability of the approach developed in chapter V, one is faced with a practical problem of presentation. One course would be to take each of a number of major languages, of different basic types or with important differences of detail even though they belong to the same type as English, to set out the syntactic principles each follows in constructing sentences and to examine, in relation to a specimen set of sentences drawn from each of the languages, how far the techniques of decoding described for English in chapter V apply and how far they need to be modified. Such an approach has to be ruled out, not only because it would require a lifetime's work to complete it but also because one would need to have at least as precise an understanding, as reliable an intuition for the syntactic functioning of each other language, as one has for one's own native tongue, that is for English.

Some simpler course must be found. This might be to start from consideration of the orthodox classification of languages into distinct types, from the syntactic and grammatical features ascribed to each type, to follow that with examination of a number of particular features of syntax in languages generally: inflection and the use of cases, word-order, parts of speech, the use of concord etc. and to conclude with some discussion, in the light of what has preceded, of the applicability of the techniques for the 'solution' (decoding) of the sentence described in chapter V.

Language types

In traditional comparative linguistics, world languages have been classified both in terms of their assumed family-relationships (Indo-European, Sino-Tibetan, Semito-Hamitic etc.) and in terms of their lexical or syntactic structure (isolating, inflectional, agglutinative, polysynthetic). There is no necessary relation between the language-family to which a particular language is said to belong and the type of language to which the same language is classified. Within Indo-European one can find languages which are predominantly isolating, inflectional or agglutinative. The family-classification of languages flourished in the 19th century but the principles of classification were always debatable and often excessively subjective. For the purposes of the present section, the more important attempted classification is by language type. The standard account is that an isolating language is one in which a sentence is formed from the combination of a number of unchanging single words (no change in the form of the word to represent singular or plural, case, gender, tense, part of speech). Classical Chinese is taken as the purest example of the type, comprising a wholly invariant limited number of monosyllables. Latin is the standard example of an inflectional language (with systematic change in the form of individual words to indicate gender, case, number, tense, parts of speech and the role of individual words in a sentence). An agglutinative language is one which indicates specific aspects (case, number, gender, person, relation) by particular word-fragments (morphemes) which are attached as prefixes or suffixes to the root word to form a longer single word expressing all the different aspects together. The standard example of an agglutinative language is Turkish. The difference in principle between an inflectional language and an agglutinative language is that where an inflectional language might express several aspects of meaning by one case-form (for example, in 'mensae' Latin indicates by the ending '-ae' that the word is feminine, plural and nominative), an agglutinative language would add on to the root word for 'table' three separate syllables to indicate the three different aspects of meaning. The fourth type of language, the polysynthetic, is rare and chiefly found among American Indian languages;

the standard example is Eskimo in which (carrying the agglutinative principle to its extreme limit) all the roots and separate aspects of meaning in a sentence are fused together to form one word (with some aspects of meaning being represented by a single phoneme rather than by a syllable); in such languages it may be impossible to distinguish between noun and verb or indeed to undertake any systematic analysis at all of the functioning of the language.

If the classification of languages by type really was well-founded and systematic, then it ought to indicate accurately the kind of principles different languages use in forming sentences. The reality is that the distinctions between the types are blurred and the classifications of languages as belonging to one type or another are often uncertain. In many languages one finds that the syntax contains forms which in some respects can be described as isolating, in others as agglutinative, in others inflectional and even indeed in some respects polysynthetic. Modern Chinese is no longer purely isolating; English is said by some linguists to be isolating (the Western equivalent of Chinese) but one can in fact find in it remnants of inflection: 'he/him' 'have/has/had', the effective use of agglutination: a word such as 'unforgettable' and, in common speech, the merging of a number of words in a sentence into what is in effect a single word phonetically: 'Whatdyouthink?', a polysynthetic formation. At best for most languages one can say that they are predominantly of one or other of the four types but to say that English is predominantly isolating tells one of little practical value about the way in which sentences are constructed and interpreted in English. An illustration of the confusion in the use of typological terms can be found by comparing what Yuen Ren Chao says about Chinese (a predominantly isolating language) that "chemistry is a model for language combination in Chinese"(58) and what Whorf (an expert in American Indian languages) said about two polysynthetic languages at the opposite extreme from Chinese: "the way the constituents are put together in these sentences of Shawnee and Nootka suggests a chemical compound . . . put together out of mutually suited ingredients"(59).

In terms of comparative syntax, the awkward fact is that different languages resemble and differ from each other in a variety of detailed aspects of sentence-formation. In the end, each language employs a unique collection of syntactic devices, even if it shares some of the devices with other languages. Perhaps the only broad classification of languages (quite different from the traditional set of types) which is of practical value is between those which rely largely on word-order to indicate the structure of the sentence (Subject, Object, Noun, Verb, Adjective etc., phrase and clause grouping) and those which rely largely on change in the form of individual words (prefixes, suffixes, infixes and vowel change) to indicate the sentence-structure. If one adopts this broad division into two classes, then the obvious question is: How, assuming that languages in the two classes are equally effective as means of communication, do languages relying on word-order make up for the absence of the convenience offered by inflection etc. and how do languages with a free word-order in fact make use of the important communicative facility that free word-order constitutes?

The differences between languages in terms of this broad classification can be examined from two points of view: first of all, it is sometimes suggested that in any language syntax and morphology counterbalance one another; a language with a complex syntax is likely to have simple principles of word-formation and correspondingly a language with elaborated principles of word-formation is likely to have a simpler syntax. This is, so to say, a static view of the relation of syntax and lexicon, of word-order and inflection. The more interesting view is that the trend in the general development of language is away from inflection and towards reliance on word-order; on this view, case is an obsolescent survival which has disappeared entirely in Chinese, has almost completely disappeared in English and is on its way out in other languages. There is a general tendency to analyse more precisely aspects of meaning and relationship and to express these aspects both by a greater subtlety in word-ordering and by the use of words expressing more sharply and narrowly the necessary 'units' of meaning and relation. Jespersen's view was that language loses nothing by shedding inflections (provided that their disappearance is compensated for by the use of word-order) and Bever(60) more recently has commented on the historical development of syntactic rules to compensate for the loss of disambiguation through inflection. At a certain point, and this point has largely been reached in English, when the rules governing word-order have developed sufficiently, one can dispense not only with inflections but also with any overt distinction of form between different parts of speech. In English nowadays there is often nothing to show, in the form of a word, whether it is a noun, an adjective or a verb, or indeed whether the word is subject, object or any other specific part of the sentence The manner in which structure is created in the sentence, in modern English and in some other languages, seems much more indirect, refined and sophisticated than was the case, for example, in a heavily inflected language such as Latin or Greek. This general trend away from rigid grammar to the use of word-order and to a more finely developed lexicon may well be the result of progressive intellectual development, a sharper analysis of the concepts to which language relates. If this is so, then one can understand how it would be possible to translate any sentence in an inflected language systematically into a sentence-form appropriate to a language depending on word-order and on the refinement of its lexicon to replace inflections.

The important proposition which results from the above discussion is that in the construction and interpretation (decoding) of the sentence in any language, one cannot concentrate either on the syntax alone or on semantics (the lexicon) alone; construction and comprehension of the sentence depend upon the interaction of syntax and semantics, of word-order rules and lexical structure. This is not a suddenly perceived new truth. Essentially the point is the same as that made by Saussure who argued that one ought to analyse the functioning of language in terms of a theory of syntagma and a theory of associations, that is, rules relating to the way in which words can be arranged in serial order in a sentence and structural rules by which words in the lexicon are associated together and formed into groups: "Functionally, therefore, the lexical and the syntactical may blend . . . innumerable relations may be expressed as efficiently by words as by grammar" not only if one compares one language with another but "the interchange of words and phrases within the same language also occurs very frequently"(61). In the examination which follows of the particular features of syntax found in language generally, and in the discussion of the techniques for 'decoding' the sentence with which this section concludes, it will be very relevant to see how one language may achieve by a grammatical device (inflection or concord) what another achieves by word-order rules or by the addition of words to its lexicon expressing more precisely aspects of meaning or relationship.

Syntactic devices

Though every language may have, considered as a totality, a unique syntax (as it has a unique lexicon), there is only a limited number of distinct syntactic devices which any language can employ. These can include, most obviously, inflection (cases and tenses), word-order rules, the distinction of parts-of-speech, sentence-patterns (Subject Verb Object and variant orders), the use of concord (agreement of adjectives and nouns etc.), consonant or vowel harmony (the use of similar consonants or similar vowels within a sentence to indicate sentence-structure), the use of affixes (prefixes, suffixes and infixes). The following paragraphs consider the use of the various devices in different languages:

Cases and tenses Apart from the classical examples of Latin and Greek, a number of important languages still make extensive use of inflection either in the form of the case-declension of nouns and adjectives or in the form of conjugation of tenses to express person, number, tense-category or mood. The most important examples of fully inflectional systems are found in German and Russian but there is a substantial inflectional content (particularly for tense-conjugation) in French, Spanish and Italian; and there are full inflectional systems in Finnish and Hungarian. Inflectional languages can be arranged in a spectrum from those which rely on the device most heavily to those which have only much reduced traces of inflection. Including the classical languages, the order runs probably from the most highly inflected Sanskrit with 3 genders, 3 numbers, 8 cases and over 700 formal variations of the verb, through Greek and Latin to, amongst modern languages, Russian (which retains an inherently archaic system of inflection), German, Hungarian and Finnish, followed by French, Spanish and Italian with much reduced inflectional systems. The number of cases of the noun or pronoun can vary widely between languages, from 2 in English ('he/him') up to 16 or so in Finnish; the range of variation in the elaboration of tenses is equally great.

There are varying view about the usefulness of a highly-developed inflectional system as a syntactic device; Humboldt, as a German, rated it highly and thought that the inflectional method "preserves in itself the pure principle of linguistic structure, a principle of genius proceeding from the true intuition of language"(62). French authors have argued that the structure of their language is the most perfectly adapted to accuracy and clarity of thought. Classicists have suggested that Latin constituted a clear structural analysis of experience, which not only analysed relation and time through the case and tense system but by its forms of words, allowing one to distinguish nouns, verbs, adjectives, prepositions and conjunctions, eliminated ambiguity in the structuring of a sentence. Certainly an inflected language is more independent of context for determining the role played by individual words in a sentence or the way in which words in a sentence should be associated with one another.

If one puts on one side these perhaps rather chauvinistic views, the fact is that in the struggle for survival between different syntactic devices, inflection (the elaboration of cases and tenses by modification of the individual word form) has consistently been losing ground; in modern Greek most of the complexities of Classical Greek have disappeared. The Romance languages have quite generally moved away from the use of Latin inflections to reliance on a more analytic syntax, dependent directly on word-order. Many linguists have noted that there often is little system and much confusion in individual inflectional languages and as between different inflectional languages, in their use of cases and tenses. In many modern languages, cases survive but serve no useful purpose. in Russian the locative is always accompanied by a preposition and is thus redundant; in French, whilst for some pronouns case distinctions have been preserved, for others they have disappeared (compare 'tu/te' and 'vous/vous'). In an individual language, however elaborate the case-system, it will not cover except imperfectly the infinite variety of possible relations; others have said that cases may resemble various situations of the practical world but never with any consistency and one cannot correlate case-functions with logical or psychological constants.

Between languages which nominally have similar case-systems, the actual functions of particular cases vary widely. According to Palmer(63) the apparent clarity of the Latin case-system was an illusion; no single clear-cut functions attached to any of the cases and it is impossible to arrive at the primitive function of a case; the picture was one of bewildering multiplicity of functions for which different cases were used—and in colloquial Latin, from a very early date, there was a tendency to use prepositional phrases rather than rely simply on the use of case. From then on, in vulgar Latin, the process of simplification proceeded continuously (and, of course, led to the simpler structures found in present-day Romance languages). If, however, one takes classical Latin as one's reference system, surviving languages with case-systems cannot be correlated in any precise way with the Latin case-system or with each other. Though in a number of inflectional languages, the accusative, genitive and dative cases remain, they are used to express different relations or with different prepositions from one language to another. One author comments: "Why (in German) should some prepositions favour the dative whilst others equally capriciously take the genitive or accusative? . . . If we venture as far as Slavonic (e.g. Russian), we lose all sense of order and begin to suspect that assignment of gender, number and the use of cases is entirely arbitrary and nonsensical—and that is precisely what it is"(63).

Much the same comments have been made about the use of tense in different inflected languages, and there is no doubt that the conceptual problems in the analysis of relative temporal order are great, so that it is hardly surprising that the syntactic treatment of time, in the form of tense, should also be complex. An inflected language attempts to deal with the complexities of tense by changes in the form of the root-word (the verb); analytic languages deal with tense by the use of combinations of auxiliary words (e.g. in English 'would-have-been understood'). There is great variation in the fullness of the verbal system in different inflectional languages ranging from over 700 formal variations of the verb in Sanskrit to 500 in Greek and 140 in Latin and, in modern languages, from Hungarian with 3 moods, 12 tenses, 5 aspects of the verb and participles through Russian with 4 tenses, 2 aspects, participles and gerunds to German with 2 moods and 2 tenses. In modern languages, other tenses are supplied by constructions using auxiliaries rather than by inflected forms (in the same way as happens in English). At the opposite extreme to the expression of tenses by inflection, there is a Semitic language such as Hebrew which has no inflectional means at all for distinguishing different tenses of the verb; it does not by any change in form recognise the fundamental distinctions between past, present and future though it has a great variety of other devices for translating verbal relatives e.g. causative, intensive, desiderative, jussive, reciprocal, reflexive.

This discussion of case and tense has served one purpose, to make it absolutely clear that classifying a language as inflectional tells one little about the actual way in which its syntax operates. One cannot generalise even between inflected languages about the significance of the genitive or dative case or the use of the imperfect or future tense. The characteristic feature of an inflected language is that it retains many more variant forms of a single word than are found in an analytic or isolating language and may lack syntactically useful individual words, analysing out more finely aspects of relation or structure. The problem of decoding the sentence cannot be dealt with uniformly for inflectional languages as a whole (because of the great differences between them in their use of inflection) and, as has already been said, each language in fact employs a unique collection of syntactic devices. The 'solution' of the sentence in any language depends on identification of the mode of interaction between syntax and lexicon, between word-order and the richness of distinctions available in the vocabulary of the language. This applies just as much to an inflected language as it does to an isolating or analytic language.

Word-order The general aspects of word-order as a syntactic device have already been discussed at some length earlier in chapter V both in the section which contrasted the use of word-order in the sentence with the order of eye-movements and fixations in scanning a visual scene and in the section which considered the contribution made by word-order to the 'solution' of the sentence. Nearly the whole of that discussion applied to language in general and not to the English sentence in particular; in every language, words in a particular real sentence have to be arranged in some specific serial order, and though it is said that word-order in some languages is 'free', the speaker of a sentence in that language has to decide which order to use. Word-order is a coding device, a means of communicating information, of the greatest importance in any human language and it does not follow that because a language does not use word-order to indicate sentence structure, then word-order in that language is totally redundant. In fact, what seems to be the case is that variations in word order in 'free' languages are used to convey differences in emphasis, in attitude and in relative importance of aspects of the sentence which in English may be indicated by the overall intonation of the sentence, by stress or by punctuation.

There has been little systematic study of the implications of variations in order in particular languages. Jespersen described word-order as the most neglected aspect of linguistic science and Lord commented on how many even of the best and most complete grammars are wholly, or almost wholly, silent about word-order "and yet it presents a great many problems of high importance and of the greatest interest not only in those languages in which word-order has been extensively utilised for grammatical purposes, such as English and Chinese, but in other languages as well" (65). One knows that languages typically use different word-orders but there is no comprehensive survey of obligatory and optional variations in word-order in the range of different languages. It is also notorious that word-order in any given language may differ very much in the common spoken form of the language from that in the more formal written language; even in a language such as

English where word-order plays a key role in disambiguating a sentence, for describing a particular scene there is no single, absolutely rigid order which must be used (as Osgood's experiments described in his article "Where do sentences come from?" demonstrated conclusively). Often, such limited discussion of word-order as there has been, has confused aspects of order which ought to be distinguished; in a sentence, there is an order in which one finds the main elements in the sentence, the order of sentence-parts (Subject Verb Object or Actor Action Goal etc.), an order in which one finds subordinate clauses and phrases and, at a more detailed level, an order in which one typically finds the elements in a noun-phrase, an adverbial or prepositional phrase, and so on. Saussure went further and contended that, under the concept of order (or syntagm), one ought also to bring in the ordering of the units going to form a compound word, that is, the principles of word-order which operate at the morphological as well as at the syntactic level.

Roger Brown comments that there is something very simple and automatic for human beings about the linearisation of speech units; linear position seems to be the first aspect of syntax to which children are sensitive. Greenberg, surveying sentence-part order in a number of languages, commented that the order of elements in language parallels that in physical experience or the order of knowledge . . . "no one thinks to write a proof backwards" (66) and studies of the acquisition by children of inflected languages with free or fixed order have found that frequently there is a tendency for the word-order used by children to follow the natural visual order, even though the adult language may have a different order. The problem remains, however, that adult languages do adopt different word-order rules, at every level: in terms of sentence-parts, order of clauses, order of parts of speech in phrases and order in the formation of compound or derived words. There are variations in order not only between inflected and non-inflected languages but also between one inflected language and another and between one (predominantly) isolating language and another (for example, between English and Chinese). Questions which present themselves are: 1. Is there a single natural order? 2. How extensive is the variation in word-order between languages? 3. What variation in order is there at each of the levels: sentence-parts, clauses, phrase-order, order of parts in compound or derived words? 4. Why should word-order vary? 5, How in practice can word-order be used as a device for constructing or decoding actual sentences?

A full discussion of these questions would have to cover a great deal of ground and require extensive research. The following paragraphs attempt to deal with the questions briefly using readily available material. First of all, in chapter V it was argued that there is a natural relation between word-order and the order of eye-movements and fixations in scanning a visual scene i.e. there is a natural order for any particular sentence but there is no single universal natural order because the order of fixations in scanning a scene can vary between individuals or between members of different races or communities (or even between the different occasions on which or circumstances in which the same individual scans a particular scene). Some patterns of scanning and of word-order may be more frequent than others but the pattern adopted on any particular occasion will be influenced by context, expectation, familiarity etc. If different language-communities adopt different normal word-orders, the preference for a particular order is the result of the same influences as lead to a community's preferences for using particular speech-sounds or forming words in particular ways, that is, average genetic influences operating over a long period and consolidated through the acquisition of the prevailing community-pattern by children through the process of imprinting.

The best evidence on the degree of variation in word-order between languages is to be found in the work of Joseph Greenberg. Working with a sample of 30 languages (which he thought large and diverse enough to have a high degree of universal validity), he found that in word-order for sentence-parts (Subject Verb Object), the dominant order is almost always one in which the Subject precedes the Object (orders where Object preceded Subject were excessively rare); for the large majority of the world's languages the Subject also precedes the Verb (the only exceptions of any significance in Greenberg's sample were Hindi, Japanese and Turkish); a majority of languages also have the Verb preceding the Object with perhaps the most important additional exception being German (or at any rate standard written German); all languages which have the dominant order with Verb preceding the Subject also allow of an alternative order (sometimes the only alternative order) Subject Verb Object. For the minority of languages where the Verb follows both Subject and Object, Greenberg found that almost always these languages were inflected languages with a case system.

Greenberg's evidence is consistent with the assumption that there is something especially natural about the order Subject Verb Object; the most notable exception to this order among major languages is German but how real an exception this is in practice in spoken German or in German used in different regions is doubtful. One study of modern German prose usage commented. "The freer word order is a very old feature of German speech; in the literary language it is held to have been curbed by the influence of Latin and by scholastic modes of expression. But these influences failed to kill it; again and again it has . . . reasserted itself until in recent years it began to experience something of a renaissance"(67). As already mentioned, studies of children learning their native language point in the same direction; for example, one study of a child learning Korean, where all word-orders are possible, showed that the child commonly used the Subject Verb Object order (despite the fact that its parents in their daily speech used all word-order forms); a similar study of a child learning Finnish, where the adult word-order is free, also found that the child of its own accord used the Subject Verb Object order.

Greenberg also examined, for his sample of languages, a number of other more detailed aspects of word-order: adjective following or preceding noun, the use of prepositions or postpositions, the genitive before or after the noun to which it relates, the order of clauses, the order of words in question-sentences. He provided a list of 45 universals, near-universals or conditional universals (that is of the type: if the Verb precedes the Subject and Object in a language, then that language puts prepositions before the noun). It would be tedious to repeat here the full extent of his findings but there are several which one might quote:

— in all languages, the conditional clause precedes the main clause
— if a language uses only prefixes and not suffixes, it uses only prepositions and not postpositions
— if the Verb comes first in a sentence, then in nearly every case the adjective follows the noun

The main conclusion perhaps to be drawn from Greenberg's study of word-order is that there is evidence of some systematic relation in different languages between various aspects of word-order (at the different levels: sentence-parts, clauses, phrase order, formation of compound or derived words) and that some types of word-order are much more common than others and appear to have a natural basis in perception. No one has yet explained satisfactorily certain features of order in English or other languages, for example, why, if a number of adjectives are used in a phrase to apply to one noun, there is a correct, normal and naturally recognised order in which the adjectives are placed. One says: 'A large white Siamese cat' and not 'A Siamese white large cat' and there are similar patterns for the ordering of adjectives in other languages. If one translates this kind of word-order into the equivalent process in visual scanning, then this would equate with a specific order in the pattern of attention. Lashley, who gave some thought to this topic, said that he was able to find no consistent relation to explain the ordering found. Greenberg discussed the question in terms of 'proximity hierarchies . . . the rule that certain elements must be closer to some central element than some other satellite . . . these hierarchies are presumably related to degrees of logical and psychological remoteness from the centre". Perhaps the simplest explanation in visual terms would be that in the phrase 'A large white Siamese cat', 'cat' is the focal element; the detail represented by the adjectives is extracted as a result of fixation on the cat as focal element; 'cat' constitutes a familiar visual schema, subdivided into almost as familiar sub-schemas 'Siamese cat' and other types of cat; and the adjectives progressively narrow down the class to which the focal element belongs in terms of their proximity to the noun. A 'white' Siamese cat is a subclass of Siamese cats, a 'large' white Siamese cat is a still smaller class and 'A' large white Siamese cat narrows down the object to a single particular perceived cat, the smallest class of all with only one member.

Other features of word-order are less difficult to explain, on similar lines. In some languages adjectives follow nouns, in others nouns follow adjectives. In terms of visual scanning, it probably makes little difference whether one pays attention first to the fact that there is a white object, which is a cat ('A white cat') or to the fact that there is a cat present, which is white ('Un chat blanc'). The same sort of point can be made about the fact that the definite article precedes the noun in English, Dutch and German (and other languages) and follows it in Swedish and other Scandinavian languages (and in other non-European languages). Similarly, it may matter little in scanning a visual scene whether one identifies the Subject and the Object first and then the Verb, or one first identifies the Subject, then the Verb and then the Object. Any of these orders may be compatible with natural visual scanning patterns.

The final question is how word-order can be used in constructing or decoding an actual sentence; this is something for discussion in the concluding section of this chapter (on the comparative application of the techniques for 'solution' of the sentence) but, quite simply, if in any language there are accepted word-order rules or predominantly followed word-order patterns, then these immediately will provide clues to the function, category and relation of each word presented in the serial string which a sentence constitutes. If, in an inflected language, word-order is not required to identify parts-of-sentence, sentence-structure or parts-of-speech, then word-order will serve to provide clues to other aspects of the total meaning to be communicated by the sentence, that is the relative importance of different elements, the stress or emphasis placed on a particular aspect by the speaker, the newness or familiarity of an object or feature referred to in the sentence. It seems highly improbable that in any language the valuable communication facility that word-order offers will be totally disregarded and, in effect, redundant.

Parts-of-speech

Chapter V discussed at considerable length the range of problems associated with parts-of-speech as a syntactic device, Because in English the part of speech category to which a word belongs is often not indicated in any way by the form of the word and has to be deduced from the position and role of the word in the particular sentence, the discussion in chapter V had to range rather wide and consider the significance of parts-of-speech categorisation in language generally; as a result, most of what has already been said has been framed in comparative terms, that is, has involved discussion of the role of parts of speech in other languages as well as in English. There is no need to repeat the discussion in full here but it may be useful to recall a few of the main points which were made or emerged. Parts-of-speech have to be distinguished as a topic from parts-of-sentence (the immediately preceding paragraphs have dealt with the order in which parts-of-sentence are arranged in different languages). There is, however, a complex relation, certainly in a language such as English, between parts-of-speech and parts-of-sentence because, with no overt marking of a word in a sentence as being a noun or as being the Subject, decoding the sentence to establish that a word is a noun may in fact at the same time establish that it is the Subject of the particular sentence; correspondingly decoding to discover that a word is the Subject may at the same time demonstrate that the word in that sentence is functioning as a noun.

There is an unsettled dispute amongst linguists about the very existence of parts of speech and certainly about the significance of the classification of words into traditional parts of speech in a language such as English. In comparative terms, there are considerable variations in the number and categories of parts of speech which orthodox grammars of the different languages recognise. Despite the disputes among linguists, survey of other languages (again one must rely largely on Greenberg) provides evidence that all languages have nominals and verbals, all have adjectival expressions and adverbial expressions, all have conjunctions such as 'and' 'or' and many languages have elements analogous to pronouns and demonstratives. No language wholly fails to distinguish noun and verb and there seems adequate evidence for thinking that these at least as parts of speech have a natural basis in all languages. Though the traditional classification of words into parts of speech by grammarians (based on Latin and Greek) may have been defective or have ceased to correspond to what was required in modern languages as they moved from reliance on inflection to reliance on word-order, it seems undeniable that, quite apart from language, human experience can be divided into real categories, shapes and objects, movements and actions, detailed aspects of particular elements in the visual scene, spatial and temporal relationships, and that it is this categorisation of human experience which provides the natural basis for some parallel system of parts-of-speech. The parts of speech found in different languages reflect, however imperfectly, the parts-of-vision and parts-of-action of which human experience is composed.

The comparative question, in terms of other languages, is why and how some languages have fewer or more parts of speech (according to their grammars) than others; in Chinese it is a principle of grammar, in effect, that there should be no distinct parts of speech (i.e. distinguished as such by their form or by their systematic use). Other languages have parts of speech recognised as being of the traditional kind but also have particles which perform functions not classifiable in terms of the familiar set of parts of speech, for example, the particle in Japanese which indicates that a noun is the subject of a sentence. Even in English, some linguists have recognised not only the traditional parts of speech but subdivisions of those parts of speech: they have treated mass-nouns as a distinct category from count-nouns, transitive verbs as a distinct category from intransitive verbs. Once one starts to define parts of speech in terms of the distinct functions which words may have in different sentence contexts, there is almost no limit to the number of divisions and subdivisions of parts of speech one can postulate. In the other direction, most languages formally distinguish a smaller number of distinct parts of speech than one finds in traditional grammar, sometimes only three (rather than eight or nine): substantives, verbs and adjectives. Other languages lack parts of speech which most languages find indispensable: Russian and Japanese manage without definite or indefinite articles; Japanese has no true pronouns; a fully inflected language should need no auxiliary verbs, no pronouns and no prepositions. Where the same parts of speech are found in different languages, the relative number of nouns and verbs may vary greatly from one language to another, and the same may be the case for the number of prepositions, pronouns or conjunctions

There is nothing complicated or inexplicable about the variation in the number of distinguishable parts of speech between languages. The real distinctions which have to be made in a language must correspond to the distinctions in human experience, the natural categories of vision and action. The variation in parts of speech between different languages is largely illusory; the point has already been made that in language syntax and lexicon intersect and are inseparable. One language may represent a particular category of experience by the formation of a particular word-class (that is, by an addition to its lexicon) whilst another may represent that category of experience by a combination of existing words, by an essentially syntagmatic method (as Saussure would describe it). Another device by which one can dispense with a distinct part-of-speech category is by compound word formation; if one uses prefixes and suffixes, one may be able to dispense with prepositions; if one converts relational words into substantives, one can eliminate other parts of speech. So in English, instead of 'he came to the house' one could say 'he reached the proximity of the house'; the local relation has been nominalised and one has eliminated the need for the preposition 'to'. Prepositional aspects can in fact be incorporated in verb-forms as happens in English not only with the word 'reach' but with other words such as 'enter' 'leave' 'accompany' and so on. If other languages have no separate parts of speech as adjectives or adverbs, we also can in English freely use nouns as adjectives by apposition or treat adjectives as adverbs (as in 'Go quick'). How many nouns a language may have and how many verbs is again of no real significance; it depends on the availability of processes for converting nouns into verbs or verbs into nouns.

Other syntactic devices

In various languages, other devices are found which, for the most part, are of less general significance than the syntactic devices already considered above. Sometimes affixation is considered separately as a syntactic device, that is, the use of prefixes, suffixes or infixes; affixing is by far the most frequently used grammatical process (according to Sapir), with the use of suffixes much more common than the use of prefixes. Languages of many different types, Turkish, Hottentot, Eskimo, make use of suffixes. American Indian languages have, or had, hundreds of suffixed elements, "many of them of a concreteness of significance that would demand expression in the vast majority of languages by means of radical elements"(68). But in reality affixation is not a distinct device; every inflectional language and every agglutinative language must form its word variants as word-compounds by the use of prefixes, suffixes or infixes and affixation is only one normal expression of what Saussure called the syntagmatic method, that is, the serial ordering of words or word-fragments. Affixation accordingly can be treated, not as an independent syntactic device but as an aspect of the major device constituted by word-order.

Amongst the minor syntactic devices, one might include the use of gender, agreement or concord between different parts of speech, vowel and consonantal harmony and the use of 'classifiers' (as in Chinese):

Gender Distinctions of gender between nouns are found in very many languages (not only in the classical languages, Latin, Greek and Sanskrit, but also in important modern languages such as German, Russian and French). On the other hand, many important languages have no trace of any distinction of gender (Chinese, Japanese, Turkish, Hungarian, Finnish, Malay and many others). There is no consistency in the use of gender between languages which have gender systems; some languages have two genders, others have three; the division of nouns between the masculine and feminine gender follows no uniform pattern between different languages. the word for 'sun' is masculine in French, feminine in German and neuter in Russian. Even within a single language, the allocation of nouns to different genders may be inexplicable: in German the word for 'girl' ('m„dschen') is neuter, the word for 'boy' is masculine; in Russian, the word for 'day' is masculine and that for 'morning' is neuter. Within a single language, words which were once masculine are later classified as feminine or neuter or vice versa. In Greek, whole classes of words which had been feminine in ancient Greek were converted into masculine nouns as the language developed into modern Greek. There are other peculiarities: some languages which have no division into genders in the usual sense (masculine, feminine and neuter) have a system parallel to gender: Dravidian languages divide nouns to distinguish caste but not sex; in Masai there is one gender for big, strong things and another gender for small, weak things; in Japanese there are distinctions parallel to gender to express differences in rank.

Given this extraordinary picture of diversity and apparent confusion, the question is what importance should one attach to gender as a syntactic device. Most languages manage without it; English has almost entirely eliminated the grammatical use of gender except in the limited and perhaps more justifiable form of the distinction between 'he' and 'she', 'her' and 'him', 'hers' and 'his'. Many linguists would say that gender is a survival of primitive ways of thought (primitive animism) and is now purely vestigial, without any syntactic importance. If this is so, one wonders why a completely useless grammatical distinction should show such continuing vigour and remain in use in major world languages, despite the difficulties it involves both for native speakers and for foreigners in learning the appropriate gender to which a particular word belongs. Certainly if, in a language, classification of a word as of one gender or another makes no difference whatsoever to any other words going to form a sentence, then gender is pointless and surely cannot survive. What however gives vitality to gender is not that in some sense nouns are recognised as being characteristically related to the masculine or feminine sex or to neither but that gender is a basis for dividing the complete set of nouns in a language into two or more distinct classes—and the same applies to parallel systems such as those found in the Dravidian languages, Masai etc. Gender makes sense as a syntactic device if it is associated with rules about concord or agreement; for example, if a feminine form of the adjective must agree with a feminine noun, or a masculine pronoun must be used to refer to a masculine noun. From this point of view, gender is one more device (an extremely primitive one perhaps) for assisting the disambiguation of words in the serial string formed by the sentence, a way of helping one to decide what the correct structure and interpretation of a particular sentence is. So, through the surviving remnant of gender in English, in a sentence such as: 'Mary and John both wanted the book but it was hers', the gender form of the personal possessive 'hers' immediately determines the correct interpretation of the sentence.

Concord. vowel and consonantal harmony Agreement in case-endings between noun and adjective or between noun and tense-ending are examples of concord serving the same sort of purpose in disambiguating a sentence as has just been described for gender. There are analogous systems of concord in other languages: Swahili, as a typical Bantu language, classifies nouns into about a dozen classes, each of which has a distinguishing prefix which must be attached to all nouns of that class and to any other words describing or otherwise associated with them in a sentence; for each class the prefix is normally different for the singular and the plural. One of the Swahili noun classes, that for things, uses:the prefix 'ki-' in the singular and 'vi-' in the plural. The effect of Bantu concord can be seen by comparing two sentences formed from the words for 'knife' 'one' 'three' and 'enough' ('kisu' 'moja' 'tatu' and 'tosha'): 'kisu kimoja kilitosha' means 'one knife was enough' whilst 'visu vitatu vinatosha' means 'three knives were enough'. The method may seem cumbersome but no more so than systems of suffixes employed in major inflectional languages. It serves the same purpose in allowing one to determine the relation of the words in the sentence and the sentence-structure. Systems of vowel harmony are in principle used for much the same syntactic purpose and are comprehensible in terms of the decoding approach to the disambiguation of a sentence described in chapter V. For example, in Turkish the plural of a word is indicated by adding a standard suffix; the vowel used in the standard suffix changes depending upon the vowel in the word to which it is added: the plural of 'ev' ('house') is 'ev-ler', the plural of 'bas' ('head') is 'bas-lar'. In an agglutinative language like Turkish, vowel harmony again reduces the uncertainty of the relation between the root word and the suffix.

A final and very important example of a parallel syntactic device to reduce ambiguity is the use of 'classifiers' in Chinese (also found in other Sinitic languages, in American Indian etc.). In Chinese, there are very few distinct words (there are many homophones with a large number of different meanings) and the risk of confusion and ambiguity is accordingly very great. Ambiguity is reduced by dividing words referring to things into a large number of distinct classes and marking each class by the use of a particular class-word which precedes the object referred to. The basis for the division of things into classes is not much more systematic than the basis on which in other languages nouns are classified to different genders. In part, the classifications seem to be in terms of the shape of the object, small round things, thin long things, flat layers of things, containers and covers; and in part the classifications are based in other ways: animals, large objects such as hills, towers and temples, items of pottery or glass, furniture and so on. In the similar system in American Indian languages such as Navaho, some of the classes have a straightforward visual basis: round (or roundish) objects, long objects, but otherwise the classes used and the allocation of words to classes are as unsystematic as in Chinese. Nevertheless, to have some classification of nouns, marked in a particular way, can serve a useful syntactic purpose, regardless of the basis on which words are allocated to different classes, and this no doubt equally explains the survival of gender, of concord, of vocal harmony and of the use of classifiers.

'Solution' of the sentence—application to other languages

So far this section has considered what guidance can be derived on the construction and interpretation of sentences in other languages (in relation to the discussion in chapter V) from surveying the different language-types into which the world languages are traditionally classified and the different syntactic devices used in other languages, some of which are familiar to us in English: word-order and parts-of-speech. and others less familiar: the systematic use of inflection (variant case and tense forms), gender and concord, vowel and consonantal harmony. The remaining question, of outstanding interest, is how far, in comparative terms, what was said in chapter V about the,' 'solution' (decoding or disambiguation) of the sentence can be applied to languages other than English or adapted to be of use in determining principles for the systematic interpretation of sentences in other languages. How are other languages successful in conveying by way of different syntactic devices from those used in English the same coherent and unambiguous meaning (description of a scene or action, expression of a thought or intention and so on) as would be conveyed in a parallel English sentence? How in other languages is the meaning accurately represented by and extractable from a collection of words arranged in a serial string but using a word-order different from any that would be possible in English?

Most of what has been said about the 'solution' of the sentence in chapter V was of general application and not related specifically to the English sentence. The main points made were: that we do not just want to parse a sentence to find a correct solution; that the solution of a real sentence (one spoken in specific circumstances) depends on full knowledge of the context and the most one can look for is a general solution, a general approach to the interpretation of a sentence, which can be applied, together with knowledge of the specific context, to arrive at the unique meaning of an actually-uttered sentence, that is, the initial problem of the sentence is ambiguity and solution of it is a process of progressive disambiguation; that the aim is to be able to say for each word in the sentence which out of the various possible meanings is the particular meaning it has in that sentence, with which other words is the particular word in fact closely associated, which out of the possible range of functions does the particular word have in the particular sentence, what role as a part of the sentence does it have. At the same time as one establishes the precise meaning, grouping, function and role for each individual word, one must perform the same process for each word-grouping and each clause, and finally for the sentence itself as a whole, determining the kind of material the sentence refers to, whether it is a concrete or a metaphorical sentence and what its function is (as question, description, imperative etc.). Beyond that, chapter V referred to the different possible sources of ambiguity in any sentence: words with the same sound but different meanings, the same word with different functions (as noun, verb or adjective) or with different roles in the sentence (as Subject, Object, Actor, Action, Goal and so on), the presence of 'referential' words like pronouns and demonstratives. Chapter V approached the solution of the sentence in terms of the need to make an inventory first of the 'operational processes' for decoding and secondly of the 'material resources' available for use in decoding (our general knowledge of the lexicon in a particular language, of the patterning underlying our normal everyday experience of perception and action, our knowledge of the sentence-structure usually used in the language and of the specific syntactic features of the language).

The 'operational processes' described in chapter V for disambiguating a sentence apply without any modification to sentences in other languages. What they amount to is that both the syntax and the semantics of the sentence must be explored in parallel; we look for clues, which may be provided semantically, and also for short-cuts to disambiguation which syntactic processes available in the language may offer. In considering each word in the serial string constituted by the sentence, we aim at continuously narrowing down the range of possible interpretations of each word, each phrase and each clause until we arrive at the unique meaning of the sentence as a whole. We come to any sentence with a set, a pattern of expectations, identify by rapid processes familiar elements and use them to assist in the disambiguation of less familiar elements; the process does not necessarily proceed straightforwardly from the first word to the last, taking each in order; there can be backward and forward checking for consistency, with provisional interpretation at each point setting up hypotheses which can be checked against the remaining parts of the serial string. Once a highly probable interpretation has been reached, the need for further semantic or syntactic examination ceases and that interpretation is taken as the meaning of the sentence.

In terms of the comparative application of chapter V to solution of the sentence, whilst the 'operational processes' seem to raise no particular problem in relation to other languages, the real difficulties arise with difference in what has been described as the 'material resources' brought into play in disambiguating a sentence. For the English sentence, the chapter identified these as including, principally, English rules of word-order, supra-segmental features, punctuation, pauses and intonation, context, the typical structure of the English Primitive Vocabulary and of the English lexicon (the frameworks of position or action within which particular words are normally found), semantic markers (words in English with a narrow range of meaning or function), typical sentence-patterns and sentence-types in English (both in terms of the experience to which sentences may refer and the forms used for sentences serving different functions: as questions, statements, orders etc). Whilst the categories of material resources used for the disambiguation of sentence in English are categories which also form part of the material resources in other languages—other languages have their word-order rules, supra-segmental features, context, the structures of their lexicon related to the structuring of their Primitive Vocabulary, their typical sentence-patterns and sentence-types—obviously the content of the different categories is bound to be very different, and there may be additional categories of material resources in other languages which are not available or used in English, such as case—and tense-systems, concord, gender, consonantal or vowel harmony.

Other languages rely to different extents in disambiguating sentences on the different categories of 'material resources' identified; a fully-inflected language may not need to use word-order at all to arrive at the surface meaning of a sentence; languages where parts-of-speech are marked by differences in form from other words do not need to rely on the complex processes by which in English one determines that a word is a noun rather than a verb or an adjective. Languages which use concord make it easy to decide which adjectives go with which nouns (and the simplicity of disambiguation is increased if the language has a gender system or a classification of nouns parallel to the gender system such as is found in the Bantu languages). Perhaps one provisional conclusion may be that English as a predominantly isolating language with little marked differentiation of parts of speech and no markers to indicate Subject Object and Predicate, is probably one of the languages which present the greatest tests for disambiguation and requires the greatest subtlety in the underlying word-order rules and structuring of the lexicon, possibly only matched in prosodic difficulty by classical Chinese (which has the additional problems resulting from the degree of homophony, the limited number of word-sounds and from the total absence of inflection). Modern Chinese has developed a number of lexical forms which simplify the process of disambiguation and in some instances come close to establishing categories of parts of speech marked not by changes in individual words but by the association of particular particles with unchanging word-forms: a particle of emphasis (which distinguishes the use of a word as an imperative or as the object of a sentence), particles to mark a sentence as a question, particles used to indicate that a word is used as a verb in the past or future tense or as a present participle and so on. In fact, one might describe modern Chinese as a language which makes combined use of word-order and an extensive set of refined semantic markers to facilitate disambiguation of a sentence. However, in the absence of use of specific particles as semantic markers, the meaning of a Chinese sentence depends solely on word-order (and the deductions drawn from the way in which the range of meanings associated with each word might be combined).

This section has been concerned with how far what was said in chapter V about the general approach to the 'solution' (decoding) of the sentence can be applied to other languages. There seems no doubt that the techniques of disambiguation proposed could be applied to any language. One would need to prepare a catalogue for each of the syntactic devices discussed earlier in this part of the chapter of the specific rules that each particular language has as part of its syntax: for English, for example, one might include in the list of semantic markers the word 'the' and in the list of word-order rules note that where 'the' precedes a word or group of words, the immediately following word is a noun if it is succeeded by a semantic marker such as 'is' or 'of' etc. etc. In fact, a large number of rules of this kind have already been worked out for the parsing of sentences by computer programs (of the kind developed by Winograd(69)). Similarly, for each language one would need to prepare a list of standard sentence-patterns and sentence-types (patterns for descriptive sentences, for sentences referring to action, for interrogative sentences and so on). Again this kind of information has been analysed comprehensively for English in such work as Halliday's systemic grammar. The preparation, on a comparative basis, under the heading of the different syntactic devices identified, of the specific features of each major language is a task for the future, not so far attempted, but one that workers in the field of artificial intelligence are at this moment tackling. It is hoped that the discussion in this chapter may have provided a more integrated and systematic basis for this work to be extended beyond the English language (where it has so far been mainly concentrated) to a wider range of languages. This new comparative investigation will be founded on a firm central hypothesis, that each language, in its coding 'devices', is structured so as to convey the elements, relations, ordering and qualities found universally in human behaviour and experience and structurally integrated with the organisation, physiological and neurological, of visual perception and voluntary action.

ANNEX TO CHAPTER VI

Words selected from Primitive Vocabulary

English	French	German	Russian	Malay	Basque	Japanese

ACTIONS

English	French	German	Russian	Malay	Basque	Japanese
YAWN	BAILLER	GAHNEN	ZEVAT	GUAP	AHARROSI	AKUBI
LICK	LECHER	LECKEN	LEEZAT	JILAT	MILIKA	NAMERU
TOUCH	TOUCHER	TASTSINN	KASATYA	SENTOHAN	HUNKI	SAWERU
PUT	METTRE	STELLEN	KLAST	BUBOH	EMAN	OKU
PUSH	POUSSER	SCHUB	TOLKAT	TOLAK	PUSATU	OSU
HIT	FRAPPER	SCHLAGEN	UDARYAT	PUKUL	JO	UTSU
GO	ALLER	GEHEN	EETTEE	PERGI	JOAN	IKU
SEW	COUDRE	NAHEN	SHEET	JAHIT	JOSI	NUU
NEEDLE	AIGUILLE	NADEL	EEGOLKA	JARUM	ORRATZ	HARI
WORM	VER	WURM	CHERVYAK	CHACHING	CHICHARI	MUSHI
POINT	POINT	PUNKT	TOCHKA	NOKTAH	PUNDU	TEN
UP	DESSUS	AUF	VVERKH	ATAS	GAIN	UE
MEET	RENCONTRER	VERSAMMELN	VSTRECHAT	TEMU	AURKITU	AU
SAME	MEME	SELB	SAMYII	SAMA	BER	ONAZI
HAMMER	MARTEAU	HAMMER	MOLOTOK	MENUKUL	MAILU	KANAZUCHI

English	French	German	Russian	Malay	Basque	Japanese

POINTING

English	French	German	Russian	Malay	Basque	Japanese
EAR	OREILLE	OHR	UKHO	TELINGA	BEHARRI	MIMI
HEAR	OUIR	HOREN	SLUKH	DENGAR	ADITU	KIKU
EYE	OEIL	AUGE	GLAZ	MATA	BEGI	ME
I	JE	ICH	YA	AKU	NIK	(WATASI)
HAND	MAIN	HAND	RUKA	TANGAN	ESKU	TE
HAIR	CHEVEUX	HAAR	VOLOS	BULU	BILO	KAMI

English	French	German	Russian	Malay	Basque	Japanese

POINTING

English	French	German	Russian	Malay	Basque	Japanese
EAR	OREILLE	OHR	UKHO	TELINGA	BEHARRI	MIMI
HEAR	OUIR	HOREN	SLUKH	DENGAR	ADITU	KIKU
EYE	OEIL	AUGE	GLAZ	MATA	BEGI	ME
I	JE	ICH	YA	AKU	NIK	(WATASI)
HAND	MAIN	HAND	RUKA	TANGAN	ESKU	TE
HAIR	CHEVEUX	HAAR	VOLOS	BULU	BILO	KAMI
THAT	CA	DASS	TOT	ITU	HORI	ANO
THE	LE/LA	DER/DIE/DAS			A	
YOU	VOUS/TU	SIE/DU	VIY/TIY	KAMU	ZUEK/ZU	ANTA
IT	IL/LE	ES	ETO	IA		

VISUAL

English	French	German	Russian	Malay	Basque	Japanese
EDGE	BORD	RAND	KRAE	TEPI	BAZTER	FUCHI
CIRCLE	CERCLE	KREIS	KRUG	LENGKARAN	ERRUNDA	MARU
HEAP	TAS	HAUFE	GRUDA	TIMBUN	META	YAMA
CUP	COUPE	TASSE	KUBOK	CHAWAN	GATILU	CHAWAN
HOOK	CROC	HAKEN	KRYUK	KAIT	MAKO	KAGI
LAMP	LAMPE	LAMPE	LAMPA	PELITA	ARGI	RAMPU
ARCH	ARCHE	BOGEN	ARKA	RELONG	UNTZI	HASHI
FALL	TOMBER	FALLEN	PADAT	JATOH	ERORI	OCHIRU
WIDE	LARGE	WEIT	SHEEROKEE	LEBAR	ZABAL	HIROI
NARROW	ETROITE	ENG	UZKEE	SEMPIT	HERTSI	SEMAI
HIGH	HAUT	HOCH	VIYSOKEE	TINGGI	GORA	TAKAI
CLAW	GRIFFE	KLAUE	KOGOT	KUKU	AZTAPAH	TSUME
BOUGH	BRANCHE	AST	SUK	DAHAN	ADAR	EDA

English	French	German	Russian	Malay	Basque	Japanese

INTERNAL

English	French	German	Russian	Malay	Basque	Japanese
THINK	PENSER	DENKEN	DUMAT	FIKIR	PENTSATU	OMOU

English	French	German	Russian	Malay	Basque	Japanese
EDGE	BORD	RAND	KRAE	TEPI	BAZTER	FUCHI
CIRCLE	CERCLE	KREIS	KRUG	LENGKARAN	ERRUNDA	MARU
HEAP	TAS	HAUFE	GRUDA	TIMBUN	META	YAMA
CUP	COUPE	TASSE	KUBOK	CHAWAN	GATILU	CHAWAN
HOOK	CROC	HAKEN	KRYUK	KAIT	MAKO	KAGI
LAMP	LAMPE	LAMPE	LAMPA	PELITA	ARGI	RAMPU
ARCH	ARCHE	BOGEN	ARKA	RELONG	UNTZI	HASHI
FALL	TOMBER	FALLEN	PADAT	JATOH	ERORI	OCHIRU
WIDE	LARGE	WEIT	SHEEROKEE	LEBAR	ZABAL	HIROI
NARROW	ETROITE	ENG	UZKEE	SEMPIT	HERTSI	SEMAI
HIGH	HAUT	HOCH	VIYSOKEE	TINGGI	GORA	TAKAI
CLAW	GRIFFE	KLAUE	KOGOT	KUKU	AZTAPAH	TSUME
BOUGH	BRANCHE	AST	SUK	DAHAN	ADAR	EDA

English French   German   Russian Malay   Basque   Japanese

INTERNAL

THINK	PENSER	DENKEN	DOMAT	FIKIR	PENTSATU	OMOU
KNOW	CONNAITRE	KENNEN	ZNAT	KENAL	EZAGUTU	SHIRU
ME	MOI	MICH	MENYA	AKU	NI	

SOUND

THUNDER	TONNERRE	DONNER	GROM	GUNTOR	DURRUNDA	KAMINARI
CALL	CRIER	RUFEN	KREECHAT	TERIAK	HEITATU	YOBU
SPEAK	PARLER	SPRECHEN	SKAZAT	CHAKAP	MINTZATU	HANASU
CRACK	CRAQUER	KRACHEN	KOLOT	RETAK	KRASKA	KOWASU

TIME ASPECTS

NOW	MAINTENANT	NUN	TEPER	TADI	ORAI	IMA
THEN	PUIS	DANN	TOGDA	KETIKA	ONDOAN	SONO TOKI
WHEN	QUAND	WANN	KOGDA	WAKTU	NOIZ	IYSU
BEFORE	AVANT	VORHER	PERED	DAHULU	AINTZIN	MAE

o

CHAPTER VII

Language, Perception and Action:
Philosophical Issues

The earlier part of this book has been concerned with very specific questions arising in the field of linguistics (phonetics, semantics and syntax), with the results of research into visual perception (physiological and neurological) and with rather wider speculation about the organisation of bodily action and the relation between the bodily processes underlying action, vision and speech. The hypotheses, arguments, evidence and conclusions reached have not depended to any significant extent on philosophical doctrine or concepts and the question may be asked why should a book essentially concerned with linguistics conclude with a chapter devoted to philosophy. To this question there is a broad answer and a more specific one; the broad answer is that there has been prolonged and difficult discussion between philosophers over many centuries of the subjects dealt with earlier in this book, the origin and nature of language, the relation of language to reality, perception as based on sense-experience and providing the main basis for veridical knowledge, and voluntary human action (the notions of free will and determinism, of reasons and causes of action). The narrower answer, as an occasion and justification for having a philosophical chapter, is that in some respects totally new broad and specific hypotheses are presented about the functioning of language, perception and action, and particularly about their interrelation in human behaviour, and it is worth considering

345

what implications these hypotheses, if true, may have for traditional or current philosophical views. It may be that they ought to involve some radical review of current theory but. in any case, it would be unsatisfactory simply to present a whole range of ideas bearing on language, perception and action without having regard to what relevant to these subjects has been said by philosophers (as in the same way it would be unsatisfactory not to have regard to work that has been done on these subjects by experts in the field of Artificial Intelligence).

Philosophical discussion. in ancient and modern times, has tended to deal separately with language, perception (including knowledge based on perception) and voluntary action, and at different periods the focus of attention in each of these fields has tended to be significantly different. The pattern followed in this chapter is to treat first the philosophical concern with language, and then philosophical discussion of perception (and knowledge derived from perception) and voluntary action. It seems appropriate to deal first with language not only because this is a book about linguistics but also because in the present century philosophy has taken what some have described as 'the linguistic turn'; far more than in any preceding period of philosophy, philosophers have concentrated their thought on language in one way or another. (see Rorty(1)). Indeed, in so many respects have philosophers dealt with language that it becomes something of a problem to classify the separate approaches. Conventionally, one can distinguish between: 1. the philosophy of language 2. linguistic philosophy (in the sense of various uses of linguistic methods in investigating philosophical questions 3. the philosophical aspects of modern linguistics 4. the unavoidable dependence (regardless of any theories about language) of philosophy on language as the medium for philosophic exposition and debate 5. the specialised use of language as a philosophical device in modern logic and the construction of formal languages (rather different in approach from what is described above as linguistic philosophy). Besides these wide classifications, there are other topics which do not fit neatly into the categories: language universals, innateness of ideas, the interaction of language and culture or of language and thought, the dispute about private language, language as a form of action (Austin), Obviously, together these categories and topics constitute an immense field which it would be presumptuous to attempt even to describe, quite apart from venturing on any detailed discussion or assessment. What makes the position more complicated is that the distinctions between the different approaches to language in philosophy are ones which cannot be made sharply; there would be disagreement amongst philosophers about whether what they have done or are doing should be described as philosophy of language or linguistic philosophy or simply as just philosophising. One view is that (partly because of the rapid growth of analytical philosophy relying on linguistic methods) the philosophy of language (as part of the subject-matter of philosophy) has occupied the central place in the entire enterprise of philosophy in the twentieth century; another is that linguistic philosophy, that is the general use of linguistic methods, has succeeded in putting the whole previous tradition of philosophy (from the Greeks to the modern metaphysicians) on the defensive. The list of philosophers who have in fact concerned themselves heavily with language (even if some of them would reject any description of their work as philosophy of language or linguistic philosophy) includes virtually all the most familiar names in this century in English or American philosophy (Russell, Moore, Wittgenstein, Strawson, Quine, Austin, Ryle, Ayer) and, though Continental philosophy for the most part has found the Anglo_Saxon preoccupation with language odd or incomprehensible, there has also been a substantial contingent of German, Austrian, French and other European philosophers occupied with language in one way or another (Frege, Carnap, Schlick, Derrida, Merleau-Ponty and, earlier of course, Humboldt and Herder).

Whilst detailed treatment of linguistic philosophy (in the broadest possible sense) is, as has been said, impracticable, some brief description is needed to make it possible to establish points of contact between themes and debates in current philosophy involving language and the hypotheses and discussion about the functioning of language expounded in the earlier chapters. Though the exact nature of philosophy as an activity is itself still one of the disputed issues—to reveal the nature of the world (as traditional philosophers believed) or to bring order into one's conceptual structure as some modern philosophers would say—linguistic philosophers would nevertheless see themselves as a continuation of the philosophical tradition and part of the perennial philosophical enterprise. The progression in philosophy in this century has, in general terms, been away from the grand metaphysical structures of the 19th century, to a search for reliable knowledge of the world through language and logic, then to the attempt to construct criteria for the truth of propositions by linguistic methods, then to a more modest attempt to clarify intellectual concepts through the study of ordinary language and finally perhaps to a disenchantment with language and linguistic methods, with signs of a reversion to a larger view of the objectives of philosophy (including the revival of what some might describe as more traditional metaphysical approaches). In terms of particular philosophers, the trend has been from the idealism of Bradley to the attempt to reform language (coherently with mathematics) of Russell and Whitehead(2) and the early Wittgenstein(3) (later developed by Carnap), to the Vienna school and the logical positivism of the early Ayer (using analysis to banish metaphysics), to the ordinary language approach to philosophy of Austin and Ryle and finally to the disenchantment with philosophy of the later Wittgenstein. The swing back to a larger view of philosophy can be seen most clearly in Continental philosophy (an interest in Hegel, the strength of phenomenology) but also (prematurely so to say) in Whitehead and most recently in some of the work of Strawson.(4) The immediately following paragraphs contain not an exposition but some representative statements indicating the different approaches there have been to language and its significance for philosophy.

Russell and Whitehead (and the early Wittgenstein) were, in the use and function of language, concerned to construct a new logic of propositions (of sentences asserting truths or falsities), as distinct from Aristotle's logic of classes; they were in a sense concerned with syntax rather than with lexicon. They saw the proper mode of philosophical analysis as the rewriting of natural sentences to exhibit the correct logical form so that their meaning would become clear and philosophical perplexities would be eliminated; their objectives were those of traditional philosophy but the linguistic method was new. Russell's aim was, by this kind of analysis, to arrive at the universal syntax of knowledge, the universal structure of knowledge underlying the grammar of ordinary language. The tool Russell and Whitehead found, or constructed, for the task was the application of mathematical logic to language; with this tool, and the assumption that the structure of the world, and thus the underlying structure of language, was of the same nature as the theoretical structures of physics (elementary facts forming atomic propositions which then combined to form 'molecular' complex propositions), their belief was that, from the reform or reconstruction of ordinary language, one could arrive at reliable knowledge of the structure of the world. As Wittgenstein put it, in his early philosophy, a perfect language is like a map; it pictures the structure of reality, mirrors the world as a map mirrors it. Philosophy tells us about the structure of the world. Though Russell firmly rejected any classification of his work as linguistic philosophy, it was in fact very closely based on current ideas about the structure and grammar of language; for example, atomic propositions were said to be always in the 'Subject—Predicate' form and the elements to which the atomic propositions related were the 'facts' of which the world is said to be formed.

Technical difficulties (Russell's problems with the theory of descriptions and the paradoxes) as well as the trend away from traditional metaphysics of which logical atomism in Russell and Wittgenstein's formulation represented the last wave, led to a loss of interest in this kind of linguistic analysis and its supersession by a new but still basically linguistic approach, that of logical positivism. The new analysis shared with logical atomism the objective of clarifying language (scientific and colloquial) but with a much more limited end-product, that of showing whether or not propositions or sentences were of a kind which could be meaningful or not; sentences, on this new approach, could be analytic (true because of their structure), empirical (typically scientific propositions) or non-empirical. Mathematical and logical propositions were classed as analytic and there are potentially true and meaningful; the meaningfulness of empirical sentences depended on whether they could be verified by observation or at least a theoretical method of verification by observation could be proposed. Whilst attaching a central importance in philosophy to the use of language and logic, neo-positivism in effect involved the destruction of most traditional philosophy; analytic propositions (of mathematics and logic) survived but could not refer directly to the world; empirical statements could be meaningful, if verifiable, but the methods of verification were scientific rather than philosophical or linguistic; all non-empirical statements, those for which no method of verification could be proposed, were, on the neo-positivist view, meaningless, incapable of being true or false and in fact nonsensical. This last category covered in effect the whole of traditional metaphysics (and indeed the metaphysical implications of Russell and Wittgenstein's logical atomism).

However, as a use of language for philosophical purposes, logical positivism proved to be as vulnerable to attack as had been logical atomism or traditional metaphysics. It was pointed out that until we know the meaning of a sentence, we cannot start to say what kind of sentence it is and therefore whether it is analytic or empirical, or, if it is potentially empirical, what kind of verifiability should be looked for, that is, we cannot make the meaningfulness of a sentence depend upon its truth or falsity or even upon our ability in principle to demonstrate that it is true or false. The meaning of a sentence must be prior to the question of its truth. Apart from this, neo-positivism concentrated its attention on a peculiarly narrow section of language, that is descriptive or assertive sentences; in fact, language is used in many other ways, and used effectively, but for sentences of these other kinds, the issue of truth or falsity need not arise. Indeed, even though a sentence is of a kind which may be false or true, it can be unsuccessful in conveying anything true or false but still not meaningless. Finally, and perhaps most decisively, neopositivism is open to the fundamental attack that, on its tenets, no generalisation can be shown to be true because we cannot test an infinite number of instances; not only is it awkward to have a philosophical or logical theory which rules out as nonsensical the greater part of intellectual and scientific theory and discussion, but, more devastatingly, the tenets of logical positivism are, of course, themselves generalisations ('All propositions which are not analytic or empirically verifiable are meaningless') and there is no empirical method which conceivably could be specified for demonstrating the truth of these non-analytic generalisations. As Karl Popper(10) later pointed out, generalisations can be falsified, though they may not be verifiable—and the generalisations of logical positivism are open to falsifiability by, for instance, any simple proposition of which we understand the meaning but for which we cannot, for the present at any rate, indicate how, empirically, the truth or falsity of the statement can be established.

If logical atomism and logical positivism had proved unconvincing as methods of using language for philosophic purposes, the next step was overtly less ambitious but potentially more fruitful, that is, the development of the 'ordinary language' school (chiefly in Oxford). This was based on two main ideas: first, that ordinary language is more subtle and less confused than the earlier linguistic philosophers had supposed and something could be learnt from the study of use in ordinary language of key terms in philosophy. Austin was the principal exponent of this method and indeed went so far as to believe that philosophy was on the point of giving birth to a new science of language, through a systematic study of the functioning of colloquial language. The second main idea was that many of the problems of philosophers derive from their own misuse of ordinary terms in language; in particular, Ryle's position was that if one corrected the misuse of words like 'know' and 'mind', charted the logical geography of 'believe', 'doubt', 'infer' and so on, misconstructions and absurd theories would be revealed and many so-called philosophical problems would disappear, taking with them the 'ghost in the machine' which philosophers had constructed for themselves from the use of the word 'mind'(5). Beside the optimistic view of the 'ordinary language' approach to philosophy, there was also a pessimistic view, espoused by the later Wittgenstein, after he had rejected the earlier certainties of the Tractatus Logico-Philosophicus; he saw the main problem in philosophy as being to escape from the 'bewitchment' of philosophy by language and at the same time the need to disabuse philosophers of their belief that philosophy could in reality achieve any substantial results. The insignificance of language for philosophy he explained through developing his view of 'language games', that the meaning of a word is no more and no less than the way it is used (in effect a symbolic convention within a particular group or community). Philosophy, according to the later Wittgenstein, is not a theory (or a system of theories) but just one kind of activity; its object is simply to help to clarify one's thoughts; it has no application to reality and it is meaningless to enquire whether one's conceptual scheme mirrors reality correctly or not(6). At best, on this pessimistic view, linguistic analysis is a therapy to correct disordered thought and to recover from the intellectual malaise which an addiction to philosophy constitutes. But in the end Wittgenstein was uncertain whether even this pessimistic conclusion was correct; in his last work, published posthumously under the title 'On Certainty' (and largely concerned with the nature of 'knowing'), amongst a variety of scattered thoughts he included: "If you tried to doubt everything you would not get as far as doubting anything. The game of doubting presupposes certainty" and "Our knowledge forms an enormous system. And only within this system has a particular bit the value we give it"(7)—which seems to imply a final reconversion to the significance of philosophy as the enterprise in the sense of seeking to understand the world.

The most recent turn in the relation between language and philosophy has come partly from Austin's development of ordinary language philosophy into a view of language as action, partly from a new interest in the problem of meaning and partly from the change of direction in linguistics (Chomsky's ideas on the 'deep structure' of language and the innateness of grammar). Austin's views on language as action precede but fit well with views developed in linguistics of the functional basis of language. Whilst the categories of action which a sentence performs were at different times analysed in somewhat different ways by Austin, his key point was that "the basic unit of study is not the word or the sentence but the act which a person performs with the aid of words or sentences; the theory of language is to become, as it were, a branch of the theory of action . . . the total act performed by the speaker with the aid of the sentence"(8). Eventually, his view was that all sentences are performative, whether they convey information (which he previously classified as 'constative'), induce action (by warning or persuading) or constitute an action in their very utterance (as in promising). The impact of linguistics on philosophy has come both from the discussion of meaning and from the investigation of syntax; Quine at one point commented that pending a satisfactory explanation of the notion of meaning, linguists in semantic fields were in the position of not knowing what they were talking about—but the problem of meaning is now being tackled from a number of directions by philosophers, logicians, linguists and others. It is becoming apparent that the problems of meaning and the problems of syntax are not separate but interlocked, and that the problem of meaning is (as already noted in a previous paragraph) separable from the problem of truth and knowledge. It is again becoming possible to be at the same time a linguistic philosopher and a metaphysician; Strawson has pointed out that the actual use of linguistic expressions remains the philosopher's sole and essential point of contact with the reality which he wishes to understand . . . language proceeds directly from the concrete object somehow engendered by life itself; the objective is to understand the foundation of our concepts in natural facts and for this purpose "ordinary language is not a crude, rough and ready instrument but an enormously sophisticated instrument for thinking". In the attempt to show the natural foundations of our logical, conceptual apparatus in the way things happen in the world, and in our own natures, and how the fundamental categories of our thought hang together, "study of the relation between our whole articulated conceptual scheme and language, in other words linguistics, would be a source of the sort of questions and problems that philosophers are characteristically interested in"(9).

Of course, this revival of interest in the structure and functioning of language as an aid to philosophical advance is by no means universal or unchallenged. The contrary view is still held that philosophical problems are only muddles into which we are enticed by our misuse of language and that it is only with the use of language that truth and error, certainty and uncertainty, come fully upon the scene; only things expressible in language are capable of being true or false. Philosophers like Popper still reject any assumption that the subject-matter of philosophy is linguistic and, in Popper's phrase, consider that problems of language are secondhand problems, that philosophers who are not interested in science, rather than language, are no true philosophers(10). Or they agree with Max Black that the refinements of latter-day linguistics are impressive without being philosophically useful. "the conception of language as a mirror of reality is radically mistaken. Language must conform to the discovered regularities and irregularities of experience . . . No roads lead from grammar to metaphysics"(11). Certainly, European philosophers for the most part would not concede the central role of language or that language is the sole point of contact with the reality which philosophy wishes to understand; their view would be that the behaviour of things is the foundation of our conceptual structure and at most language expresses hypotheses and inferences about the foundation of things (see the discussion of Strawson's view at the Royaumont colloquium between English and Continental philosophers)(12).

The philosophical views of language and its significance outlined above bear, of course, quite directly on many of the hypotheses and proposals advanced in the earlier part of this book and it would be possible to comment specifically on them at this stage in that light. However, since the fundamental thesis in the book is the integral relation between language, perception and action, a better course is first to review, again briefly, philosophical views on perception, and then to consider how the philosophies of language and perception taken together relate to the hypotheses about language, perception and action presented earlier in this book.

In philosophy, theories of perception have normally been derived directly from epistemology, from theories of knowledge. Epistemology has for centuries been a central interest of philosophers; the means by which knowledge is acquired, the extent of our knowledge and of our possible knowledge, and the criteria for judging reliability, truth or falsity. In examining knowledge, philosophers traditionally have been divided into two camps, the rationalists and the empiricists. The rationalists' view is that the only reliable source of knowledge is human reason; mathematics is the paradigm example of reliable knowledge arrived at purely by reason; all sense experience can be delusory and is therefore not a reliable source of knowledge; true knowledge is the result of the inherent properties of the human understanding (or, in the case or Plato and some other philosophers, of our gradually coming to grasp the true ideas with which we are innately provided). Much of the discussion has been in terms of what it means to say that we 'know' something; there has been much rather fruitless argument about the extent to which to say one 'knows' something must mean that the thing known is objectively so, that knowledge is a guarantee of certainty, a confusion between the subjective and objective aspects of 'knowledge'.

The more influential school, certainly in English and American philosophy, has been that of the empiricists, those who follow Locke in denying the existence of any innate knowledge and derive all knowledge from sense-experience. Apart from analytic truths, such as those of mathematics or logic, whatever a person claims to know must, however he may explain his acquisition of the knowledge, ultimately depend upon direct experience by some human being; empiricists admit that sense-experience can be misleading but absolute rational certainty is unachievable and though we may be deceived on occasion, normally we are not; the search for regularities and uniformities in the world of appearance is a worthwhile endeavour and has provided the basis for the great and rapid progress of science. Adherence to a philosophy of empiricism leads directly to a belief in the central philosophical importance of perception; Locke's prime assertion is that all our ideas (our notions, all the materials of reason and knowledge) come from experience only: "our senses . . . convey into the mind several distinct perceptions of things; the second source of our ideas is the perception of the operations of our own minds" on the ideas it has got from sensation, "perception . . . being the first step and degree towards knowledge and the inlet of all the materials of it".(13)

The discussion of perception, as a philosophical topic (in the empiricist framework) has for the most part proceeded completely independently of physiological or psychological research into perception. It has been in terms of sense-impressions as the basic particulars, of objects which have spatio-temporal position and those which, like qualities, do not. For Hume, the only items exempt from his universal scepticism were sense-impressions and mathematical concepts. The philosophy of perception in modern times was largely developed as a theory of sense-data (such as a patch of colour, a rap of sound, a felt surface or a smell); on this view, every external object is the source of a set of sense-data which fit together in a family, to form the perceived object, and any description of a material object inevitably involves the description of the sense-data which compose it. This account of perception, as an operation for combining and organising sense-data (such as colour, shape and so on) has been attacked from many points of view. How, it has been asked, does one distinguish what is experienced as a sense-datum from what is supplied by the mind in the perception of the object? Gradually, the sense-datum theory has been amended in an attempt to meet criticism; the amended sense-data are not independent realities but factors in a process of interaction between each person and other things in the world around him; or sense-data are pseudo-entities which stimulate us to perceive the presence of the colour of the object without themselves being the colour. Austin and Ryle both rejected the view that sense-data are the basis for perception and the foundation of knowledge (a view largely developed by their Oxford contemporaries, Pritchard and Price). Ryle(14) argued that the whole theory rested on a logical error, the identification of the concept of sensation with that of observation: "impressions (sense-data) are ghostly impulses, postulated for the ends of a para-mechanical theory, an invention of philosophers"; the notion of a sense-datum is not precise and cannot be explained in familiar terminology. Statements about physical objects are not formally translatable into statements about sense-data and the phenomenalist programme cannot be carried through.

But beyond this rather unsatisfactory philosophical treatment of perception as a source of knowledge, there are the profounder issues raised by the scepticism of Hume and the philosophies of Berkeley and Kant; can perception lead us to the knowledge of anything 'outside us'? Berkeley denied the existence of anything other than our ideas; Hume denied that there was any way in which we could know anything about the outside world and external objects and Kant, whilst postulating a priori knowledge consisting in the forms of understanding, by which external objects become known to us, denied that we could ever make any real contact with the transcendental objects of which the world is composed. Each of these philosophies leaves the nature of perception, as a relation between the human subject and the external world, unresolved—or resolved in ways which eliminate the notion of an external world or the possibility of knowing an external world if it in fact exists. The conundrums for the philosophy of perception that these 'idealist' doctrines present have, of course, been subjects for unending and inconclusive speculation, attempted refutation and, finally, indifference. One popular philosophical reaction has been to move towards a belief in 'naive realism', that is, regardless of the sceptical arguments of Hume, and the idealist positions of Berkeley and Kant, the common sense view that there are real physical objects outside us and we do establish contact with them through perception and action. Naive realism is a reaction shared not only by some philosophers (including the pragmatic philosophers) but also by most scientists and the common thinking man. The position is, no doubt, strictly philosophically indefensible but, in practice, the only possible one—the idealist philosopher may deny the existence of an external world but, in his everyday behaviour, act as if he were fully convinced of its existence. At the same time, the 'naive realist' may be no more interested in the scientific basis of perception than is the idealist; when Ryle's first book was published, he said that he knew nothing about psychology (though he was writing about the mind) and when he was criticised for having no knowledge either of neurology said: "It doesn't seem to me that one is not at home in the field of perception . . . I do not want to know anything about the rods and cones in the eye".(16)

As Sloman has pointed out in connection with machine-vision, philosophers have normally ignored the complexities which come to light if one begins to design a working visual system, and even what are taken to be simple sense-data (patches of colour, lines, shapes) are found to be the result of complex processes of analysis and interpretation. Konrad Lorenz(15) has similarly commented that the barrier between philosophy and science has obstructed human knowledge in the very direction where it was most necessary i.e. the objective investigation of the interaction between the perceiving mind and the object of perception. Hume and Kant between them might both qualify for the description of 'destroyers of metaphysics', Hume because he treated our beliefs about the external world as 'a peculiar set of mental habits or customs' and denied the reality of external causation: 'necessity exists only in the human mind' and Kant because of the sharpness of the distinction he drew between the phenomenal (what appears to be the case to our perception and understanding) and the noumenal (the world of things-in-themselves). Kant's view was that we can know nothing about a real spatial or temporal world, the objects in it or the causal relation between events nor, even more constricting, can we discover within ourselves the cause of our a priori categories and system of perception, the source or cause of the organising principles of our mental machinery. As in the case of language, so in the case of perception and knowledge of the external world, philosophy has reached an impasse. Whilst, as someone has commented, it is not excessively uncomfortable to hold to a belief in 'naive realism', it is not a position defensible in philosophical terms. Meanwhile, the central problem of perception, the justification of our belief in the existence of perceivable physical objects, remains; the common sense view of ordinary men and of professional philosophers is that both the perceiver and the perceived exist and are related to one another through perception and action. Science, as in practice a supremely effective intellectual process, bases itself on the reliability of perception and the regularity of relations between events (that is, necessary causation), despite Kant, Hume and Berkeley.

There are ways out of the philosophical impasse. There is the way of pragmatism, to say that truth is determined by experience; the pragmatic test of meaning is whether ideas in fact serve as effective tools for coping with experience, for survival and successful action. By the pragmatic test of truth, universal scepticism and the unsurmountable separation between the perceiver and the perceived world must at some point involve fallacious ideas; Kant's view that the nature of things must always necessarily be unknown to us is 'a kind of nonsense'. Popper's way of dealing with the impasse in the philosophy of language is rather similar; language is no more than a kind of spectacles through which one looks at the world: "one shouldn't waste one's life in spectacle-cleaning or in talking about language . . . To be only interested in language is a philosophical mistake . . . leading to scolasticism"(10)

But the more convincing roads out of the philosophical impasse are those suggested by three authors who belong to quite different philosophical schools but resemble each other in having interests, in science or mathematics, going wider than academic philosophy. The first of these is Whitehead: the starting point for him is perception considered as a grasping, 'prehension', of its environment by an organism. For him, perception does not present us with isolated sensations; perception is experience from within nature of the system of events which make up nature, the self-knowledge enjoyed by an element of nature respecting its relations with the whole of nature in its various aspects; his theory of perception is a biological one, the perceiver as a natural organism reacting to the world around him. The views of the second author, Merleau-Ponty, a leading figure in French structuralism and phenomenology, are strikingly similar, though reached by a quite different route. His overriding theme is 'back to perception, restore the primacy of perception in philosophy'. His philosophy offers a middle way between rationalism and empiricism, between realism and idealism, in his concept of the 'body-subject', which encounters a world which already has 'meanings' incorporated in it, that is, a world in which this object is recognised as food, that as inedible and so on. At the same time as his concept of the 'body-subject' resolves the impasse in the philosophy of perception, it also, according to Merleau-Ponty, extricates us from the impasse in the conception of language: "language is itself an illustration of the dialectical relation between ourselves and the world and originates from the mixture of the world and ourselves" which precedes all reflection; for the child the name is the essence of the object and the child does not name the object but recognises it. Language is not composed of conventional signs but to Merleau-Ponty is seen as a form of 'psychic gesticulation', with meaning rooted not in abstract intellect but in real bodily gesture and behaviour. The understanding of a speaker's message (the psychic gesticulation which his words constitute) takes place in the same way as we understand his bodily gestures, which 'intermingle with the structure of the world that the gesture outlines',

Though Merleau-Ponty's terminology has some of the cloudiness associated with Continental phenomenology, the essence of what he says is not far removed from Whitehead's views, Nor again are these far removed from the much more straightforward and convincing exit from the impasse proposed by Konrad Lorenz, as an ethologist interested in human as well as in animal behaviour, For him, both the perceiving subject and the object of perception are equally real and all knowledge derives from the interaction between them. Leibniz at one stage had suggested, but not pursued, as a possible philosophical reconciliation between idealism and realism 'preestablished harmony' between knower and known. Essentially, this is what Lorenz as a biologist familiar with the facts of evolution suggests as the obvious answer to the Kantian dilemma: "the cognitive apparatus is itself an objective reality which has acquired its present form through contact with and adaptation to equally real things in the outer world . . . The 'spectacles' of our modes of thought and perception, such as causality, substance, quality, time and place (the Kantian categories) are functions of a neurosensory organisation that has evolved in the service of survival . . . What we experience is a real image of reality, albeit an extremely simple one, only just sufficing for our practical purposes"(15). For the individual human being, the cognitive apparatus, the modes of perception, are given a priori and determine the manner in which the real world is perceived or experienced. Though Kant might not have been able to see it as such, the 'perceiving apparatus' can be unconditionally equated with the Kantian synthetic a priori. But for the human race as a whole, the mode of perception is not a priori but the result of physiological and neurological evolution of the system of sense organs and nerves. The philosophical impasse of perception is resolved by the evolutionary and historical convergence of the organisation of the perceiving subject and the real perceived world.

The original plan of this chapter was first to give a necessarily summary account of philosophical theory and discussion bearing on language and perception as primary topics dealt with in this book and secondly to consider whether the broad and specific hypotheses advanced on the integration of language, perception and action in human behaviour have any implications for traditional or current philosophical views or whether they leave philosophical theory completely unaffected. Before the chapter tackles this second issue, it may be convenient to recall, briefly, what the hypotheses and proposals have been in the various earlier chapters:

— words, syntax and speech-sounds are not arbitrary. They are determined by anatomical, physiological and neurological structures and for each language, the structures of the language are derived from and directly related to other major segments of human behaviour (perception and action)

— the selection made by a language-community of its specific syntax, words and speech-sounds is not arbitrary or conventional but a selection from a range of possible sounds, words and syntaxes, with the community's preferences being determined by the pooling of genetic features of the population over time. Stability of a language is a result of stability in the genetic composition of the population coupled with the acquisition of a child's particular language by a process analogous to imprinting in animals and depending on the special character of the language as human behaviour

— language was not invented but emerged as part of evolutionary development, in parallel with the physiological, behavioural and social evolution of the human being and human communities

— languages are isomorphic because they are intertranslatable and their isomorphism derives from the integration of language with the general underlying structures and processes of perception and action

— the key to the evolutionary survival of the animal and of the human is the effective organisation of action (action appropriate to the environment). Perception developed from action and to serve action

— language, as a further stage, developed in groups and communities of human beings as a system for precise and flexible communication at a distance of the contents of perception of one individual to another i.e. language developed to serve perception and thus at one remove to serve effective action

— for perception to be an effective adjunct to action it must be integrated as closely as possible with the organisation of action (seeing and grasping must be physiologically and neurologically precisely aligned with each other), In the same way for language to be precise and effective in conveying the content of perception or in referring to action, it must, physiologically and neurologically, be fully integrated with the structures underlying perception and action (looking and speaking must be aligned with each other)

— each language forms a coherent system at each level (that of speech sounds, words and sentences). At each level, the forms and processes of language derive from and are integrated with the structures and processes of the corresponding levels of the systems of perception and complex voluntary action

— besides being integrated with the organisation of action, both perception and language are themselves forms of action (muscular movement in articulation and eye-movements) and form part of the total organisation of action in the human being

— the unity of the organisation of speech, perception and action rests in the neurological patterning of motor-control programmes in the cortex. One can conceive of the relation as three intersecting circles of speech-control, vision-control and action-control, with a shared central area where each intersects with the other and which, together with the self-reflexive character of language and perception and the fundamental unity of total action-organisation, provides the basis for the essentially unified character of human mental processes and behaviour

— research in vision and action-organisation (both in physiology and neurology) can throw light on research in language—and vice versa. Speech, vision and action all appear to be organised hierarchically in much the same way, starting from elementary units which have a specific relation to the construction in parallel of words, visual shapes and action-routines and then to the parallel syntaxes of the sentence, the visual scene and the complex action

— neurological research has provided a detailed basis for understanding the process of visual perception (at the more elementary levels) by identifying the relation between cells in the visual cortex and typical units which go to form a visual shape or the visual scene (lines, angles, curves etc.). Visual shapes appear to be constructed from a combination of the elementary units (in the first instance) with the formation of progressively more complex visual schemas (patternings in the cortex related to the sequence of eye-movements and fixations in scanning a visual shape or scene). The innate characteristics of the visual apparatus are the result of genetic influences (the product of evolutionary pressures); the predisposition to perceive the elementary units and patternings of the actual world is the result of 'imprinting', neurological pretuning to respond to a range of possible types of visual patterning. In the course of visual experience, the animal or the human being builds up more complex persisting neurological structures, schemas, which serve as short-cuts to the recognition of elements in a visual scene. The source of all the structuring found in a visual scene is in the physical visual stimuli, the stream of light energy falling on the eye, but the visual apparatus has evolved, both phylogenetically and in the individual animal or human development, so as to be predisposed to recognise the patterns most probably to be found in the environment

— analogous processes to those postulated for visual perception seem to operate in the production and comprehension of speech and the planning and execution of complex action. The meaning of a sentence can be treated as an equivalent simultaneously present neural patterning to the patterning which constitutes the interpretation, the meaning, of a visual scene, or to the plan of a proposed action. In each case, the translation of the meaning into a sentence, of a plan into an executed action, the comprehension of a heard sentence, the understanding of a perceived pattern of action or of a visual scene, can be analysed as a process of translating the simultaneous (present neural pattern) into a serial form (the spoken sentence or the executed action) or translating the serial (the heard sentence, the scanned visual scene or the perceived external action) into the simultaneous (a return to a cotemporaneous neural pattern)

— at the word level and at the sentence level, the integration between speech, vision and action operates equivalently. Each primitive word (that is, each word whose meaning is learnt from experience and not solely from explanation in terms of other words) has directly associated with it visual or action contours which indicate or give a natural clue to the meaning of the word. There is evidence for all languages of awareness of a natural relation between word-sound and word-meaning (sound symbolism) and considerable evidence that, for all except tonal languages, some kind of sound symbolism operates. "The word falls, one is tempted to explain", according to the early Wittgenstein, "into a mould of my mind prepared for it".

— at the sentence-level, the process of constructing a sentence or planning a complex action and of understanding (decoding or disambiguating) a heard sentence or perceived scene are analogous. They can be analysed in parallel. The key operation is disambiguation, the progressive narrowing down of the possible significance and role of the elements in a sentence or a visual scene. In this process, syntax and semantics operate together (both in vision and in language) to identify the word or visual schemas present and their interrelationship in the sentence or scene. In the operation (which is in effect one of problem solving), the interpretation is arrived at via a series of provisional hypotheses on the meaning and the relation of the elements and depends for its final certainty on the adequacy of the linguistic, perceptual or experiential context in which a particular sentence is uttered or a particular scene is perceived

— the total set of words in a language (the lexicon) and the total vocabulary of an individual are built up from a central core of primitive words (words learnt from experience only). The underlying structure of the lexicon or vocabulary reflects the structuring of the perceptual and other experience of the child or, primitively, of the language-community. The total lexicon is developed by regular processes of composition and extension of the meaning of words, by the borrowing of words from foreign languages (originally founded on the primitive elements in the vocabularies of the other languages) and, most importantly of all, by the vital process of metaphor, that is, the transfer of the structure of the percept to which a word or sentence refers to apply to more abstract, intellectual material. Metaphor is the source of virtually all abstract words in philosophy and science and is the main link between the concrete vocabulary (founded on the primitive words of the child or the community) and the total vocabulary of a language. The structuring of the primitive vocabulary is the basis for the structuring of the total vocabulary of concrete words and, at one remove via metaphor, for the structuring of the abstract lexicon. Disputes about the use of abstract terms are the expression of an attempt to relate them to the strong, natural structure of the concrete lexicon (based ultimately on the categories of human perception and action)

— the 'deep structure' of language is not linguistic but is in fact the structure of reality (as experienced in perception and action). Language can, however, only offer a mapping of human experience (perception or action), not a detailed picture—in effect a 'skeleton' of the particular perceived scene, proposed action or intellectual construct (in the same way as perception presents only a selection, a mapping, of the fullness of the content in any visual scene). 'Competence' and 'performance' are reinterpreted as the ability to comprehend and the ability to express—we can understand more than we can explain in language. The 'open-endedness' of language is not in any way a special property but an inevitable consequence of language's function in matching the open-endedness of human experience, of human perception and of human action.

— other languages, with different syntaxes and different lexicons (derived from originally genetic differences in the 'preferences' between possible forms of the structures of articulation, perception and action) arrive at equally valid representations of the world in words by different, equally natural routes. The extension of these hypotheses on the relation of language, perception and action to other languages is the starting-point for assuming that the hypotheses may have wider philosophical applications or implications.

The summary of the hypotheses and proposals advanced in the earlier chapters of the work is inevitably greatly compressed and may do no greater justice to the important details of the argument than the summary in the first part of this chapter does to conventional philosophical discussion of language and perception. However, in the light of the summaries furnished, one is now in a position to comment on the acceptability or relevance of the philosophical notions and approaches described for the hypotheses in this book and, equivalently, on the implications, such as they may be, of the hypotheses presented for the philosophical treatment of language, perception and knowledge. The discussion cannot possibly be a full one and the comments are framed as briefly as is consistent with their intelligibility. The comments on the philosophical summary are separated into those on the philosophy of language (or linguistic philosophy) on the one hand and those on the philosophy of perception (and knowledge) on the other.

Significance of language for philosophy

Philosophical discussion can only be conducted in language and this is the prime source of the importance of language for philosophy. Different schools of philosophy, if one accepts the hypothesis in this book that language derives its structure from the structures of perception and action and has as its function the representation, in outline, of the content of perception and action, have attached either too much or too little importance to language as an instrument to assist or obstruct the progress of philosophy. Language is validated by perception and action, not the other way round. Language is not 'the sole and essential point of contact for the philosopher with reality'—and the most pressing contacts with reality impose themselves without any intermediation of language. Language is not, on the view in this book, an abstract rational structure but one built on the most mundane of foundations, in human neurophysiological structure; it is subsidiary rather than primary in human behaviour and thought. Accordingly, because language is a secondary coding of experience, one should not expect much certainty or philosophical illumination from the analysis of language in isolation.

On the other hand, philosophical comment on the confusion and deception arising from language has been much overstated. Language originated and was designed, by evolution, for the accurate representation of the ordering of the concrete world of perception and action, and for this purpose it functions well, to the extent that it mirrors reliably the external world in which the human being has to act Between men with a shared approach to an area of knowledge or science, a shared practical objective or a shared skill, language has proved an indispensable and reliable instrument. Difficulties with language, as an instrument, have arisen rather from those who have attempted to make use of it for purposes for which it was not designed, primarily philosophers themselves and linguists. Amongst philosophers, verbal confusions and debates have proceeded from the use or invention of terms with no precise meaning and no clear relation to the central reliable core of the lexicon (founded in the original relation between words, perception and action). If philosophers choose to disregard the essentially social and natural foundations of words and organisation of words into sentences, to formulate their own idiosyncratic terms and syntactic procedures, then agreement and a shared clear view of what is true or at least probable becomes impossible or highly unlikely. Wittgenstein might have been more successful in struggling against the 'bewitchment of our intelligence by language' if he had not fabricated, with Russell, new unexplained terms (atomic facts, molecular propositions, logical space and so on) and if he had turned his attention away from language as a structure in its own right to human behaviour, the normal functioning of perception and action.

Even the terminology of 'ordinary language' philosophers was in its way obfuscating. Austin's perlocutionary, illocutionary and constative classification of utterances—and, of course, much earlier Kantian and Hegelian terminology—created a cloud of linguistic obscurity which no one can be said to have penetrated with confidence. Another source of confusion, due to philosophers rather than to language, has been the assumption, by Anglo-Saxons, French and Germans, that the special features of the syntax or structure of the lexicons of their native languages offer a direct insight into underlying universal truths. Whole philosophies in German and in English have been erected on distinctions of meaning or on differences in grammatical structure which are idiosyncratic to the particular language. Even on the ordinary language approach, the range of meaning of common words such as 'know' and 'believe' and their mode of use vary significantly from language to language. No absolute philosophical understanding can be arrived at by confining oneself to the particular structures of one's native language. What the hypotheses in this book contend about language is that every language certainly can achieve the same practical effect, in terms of the perception conveyed or the action indicated, but the combination of syntactic and semantic devices used to achieve the result may vary from language to language. To concentrate on one feature of syntax or vocabulary in a language is bound to result in distortion if one attempts to draw from it some general philosophical truth. A parallel kind of misdirection and confusion, but this time due to linguists rather than to philosophers, has been the over-estimation of the importance of differences between languages in syntax or lexicon, the theory associated with Sapir and Whorf that language determines perception, that people speaking languages largely differing in structure or in lexicon experience differently ordered worlds. Because in Hopi, for instance, time aspects are conveyed not by verbs but by other devices, Whorf sees the American Indian as living in a different spatio-temporal world from the European—but in reality the American Indian has to live in the world as it is, day after day, just as does the European, regardless of any differences in syntax. The real world imposes its structure on language, and language does not, cannot, impose some different, arbitrary structure on the real world.

At the other extreme, under-estimation of the usefulness of language in philosophy is as unhelpful as over-estimation of its significance. Max Black's assertion that "no road leads from grammar to metaphysics" and Popper's, that language is no more than a set of spectacles through which one looks at the world and one shouldn't waste one's time in cleaning the spectacles or talking about language, seem to go too far in the opposite direction. Language is part of human behaviour and it is a fact as much founded in neurology and physiology as any other part of the human organism. Whilst one must agree with Popper that philosophers who, on principle, disregard the content and progress of science can hardly claim to be philosophers in any true sense, the study of the functioning of language is itself a scientific study of great interest and importance. Certainly this is the case if one accepts the hypothesis that it is derived from, integrated with and structured by the neurological and physiological bases of perception and action. Even Popper needs language as a reliable instrument for expounding his own views on the methods of science and philosophy and, though he may be right to dismiss as fruitless some forms which linguistic philosophy has taken, this does not justify him in rejecting any attempt at a combined philosophical and scientific discussion of the issues which language presents. Whether, even in a narrow sense, Max Black's view on the philosophical insignificance of grammar is sustainable is doubtful. Whilst the syntax and lexicon of any single language may not point unequivocally to reliable philosophical views about the real world, insofar as languages are essentially isomorphic (that is they achieve by different coding methods the representation of the same content of perception, action or thought) and this isomorphism rests on the underlying relation of language, perception and action, a comparative examination of the different ways in which languages achieve the same results, in representing the real 'parts-of-vision' or 'parts-of-action' which correspond to traditional parts-of-speech, or achieve successful disambiguation by the combination of syntax and semantic structuring, could lead to useful general truths, or at least useful general probabilities in one's view of the real world.

Meaning as a central topic in the philosophy of language

Both in the summary account of the philosophy of language given earlier in this chapter and in the range of hypotheses presented in this book about the functioning and basis of language there has inevitably been reference in many different contexts to the concept of 'meaning'. Of all linguistic concepts the question 'What is meaning?' is the one which has been most studied and argued over by philosophers of language. 'Semantics' was originally conceived as a philosophical enquiry into meaning, though the range of application of semantics has now been greatly widened. The discussion about 'meaning' is a peculiarly apt demonstration of the self-reflexive property of language. If, it might be said, philosophers cannot agree to tell us what 'meaning' means, how can they give us reliable guidance on the meaning of any other philosophical concepts? The philosophical discussion of meaning has demonstrated perhaps more clearly than any other segment of philosophical activity both the difficulty and the confusion of the philosophical enterprise. 'Meaning' as a word has been analysed as having very many diverse meanings (one estimate was that there are over 50 distinct meanings of 'meaning') so that to the question 'What is meaning?', an almost unlimited range of answers has been possible and has been offered. Quine's comment already quoted that, until they have a satisfactory explanation of the notion of meaning, linguists in semantic fields are in the position of not knowing what they are talking about, could equally readily be applied to many philosophers. At the same time, if a satisfactory account can be constructed, by philosophers or by linguists, of the nature of 'meaning', it would carry with it the possibility of important advance in many other areas of linguistics and philosophy in so far as the techniques employed to explicate meaning could be used to tackle the relatively less complicated problems involved in understanding other philosophical terms and concepts.

Before considering how a variety of philosophers have tackled 'meaning' and how their views bear on or are affected by the references made to meaning earlier in this book, there are two preliminary clarifications. First of all, we have, at the moment, no basis for picking out any particular use of 'meaning' as the primary one; 'meaning' is not necessarily just a linguistic concept, the meaning of a word or of a sentence, but also we can, and do, speak equally readily about the meaning of an action, the meaning of something we see or perceive (e.g. the meaning of a traffic sign) or the meaning of a situation or an argument. If we assume that 'meaning' is necessarily and primitively linguistic, then we have already prejudged, and so limited, the range of theories of meaning which it is open to us to consider. The second preliminary clarification is one which has already emerged from the summary account given of linguistic approaches to philosophy in this chapter, that meaning comes before truth; the problem of meaning is separable and must, initially, be separated from the problems of truth and knowledge. Apart from 'analytic' truth (that is simply the explanation of one word or phrase in terms of other words or phrases), we must understand the meaning of a word or sentence before we can determine whether the sentence is true or false, whether the word applies or does not apply to a real object, event or situation; it is the world, not the words used or the structure of the sentence, which establishes the truth or falsity of the meaning which the sentence conveys. Truth and falsity are properly discussed, not in the context of meaning, but in that of the philosophy of perception and the philosophy of knowledge.

With these preliminary clarifications, it is possible to look briefly at and assess the relevance of discussion by philosophers of 'meaning'. Different philosophers have approached meaning from many different directions. Some have been concerned with distinguishing the range of uses of the word 'meaning'; of these, some confine themselves to linguistic meaning, others deal with wider uses of meaning. Of those concerned with linguistic meaning, some concentrate on the meaning of words (or concepts) in isolation and others believe that what philosophers should be concerned with is rather the meaning of sentences or propositions as the proper mode of conceptual analysis. Other philosophers approach the topic by seeking to categorise the proper questions to investigate about meaning: are meanings abstract entities or not? what conditions have to be satisfied for an expression to be meaningful? what is the nature of 'sameness' of meaning? why do word meanings alter? what are the smallest linguistic units which possess meaning? Or they seek to categorise the levels and diverse theories of meaning. One philosopher, for example, distinguishes three levels: the meaning of thoughts, the meaning of messages and the meaning of speech acts. Another philosopher usefully categorises theories of meaning as:

— mentalist: to be meaningful involves association with a mental
   item, an image, a thought or an idea
— behaviourist: meaning is what produces certain behavioural
   responses to utterances
— use theory: meaning is constituted by use
— verificationist: meaning is determined by how one decides the truth
   of an expression
— emotivist: meaning is the tendency of a word or phrase to produce
   a particular feeling.

This is by no means a complete list of theories of meaning and every theory
has many variants. However, some of the comments already made apply
immediately to the theories listed. If meaning is prior to truth, then one
cannot accept a verificationist theory of meaning. The theory that meaning
is constituted by use explains (almost certainly wrongly) how words
acquire meaning but does not give a philosophical account of 'meaning'
as such; ordinary language philosophy explores the meanings of words in
use but does not necessarily require that the essence of 'meaning' should
be constituted by use. Indeed Austin's concept of the speech act involved
something much closer to a behaviourist view of meaning. The objections to
a behaviourist theory of meaning are the familiar, and compelling, objections
to behaviourist theories generally; behaviourism confuses essences with
effects, structure with the expression of structure. An emotivist theory of
meaning is open to very much the same kind of objection as a behaviourist
one; meaning exists for the speaker as much as it does for the person
spoken to, and to identify meaning with feeling is to confuse thought and
feeling, information with the reaction to information. One variant of the
behaviourist theory of meaning on which more specific comment may be
useful is that put forward by Grice(19) (which has received a good deal of
attention): his ideas have been presented sketchily but involve a distinction
between 'utterer's meaning' and 'timeless meaning' of an expression (for an
individual or for the language generally); the timeless meaning amounts to
no more than the definition of the meaning of a word or group of words
by the use of other words and takes one no further forward in determining
what the nature of the 'meaning' of the explained or of the explaining
words may be. Ziff's(20) criticism of Grice's approach, that it seems to
be concerned rather with the use of an expression than with 'meaning' as
such, seems justified. To talk about how meanings are used whether of a
word or of a sentence, the effects they cause or the actions they perform,

is not to provide a satisfactory philosophical account of the concept of 'meaning' as such, any more than to describe what a machine does, where one can travel to in a car, for example, explains how the machine or the car functions, what its essential structural properties are. Finally, in this categorisation of theories of meaning, a brief reference may be made to the original views of Carnap and Neurath(21) that 'meaning' should be defined purely in syntactical terms, as referring to the properties of sentences in a formal system. If one accepts that words in isolation can have meaning, as well as sentences, then such a theory is unacceptable. Carnap himself later abandoned it and his revised view was that the problem of meaning is a semantic and not a syntactic issue.

If, as the comments in the previous paragraph have done, one rejects verificationist, behaviourist, emotivist and use theories of meaning and the other variant theories described, the only theory left on the list and not so far explained or criticised is the mentalist theory of meaning, that to be meaningful involves association with a mental item, an image, a thought or an idea. This is really not one theory but a category or collection of theories. Quite clearly, there is an intimate relation between the meaning of words and mental processes; some would say that mental processes are the manipulation of words (though there are reasons for thinking such a view mistaken) but at least words emerge from mental processes and express mental processes. But to accept the close link between word—or sentence-meanings and mental processes does not necessarily take one much further in giving a philosophical account of meaning. The concepts of 'idea', 'thought', 'mental image', are themselves as philosophically obscure and unexplained as the concept of 'meaning'. To treat 'meaning' as in some way an operation or relation of 'mind' leads one into the swamp of philosophical debate about mind and leaves one as puzzled as before about the most suitable philosophical approach to 'meaning'.

The outcome of this survey of philosophical consideration of 'meaning' is at the same time disappointing and paradoxical. Disappointing because none of the various theories offers a helpful account of meaning or is immune from straightforward and powerful destructive criticism. Paradoxical because, despite the failure of philosophical discussion, everyone, philosophers, linguists and ordinary people, uses the concept of 'meaning' without the slightest difficulty; we all know intuitively what the words we use mean (except perhaps words which are the artificial constructs of philosophers), we all understand what it is to grasp the 'meaning' of a sentence, to see what the development of some events or situation 'mean', and we all readily say: "I see what you mean" "You have understood my meaning" or "That means nothing to me". The words 'mean' and 'meaning' are some of the most familiar and frequently used by ordinary people, by philosophers and linguists. Surely there must be some way out of the labyrinth, some way of convincing ourselves that there is nothing mysterious or insoluble about 'meaning' as a central concept in philosophy, and in everyday life.

One possibility is that the problem of meaning has been approached from the wrong direction; philosophy, as a discipline inevitably founded on language and on the manipulation of the meaning of words and sentences and which can only offer explanations in terms of the meanings of words and sentences, is in no better position to explain one of its primitive concepts, 'meaning', than it is to explain, in philosophical terms, the nature of the colour 'red'. 'Meaning' was a property of perception and action long before it became a property of words or sentences; a theory of meaning is much more probably to be found through methods used to understand the functioning of perception and action than through the verbal manipulations of philosophy itself. If we can come to understand the nature of the 'meaning' of what we perceive, in a visual scene, or the 'meaning' of an action, then we may be able to extend this to understand the meaning of a sentence or word. On the hypotheses presented in this book, the meaning of a word (for a percept forming part of the primitive visual repertoire of a child) is constituted by a direct neurological and physiological link between the sound-structure of the word and the shape or identifying physical characteristics of the perceived object to which the word refers; in parallel to the neural patterning constituting the schema of a visual percept is the neural patterning constituting the sound-structure of the word. The coincidence of patterning between word and percept is the essence of the property 'meaning'. Similarly the meaning of a sentence, the meaning of a visual scene and the meaning of a plan of action, are constituted by the simultaneous neural patterning from which the expression of the integral meaning in the serial form of a sentence and the serial execution of the complex action are derived.

This account of 'meaning' is not a philosophical or a linguistic one but essentially a neurological, physiological one. It coincides, somewhat surprisingly, quite closely with the account of the origin and nature of the meaning relation given by Sayre in his book Cybernetics and the Philosophy of Mind. For him, words acquire meaning by being intentionally associated (by the individual or as a result of the shared intention of a community) with objects; an intention is a purpose operating consciously in control of an organism's behaviour, a neuronal configuration regulating behaviour through sequential stages and terminating in a particular goal. Language arises as a means of sharing intentions: "The meaning of a term is the shared intention with which the term is associated in its common use. On the one hand, a meaning is an intention, and hence a purpose, and hence a neural configuration . . . On the other hand, a meaning is a formal structure that can be instantiated in the cortexes of different individuals, and transmitted to others within the group".(22)

Thus, a meaning is what makes a difference to the neurophysiological organisation of the individual acquiring the meaning or expressing the meaning. Before expression in a particular sentence uttered in particular circumstances, a 'meaning' is a generalised pattern relating a sound-structure and a generalised visual or other schema; all words are universals (as all perceptual schemas are universals) until they are given a particular application, a particular reference by having their range of possible meanings narrowed down by the combined action of the syntactic and semantic structures in the sentence. At the same time, as a neural pattern, a 'meaning' forms part of the total complex of meanings (the total set of neural patterns) which go to form our conceptual system: in its use in a particular sentence, a word and its meaning bring with them, initially, their relationship to other words, and other meanings, the structures within which the individual word, the individual meaning and the individual percept are integrated. The process of determining the 'meaning' of a sentence is, operationally, the use of semantic and syntactic clues, derived from the serial string of words, to determine the particular meaning and role of the word, in that sentence on that occasion.

Perception as the foundation of knowledge of the real world

The summary account of the philosophy of knowledge earlier in the chapter describes the stages by which traditional philosophy had reached an impasse, being unable to give any satisfactory account of how perception (in the view of the empiricists the only sure foundation for knowledge) in fact enables us to know anything with certainty about the existence of objects in the real world (or even whether a real external world exists) or about the reality of the sequences of causes and effects which, in common understanding and in scientific theory, we rely upon to explain our experience of the world and the processes of physical nature. The idealism of Berkeley and Kant and the scepticism of Hume, not so far successfully challenged or refuted by orthodox philosophy, left philosophy in the position that we could know with certainty no more than our own ideas and the forms of our understanding (the Kantian categories of space, time, etc.) whilst reality and true knowledge would for ever remain beyond our reach (if indeed anything existed beyond the circle of our own ideas) including, according to Kant, any knowledge of the sources of our modes of understanding or of the functioning of our mental mechanisms. Attempts to develop a separate philosophical treatment of perception in terms of sense-data have not been convincing or provided a way out of the dilemma; naive realism and pragmatism react simply by disregarding the philosophical arguments of idealism and scepticism which they cannot refute. The practical common-sense philosopher, like Ryle, opines that theory about perception in philosophy can proceed perfectly well without any reference to the investigation of perception as a physiological or psychological process.

It now remains to relate the hypotheses about the functioning of perception (in relation to language and action) presented in this book to the situation in the philosophy of knowledge and perception and to the suggested routes from the philosophical impasse suggested by Whitehead, Merleau-Ponty and Lorenz. The theory advanced in this book has been that perception developed from action and to serve action; for perception to be effective, it has to be closely integrated, physiologically and neurologically, with the organisation of action. Visual perception is organised hierarchically, built up from elementary visual units (on the genetic basis provided by 'imprinting', that is, the predisposition to adapt the neural structures to the visual patterning found by the infant in the environment in which it finds itself at birth; the elementary units are then formed into visual shapes and objects (which are stored, in parallel with the words referring to them, as motor patterns, schemata, in the cortex). The comprehension of the visual scene, the unity of the act of perception, derives from the extraction from the visual stimuli affecting the retina of the familiar schemata and their relationship to form the coherent visual scene. On this view, all the structuring of perception of the visual scene is derived or extracted from the stream of light energy, the real physical patterning of the stimuli (accepting as sound the views of the well-known authority on visual perception, James Gibson(23)) but the visual apparatus has been adapted, partly genetically through its anatomical structure and neurological basis, partly through the operation of the 'imprinting' process described and partly through its ability to store visual schemata for recurrent patterns of visual stimulation, so that the functioning of the apparatus reliably and naturally is correlated with the visual information derivable from the real world of external objects.

This view of the way in which perception provides us with reliable knowledge of the world seems fully compatible with the accounts given by Whitehead, Merleau-Ponty and Lorenz: namely that perception is reliable because it constitutes experience from within the system of nature by an element in that system (the human being) of his relations with the whole of nature of which he is part (Whitehead); that perception should be given back its primary importance in philosophy; that the reliability of perception derives from the human being as the 'body-subject', from the mixture of the world and ourselves which precedes all reflection (Merleau-Ponty); that the perceiving subject and the perceived object are equally real, all knowledge derives from the interaction between them and the reliability of our perception is the result of the evolution of the human cognitive apparatus to adapt to the equally real things in the external world (Lorenz). For the human race, the Kantian forms of understanding have, as a result of evolutionary development, become embodied in our neurological and physiological structures. For Kant, human understanding 'prescribes its laws to nature'—but evolution, developing nature, had much earlier in biological history 'prescribed' to the human mind its categories and functioning, to accord with the real world.

The integration: of perception, action and language, resulting in the underlying isomorphism of all languages, combined with the true knowledge of the external world which the evolution of the cognitive and visual apparatus has made possible, opens the way to a new pursuit of philosophical truth through language. We need no longer distrust our own reasoning or our belief in the reality of causation in the external world. The intellectual development of mankind can proceed, as it is doing, but on a philosophically more secure basis and in the knowledge that language, as a flexible instrument designed to match the open-endedness of human experience (perception and action), can be a reliable medium for exploring, recording and developing man's knowledge of the external world and of his own nature.

CONCLUSION

There is something paradoxical about having a final section of a book of this kind (presenting a closely-argued thesis) under the rubric of 'Conclusion'. In any systematic theory (as a matter of history in the development of science, and possibly also in the development of philosophy), the conclusion is the point from which the author has started. Conversely, the Introduction of such a book looks to the past, to the work that has already been done, both by others and by the author himself, and indicates, as the introduction to this book does, the guiding scheme, which there seems no need to recapitulate here. The function of the seven preceding chapters has been an attempt to give solidity to the outline, to bring the reader to see the specific manner in which ideas drawn from widely separated scientific and philosophical disciplines share similarities of underlying structure. Bohm(1) has commented, in a quite different context, that the purpose of a theory is to obtain the essence or unity behind the diversity of phenomena (in his case to bring order into the multitude of elementary physical particles, which can only be accommodated, at present, by increasingly elaborate theoretical constructs resembling the Ptolemaic epicycles). Curiously, the enterprise in this book can be presented in the terms of the theory itself, that it constitutes an attempt to show how a coherent view, a new perception of the elements and relationships in the intellectual 'raw material' provided by the present-day results and speculations of linguistics, psychology, neurology and philosophy, can be arrived at, how new Figures can emerge from the Ground of current thought and theory. As with the familiar voluntary changes in perception demonstrated by the Gestalt psychologists, the book has sought to demonstrate how the whole scientific and philosophical scene changes if one chooses to see a natural orderliness in language rather than the merely arbitrary.

But if this Conclusion is to be thought of rather as a beginning, in what direction should we expect to move? Kant commented that knowledge must not remain a rhapsody but must become a system. There are obviously large gaps in current knowledge and understanding of visual perception, of the neurological co-ordination of action, of the cognitive patterning underlying language and thought—and indeed in the systematic analysis of the familiar phenomena of world languages. These are gaps which it will take many years and much effort to fill and, though the attempt made in this book to relate the structures of language, vision and action, may be criticised as premature because these gaps exist, any general theory is always in a sense premature—it has to reach out ahead of the hard experimental fact. The test of the value of a general theory is whether, whilst preserving what has already been learnt or partial theory has already validated, it suggests new questions to be asked, new directions of research to be followed, a new concreteness in the significance attached to the terms already in use in the different disciplines. Specifically, what difference would this new view of the nature of language make, most narrowly, to the practice of linguistics and, more broadly, to our attitude to language in all its uses, to the understanding of the relation of language, perception and brain function, to our view of the natural basis of social and cultural organisation and, finally, to the philosophical understanding of human nature, the relation of human consciousness and the world?

For linguistics, acceptance of a natural basis for language must mean a radical transformation. There is a growing consensus, amongst those not professionally committed to the particular dogmas of generative grammar (based on concepts of deep structure and specifically linguistic 'competence') that linguistics has reached, if not a dead end, at least a point of crisis. It has been argued, with much force, that contemporary linguistics has gone fundamentally astray, both conceptually and methodologically, and linguists now are faced with the question whether a science of language (of the language process) is possible—or whether anything as variable and intricate could ever be 'tamed' by scientific theories. "One does not make an empirical science out of a discipline merely by wishing or proclaiming it to be so . . . and to become truly scientific the "condition is that language loses its singularity, becomes one phenomenon among many . . . subject to the same principles of perception, learning and motivation, that are believed to govern all thought and behaviour"(3). The hypothesis of the natural and evolutionary basis of language presented in this book has as an immediate consequence the integration of linguistics with the rest of science, and particularly with biology, neurology and physiology. This consequence closely parallels what Darwin described as an immediate consequence of acceptance of the natural origin of species: "the terms used by naturalists, of affinity, relationship, community of type, paternity, morphology, adaptive characters etc. will cease to be metaphorical and will have a plain signification"(4). The same can be said of many of the traditional and modern terms and concepts in linguistics—the metaphorical 'genetic' relation of languages becomes a genuinely genetic relationship, the forms of words and sentences are seen to reflect real forms of neurological and physiological organisation, the 'deep structure' of syntax is seen to be literally a deep underlying structure of the physical organism as it reflects and models the external world,

But perhaps even more important than the direct impact on linguistics as a science in embryo, is the significance of the new view of language for research into brain function. The Introduction quoted Lashley's view of language as a route towards understanding the physiology of the cerebral cortex, speech as the only window through which the physiologist can view cerebral life. From quite different points of view others have commented that 'the central clue to the understanding of man is not his science but his language' and that 'language is something essential to comprehension, something at the very heart of consciousness'. At present, the neurology of voluntary action, of language and of perception, of thought and consciousness, present difficulties of 'astronomical proportions', and research into each of these has inevitably been treated as a distinct field of study. If one now assumes, on the theory presented here, an underlying functional integration of language, vision and action, then the 'window' into the brain that language affords becomes of vastly greater potential importance. One can begin to see how, neurologically, the correlation of perception, action and speech in the cerebral cortex might, against the background of awareness of the postural schema (the body image) from moment to moment, form the basis for the analogue or model of the world mapped in the brain, which Kenneth Craik(7), some years ago, put forward as a hypothesis. Such a model would serve to allow us to predict the outcome of events and to formulate and execute our own actions, to serve as the basis for all our computations. There is experimental evidence of the direct interaction of vision, speech and action with the postural schema and the brain's model of the external world. An animal that lacks information about the posture and movements of its own body, it has been found, cannot interpret visual information presented to it; human subjects with a disturbed postural model (through brain injury) may be incapable of voluntarily initiating a movement; patients suffering from aphasia 'may be able to name objects presented in their normal environment but not when they are presented in an artificial environment as part of a test'. J.Z. Young remarks that "the brain has many distinct parts but there is increasing evidence that they are interrelated to make one functioning whole"(8)—and the inter-relation of speech, vision and action proposed in this book goes some way towards suggesting, in part at any rate, the form which that integration may take, through the correlation of patterns, sensory and motor, within the cerebral cortex, At the same time, the new view of language may suggest some new directions of exploration for the efforts being made by the practitioners of Artificial Intelligence to decipher the code of the brain by imitating small parts of it. Up to now, theories proposed in linguistics and related fields have been too incomplete and too vaguely stated to be realised in computational terms and only a few tiny fragments of the spectrum of human abilities have begun to be simulated. In this book, an attempt has been made to translate a very broad theory into specific detail and this may well provide some solider grist for the AI mill.

Quine(9), in discussing the relation of word and object, at one point described a river as a process through time. Language, as a naturally based system, can be seen as a river of thought flowing through time—like all human behaviour an expression of interaction between genetic patterning and the environment within which the genes are expressed. Language is stable yet at the same time over long periods it changes progressively and systematically. Evolutionary change to track the environment (using Wilson's(10) terminology in sociobiology) can be long-term (as the genetic composition of a population shifts to a mode better adapted to long-term environmental changes) or medium-term (micro-evolution in inbred small human groups converting cultural practices into selective factors affecting the gene-pool) or fast, short-term. By this last is meant that in so far as the expression of a genetic inheritance is necessarily dependent upon the environment in which the organism is placed, and part of the genetic inheritance, in human beings, consists of potentialities for neurological structuring to match the social environment, as in the case of language, 'evolutionary change . . . is going on now from second to second, as a result of the very rapid evolution of afferent neuronal structures, produced by the intake and accumulation of information"(8) (J.Z. Young). The changes in the content of language, the concepts distinguished in the lexicon, the analysis of syntactic relationships ever more precisely and finely, on this view of language, represent real and not merely metaphorical cultural evolution—and one can conclude that in these terms all languages are not at similar stages of development; some are, evolutionarily, more advanced than others (reflecting real neurological differences between the members of different language communities). As an extreme example, one might speculate how difficult or easy it would be to translate nuclear physics or Hegel into a lexically or syntactically primitive language, such as those found among the Australian aborigines. At the same time, besides the rapidity of change in the content of language, there are factors making for stability which are directly analogous with those identified in other evolutionary processes what has been described as 'phylogenetic inertia This in social terms makes its appearance as the force of tradition. The factors which determine inertia, and so resistance to evolutionary change, include "the complexity of social behaviour. The more numerous the components constituting the behaviour, and the more elaborate the physiological machinery required to produce each component, the greater the inertia"(10). This account, which was formulated as a general sociobiological one relating to societies of creatures of all kinds, can be applied directly to explain the phenomena of stability and gradual change in language as a whole and in individual languages.

As regards the impact of the new view of language on philosophy, this has already been discussed at some length in chapter VII, particularly in terms of the significance of language for philosophy, the problem of meaning and the relation of perception and knowledge. In relation to each of these major topics, a theory of language, as deriving its natural character from structural integration with the processes underlying perception and action, can make an important contribution towards extricating philosophers from some of the impasses in which they have long been imprisoned; it may not be too optimistic to suggest that this new approach could lead to actual progress in philosophy, something which otherwise has been rather infrequent, and may provide a basis for conciliation between those philosophers who take the view that all philosophy is a critique of language and those, like

Popper, who consider that science matters and language does not (and that of Wittgenstein who, in describing other philosophers as flies buzzing in a bottle and unable to get out, was in his concern with language just as much himself the fly in a bottle). Though it is not possible to discuss the subject here because it would require too extensive a digression, there seems particular reason to think that the new view of language presented in this book ought to have a major impact on the foundations of logic; language, as has been said earlier, can only constitute a skeleton representation of the perception or action to which it relates, and logic (as historically and systematically heavily dependent on the syntactic structure of language) is no more than a skeleton of a skeleton. If language and syntax are structured by reality (as transmitted via perception and action), then logic, at one remove, also can only derive its structure and validity from perception and action, from what Royce describes as "the unavoidable structure of our experience"(13). The concepts of necessity and causation originate not in language, and not in logic, but in what Hegel describes as the 'logic of life', in the sequences of causes we perceive in our own action and, by transfer, in the action of others or of inanimate objects.

So far, this Conclusion has spoken about language as the subject-matter of linguistics, about language as correlated with vision and action in the brain, about language as an evolutionary process and language in philosophy and logic. But language in fact is multifarious. Besides the specialised languages and approaches to language which have been discussed, there is language as it is used in everyday life (the medium of social interaction), language as used in science (attempting to give a regular and permanent form to the unifying perceptions of scientists and within which there are many special sub-languages) and finally, and perhaps most important, there is language which transforms minds, changes consciousness—the language of poetry, of oratory and persuasion, of conversion. The extraordinary development of language, forming scientists of different nations into one global community, the almost miraculous power of language displayed in the ability to formulate and comprehend the most penetrating and intricate thought, reaches its culmination in the use of the total resources of language that poetry and oratory constitute. In these remarkable, special uses of language, there is a whole world for further exploration, for which the structural integration of language, sight and action, is of supreme importance. Two quotations, from Wittgenstein and from Saint-John Perse, particularly about the poetic use of language: "Worte eines Dichters können uns durch und durch gehen" (Wittgenstein Zettel (14)) and "Du savant comme du poéte, la pensée desintéressée. Car l'interrogation est la même qu'ils tiennent sur un même abîme et seuls leurs modes d'investigation diffèrent. Cette nuit originelle où tâtonnent deux aveugles-nés: le mystère est commun"(15).

To explain something—language, perception, thought—(or even to attempt to explain something) is not to explain it away. Each human function, language, perception, retains its immense potentialities. As language considers language and perception perceives perception, and the structure of what we come to know in finer and finer detail is expressed permanently in language, we are ourselves part of an unceasing development. The mind sees itself in all it sees, the world interprets itself through us and we realise that it is the nature of man to be a mirror of the world as well as a part of the world he mirrors. The individual has the privilege of seeing, from within the system, the development of the system of which he forms part—the society, the evolutionary process, the development of consciousness. He can see, and record, the ever-growing complexity of his own brain so that it can become an ever more accurate analogue of the structure of external things—and so that eventually there can develop, within his analogue of the world, an analogue of his own processes of language, perception and consciousness. The brain begins to understand its own nature, its own understanding.

Notes

Introduction

1. Kant trans. 1966: xlvi
2. Kuhn 1970: 4
3. Annals of New York Academy of Sciences Vol. 280
4. Brown 1958: iii
5. Brown 1976
6. Wittgenstein 1961: 48, 71, 26, 52
7. Locke 1965 Book III 'Of Words'
8. Lashley 1969: 516
9. Lenneberg 1967
10. Gregory 1974: 629
11. Lorenz 1977
12. Monod 1970: 11
13. Hume 1969: 320

Chapter I

1. Plato trans. 1926: 143 and passim
2. Lucretius trans. 1975: 461
3. Hörmann 1971: 216-217
4. Saussure trans. 1966: 67
5. Saussure: 10 f., 67 f., 113 f. and passim
6. Hockett 1958: 64
7. Sapir 1970: 7
8. Bloomfield 1933: 145

9. Firth 1964: 181, 187
10. Yuen Ren Chao 1970: 1
11. Englefield 1977: 172-173
12. Hormann 1971: 214
13. Miller & Johnson-Laird 1976: 116
14. quoted in Hewes: 1973: 54
15. Gregory 1976: 624
16. Wittgenstein 1958: 27-28
17. Saussure trans. 1966: 18-19
18. Potter 1966: 79
19. Lorenz 1977: 250
20. Hewes 1973: 54
21. Hubel & Wiesel 1979
22. Saussure 1966: 73, 131-134
23. Englefield 1977: 174
24. Saussure 1966: 71-72
25. Aarsleff 1976: 9-11
26. Englefield 1977: 93-94, 86-87
27. Summarised from Sayre 1976 Chapter XI: 187-207
28. Saussure 1976: 133
29. Quine 1968
30. Saussure 1976: 232
31. Lorenz 1977: 78 ff.
32. Kuffler & Nicholls 1977: Chapter 19
33. Material on bird-song in relation to infant vocalisation summarised
    from Marler 1976
34. Marler 1976: 389
35. Brown 1976
36. Minsky 1975
37. Brown 1976: 314 f. 453 ff.
38. Piaget 1973: 77-109
39. Brown 1958: 248-249, 465
40. McNeill
41. Gregory 1972: 190-191
42. Lenneberg 1967: Chapter 9
43. Teuber 1967: 205-208
44. Marler 1976:
45. Wittgenstein 1960: 470

Chapter II

1. Whorf 1964
2. Helmholtz 1865
3. Lashley 1951
4. Clowes 1970
5. Miller and Johnson-Laird 1976
6. Wittgenstein 1961: 19-20, 1955: 67
7. Chomsky 1971: 158; 1967: 85
8. Teuber 1967: 208-209
9. Osgood 1971: 527
10. Sloman 1978: 53
11. Miller & Johnson Laird 1976: 691 ff.
12. Gregory 1974: 622 ff.
13. Hubel & Wiesel 1962, 1979
14. Greenberg 1963, 1975

Chapter III

1. Hubel & Wiesel 1962, 1979
2. Kuffler & Nicholls 1976 Chapter 2; Milner Chapter 11; Young 1978 Chapter 12; Sommerhoff 1974 Chapter 9
3. Neisser 1967: 79-81; Gregory 1976: 58-60; Vernon 1971: 166-168; Dixon 1966: 64
4. Selfridge 1959
5. Waltz 1972; Boden 1977: 222-226
6. Pomerantz 1978
7. Kuffler & Nicholls 1976
8. Lashley 1969: 525
9. Bernstein 1967
10. Evarts 1979
11. Connolly 1974:
12. Rosse and Clawson 1970
13. Sapir 1970:42
14. Fudge 1970: 79-81
15. Morse 1976; Marler; Kuhl
16. Liberman 1967
17. Ladefoged 1967: 171
18. McCarthy

Chapter IV

1. Locke 1965 Vol I: 80 ff.; Vol II: 10-12, 76-77, 87
2. Wilkins 1968
3. von Slagle 1974: 43-50
4. Weisgerber 1962; Trier 1931
5. Miller & Johnson-Laird 1976: 238-40
6. Lyons 1977 I: 250-270
7. Chafe 1970:
8. Katz 1967
9. Matteson et al. 1972
10. Swadesh 1972
11. Ogden 1932
12. Wilks 1977
13. Schank 1972
14. Fillmore
15. Minsky 1975
16. Locke 1966 Vol II: 10
17. On metaphor generally: Brooke-Rose 1958; Black 1954
18. Richards 1936:
19. Saussure 1966: 51
20. Lashley 1954: 432
21. Neisser 1967: 139-146
22. Sommerhoff 1974: Chapter 9
23. Pribram 1971:243 ff.
24. Granit 1977: 171-172, 201
25. Ladefoged 1967: 143
26. Brain 1961
27. Liberman et al. 1967
28. Liberman 1976: 719
29. Penfield & Roberts 1959: 247

Chapter V

1. Luria 1975: 380
2. Lakoff 1978: 275
3. Malinowski 1930
4. Halliday 1973
5. Granit 1977: 171

6. Roberts 1978: 144-146
7. Bartlett 1958: 50
8. Crystal 1971: 200
9. Sapir 1970: 90
10. Bloomfield 1933: 170
11. Lyons in Minnis 1973: 61
12. Chomsky 1971: 6
13. Osgood 1971
14. Wundt quoted in Bever 1971: 158
15. Wittgenstein 1955: 165
16. Potter 1966:
17. Chomsky 1971: 2
18. Derwing 1973. See also Gross 1979
19. Rommetweit 1968; Wold 1978
20. Ditchburn 1975; Yarbus 1967; 1970; Noton & Stark 1971
21. Lashley 1969: 523
22. Yuen Ren Chao 1970: 54
23. Sapir 1970: 117-119
24. Yuen Ren Chao 1976: 91 summarising Greenberg 1963
25. Halliday 1973; Fillmore
26. Sapir 1970: 98
27. Lakoff
28. Fillmore
29. Winograd 1972
30. Schank 1972
31. Neisser 1967: 89-91, 141-142
32. Attneave 1971
33. See generally Bloomfield 1933: 264-270
34. Miller & Johnson-Laird 1976: 98
35. Boden 1977: 236-242
36. Chomsky 1971: 7 ff.
37. Derwing 1973: 259-296
38. Lorenz 1973: 7

Chapter VI

1. Gleason 1972: 3
2. Greenberg 1963, 1975
3. Whitney 1892 (1967: 255)

4. Jespersen: 1922: 184 ff.
5. Meillet 1964: 32
6. Thorpe 1967
7. Jakobson 1972: 299
8. Yuen Ren Chao 1970: 150, 117
9. Wittgenstein 1967: 59
10. Yarbus 1967
11. Noton & Stark 1971
12. Davidoff 1975
13. Leeuwenberg & Buffart 1978
14. Simon 1978: 314, 329
15. Dobzhansky 1955 in Sayre 1976: 109
16. Berry 1977: 22
17. Sayre 1976: 96-97
18. Wilson 1975: 144 ff.
19. Monod 1970: 149
20. Berry 1977: 25
21. Sayre 1977
22. Catford 1977:
23. Hockett
24. Yuen Ren Chao 1970: 140
25. Zipf
26. Jakobson 1972: 302
27. Brosnahan 1961: Chapter V, 181-183
28. Yuen Ren Chao 1970: 140
29. Denes & Pinson 1973: 149-151
30. Saussure trans. 1966: 50 ff.
31. Jakobson 1973: 123 ff.
32. Meillet 1964: 25
33. Darlington 1947, 1955
34. Whitney 1977: 244
35. Anderson 1973: 199-200
36. Lord 1966
37. Lenneberg 1967: 92
38. Firth 1964:106
39. Sweet 1971: 3 ff.
40. Jespersen 1922: 438
41. Sauvageot 1964: 175-197
42. Peterfalvi 1978

43. de Diego 1973 66-69
44. Brown 1958: 154
45. Jakobson
46. Jespersen 1922: 396
47. Jespersen 1922: 396
48. Firth 1964: 191-194
49. Brown 1958: 115
50. Tsuru 1933
51. Ertel Dorst
52. Whitney 1967: 251
53. Tylor 1871:
54. Firth 1964: 184-185
55. Bloomfield 1933: 156-157
56. Piaget 1973: 71 ff.
57. Lord
58. Yuen Ren Chao 1970:
59. Whorf 1964: 236
60. Bever
61. Saussure 1966: 136
62. Humboldt 1967:65
63. Palmer 1954
64. Witte 1937
65. Lord 1966:
66. Greenberg 1972: 331
67. Witte
68. Sapir 1971: 67 ff.
69. Winograd 1972

Chapter VII

1. Rorty 1967
2. Whitehead & Russell 1913
3. Wittgenstein 1955
4. Passmore 1966: 450 f. Austin 1961
5. Ryle 1949
6. Wittgenstein 1960
7. Wittgenstein 1974: 18, 52
8. Austin
9. Strawson 1967: 317-320

10. Popper. See Magee 1971: 169-171
11. Black 1967: 339
12. Rorty 1967: 321 ff.
13. Locke Book II 1965: 77 ff.
14. Ryle 1949:
15. Lorenz 1977: 7ff.
16. Magee 1971: 132, 173
17. Passmore 1966: 335 ff.
18. Passmore 1966: 499 ff.
19. Grice 1968
20. Ziff
21. Carnap 1958. For Neurath see Passmore 1966: 375 ff.
22. Sayre 1976: 196 ff.
23. Gibson 1950, 1966

CONCLUSION

1. Bohm 1980: 5, 112 ff.
2. Derwing 1973: 321-322
3. Darwin 1859 (1971: 460)
4. Craik 1943
5. Young 1978: 265, 262
6. Quine
7. Wilson 1975: 144-145
8. Royce 1919: 145
9. Wittgenstein 1967: 28
10. Saint-John Perse 1970: 241-242

BIBLIOGRAPHY

Allott, R. 1992. The Motor Theory of Language: Origin and Function. In *Language Origin: A Multidisciplinary Approach* ed. by Jan Wind et al. NATO ASI. Dordrecht: Kluwe

Anscombe, G.E.M. 1995. "Ludwig Wittgenstein". *Philosophy* 70: 273 395. Arbib, M. A., E.J. Conklin and J. Hill. 1987. *From Schema Theory to Language.* OUP.

Ayer A.J. 1985 *Ludwig Wittgenstein.* Penguin.

Bartley, W.W. 1985 *Wittgenstein.* Open Court.

Berthoz, Alain. 1997. *Le Sens du Mouvement.* Editions Odile Jacob.

Bilgrami, A. 2002. "Chomsky and Philosophy". *Mind & Language* 17: 3 290-302.

Bloomfield, L. 1933. [Reprint 1970]. *Language.* Allen and Unwin.

Chomsky, N. 1988. *Language and Problems of Knowledge: The Managua Lectures.* MIT.

Chomsky, N. 1993. *Language and Thought.* Moyer Bell.

Chomsky, N. 1993. "A minimalist program for linguistic theory" in K Hale and J Keyser eds. *The View from Building 20.* MIT.

Chomsky, N. 1995. *The Minimalist Program.* MIT.

Chomsky, N. 2000. *New Horizons in the Study of Language and Mind.* CUP.

Deacon, T.W. 1997. *The Symbolic Species: The Co-evolution of Language and the Brain.* Norton.

Decety, J. 1996. "Do imagined and executed actions share the same neural substrate?" *Cog. Brain Res.* 3: 87-93.

Decety, J. ed. 2000. "Cerveau, Perception et Action". *Psychologie Française.* 45 4.

Fadiga, L., G. Craighero, G. Buccino and G. Rizzolatti. 2002. "Speech listening specifically modulates the excitability of tongue muscles: a TMS study". *European Journal of Neuroscience* 15 : 399-402.

Fromkin, V. A. 1997." Some Thoughts about the Brain/Mind/Language Interface". *Lingua* 100. 3-27

Gallese, V. 1998." Mirror neurons: from grasping to language". In *Towards a |Science of Consciousness* (Tucson III)

Graziano Michael SA, Taylor Charlotte SR, Moore Trin. 2002. "Complex movements evoked by microstimulation of precentral cortex". *Neuron* 34, 841-851.

Hacker, P.M.S. 1996. *Wittgenstein's Place in Twentieth-century Analytic Philosophy.* Blackwell.

Hale, K. and S.J. Keyser. 1993. *The View from Building 20.* MIT.

Harnad, S.R., Steklis, H.D., and J. Lancaster. 1976. *Origins and Evolution of Language and Speech. Ann. N.Y. Acad. Sci.* Vol. 280.

Hornstein, N. 1995. *Logical Form: From GB to Minimalism.* Blackwell.

Hurford, J. R. 2002. "Language beyond our grasp: what mirror neurons can, and cannot, do for language evolution". In *The Evolution of Communication Systems: A Comparative Approach.* ed. by D. Kimbrough Oller, U. Griebel and K. Plunkett. MIT.

Iacoboni, M., R.P. Woods, M. Brass, H. Bekkering, J.C. Mazziotta and G. Rizzolatti. 1999. "Cortical Mechanisms of Human Imitation". *Science* 286 2526-2528.

Jackendoff, R. 2002. *Foundations of language :brain, meaning, grammar, evolution.* OUP.

Kenny, Anthony. "The Ghost of the Tractatus". In Vesey ed. 1-13.

Kohler, E., C., Keysers, M.A., Umilta, L., Fogassi, V., Gallese and G. Rizzolatti. 2002. "Hearing Sounds Understanding Actions: Action Representation in Mirror Neurons". *Science* 297 846-8.

Liberman, A.M. et al. 1967. "Perception of the speech code". *Psychological Review* 74: 431-461.

Liberman, A. M. and I. G. Mattingly. 1985. "The motor theory of speech perception revised." *Cognition* 21: 1-36.

Lyons, J. 1968. *Introduction to Theoretical Linguistics.* CUP.

Malcolm, N. 1958. *Ludwig Wittgenstein: A Memoir* (with a Biographical Sketch by G. H. von Wright). OUP.

Monk, R. 1990. *Ludwig Wittgenstein: The Duty of Genius.* Jonathan Cape.

Moravcsik, J.M. 2002. "Chomsky's New Horizons". *Mind & Language* 17: 3 303-311.

Mussa-Ivaldi, F.A., Giszter, S.F., Bizzi, E. 1994. "Linear combinations of primitives in vertebrate motor control." *Proc Natl Acad Sci* 2;91(16):7534-8

O'Grady, P. 1996 "Anscombe on the *Tractatus*". *Philosophy* 71: 276.

Pulvermüller F 1999. "Words in the Brain's Language". *Brain and Behavioral Sciences*. 22, 2, 253-279

Pulvermüller F., Lutzenberger, W., Preissl, H. 1999. "Nouns and verbs in the intact brain: evidence from event-related potentials and high-frequency cortical responses." *Cereb Cortex* 9(5):497-506.

Pulvermüller, F., Mohr, B., Schleichert, H. 1999. "Semantic or lexico-syntactic factors: what determines word-class specific activity in the human brain?" *Neurosci Lett* 12;275(2):81-4

Raichle, M. E. 1994. "Visualizing the Mind: Strategies of cognitive science and techniques of modern brain imaging open a window to the neural systems responsible for thought". *Scientific American* 270(4): 36-42.

Rijntjes, M., Dettmers, C., Buchei, C., Kiebel, S., Frackoviak, J., Weiller, C. 1999. "A blueprint for movement: Functional and anatomical representations in the human motor system." *J. Neurosci* 19(18):8043-8048.

Rizzolatti, G. and M.A. Arbib. 1998. "Language within our grasp". *Trends in Neurosciences*. 21(5) 188-194.

Rorty, R. 1979, *Philosophy and the Mirror of Nature*. Princeton UP.

Rowe, M.W. 1992. "The Definition of 'Game'. *Philosophy* 67: 262 467.

Russell, B. 1959. *My Philosophical Development*. Allen & Unwin.

Saussure, F. 1915. *Course in General Linguistics*. Trans. W. Baskin. McGraw-Hill 1966.

Stone, T. and M. Davies. 2002. "Chomsky among the Philosophers". *Mind & Language* 17 3 276-289.

Vesey, G. ed. 1974. *Understanding Wittgenstein*. Cornell.

Vesey, G. 1974. Foreword In Vesey ed. *von* Wright, G.H. "Biographical Sketch". In Malcolm *Ludwig Wittgenstein*. 1-22.

White, R.M. "Can whether one proposition makes sense depend on the truth of another? In Vesey ed. 14-29.

Wittgenstein, L. 1922. *Tractatus Logico-Philosophicus*. Routledge & Kegan Paul.

Wittgenstein L. 1953. *Philosophical Investigations*. Translated by G.E.M. Anscombe. Blackwell.

Wittgenstein, L. 1960. *The Blue and Brown Books*. Blackwell.

Wittgenstein, L. 1961. *Notebooks 1914-1916*. Blackwell.

Wittgenstein, L. 1967. *Zettel*. Blackwell.

Index Of Names

Subject Index

Lightning Source UK Ltd.
Milton Keynes UK
UKOW050219040212

186640UK00001B/68/P